Divorced Fathers and Their Families

Florence W. Kaslow

Divorced Fathers and Their Families

Legal, Economic, and Emotional Dilemmas

 Springer

Florence W. Kaslow, Ph.D.
Kaslow Associates
Palm Beach Gardens, FL, USA

ISBN 978-1-4614-5534-9   ISBN 978-1-4614-5535-6 (eBook)
DOI 10.1007/978-1-4614-5535-6
Springer New York Heidelberg Dordrecht London

Library of Congress Control Number: 2012950588

Printed on acid-free paper

Springer is part of Springer Science+Business Media (www.springer.com)

*With much love this book is dedicated to
my three wonderful grandchildren,
Rachel Loren, Ethan Isaiah, and Naomi
Rebecca Kaslow, and to my beloved son,
their Devoted, Attentive, and Dedicated Dad,
Howard Kaslow.*

Grandmamma and Dr. Mom
Florence W. Kaslow, Ph.D.

Foreword I

Dr. Florence Kaslow is on to something. She has brought a lifetime of diligent work as a therapist, plus a researcher's keen sensibilities, and a great deal of heart into a project aimed at reconsidering our world view of divorced fathers. This is a book about dads who have gone through divorce, yes, but it is also a meaningful book for the rest of us, male and female.

In my career as a journalist, I write a column about life transitions for The Wall Street Journal. I have frequently covered men's family issues, their rights as fathers, and their often-ignored emotional struggles. I have seen the pain men go through, silently, on a great many fronts, including the sadness that often accompanies divorce and child-custody matters. Divorce is one of the most searingly difficult life transitions for many men, even if their interactions with their ex-wives are not contentious.

Too often, divorced dads are demonized or discounted. As a culture, we do not focus enough on the valuable contributions they are kept from making to their children's lives. Dr. Kaslow's work in this book is a terrific step in correcting misconceptions, and in allowing divorced fathers to have a voice. The revelations in this book will surprise and enlighten you, and will lead to a better understanding of the divorced fathers in your family or social circles. In the end, children also will be beneficiaries of the work Dr. Kaslow has done in these pages.

This book offers stories, reflections, history, and fresh analysis of issues we would be smart to pay close attention to. It is a coincidence that Dr. Kaslow and I have similar names. It is no coincidence that we have similar views on the vital needs and yearnings of divorced fathers. I salute her for undertaking this project.

– Jeffrey Zaslow (deceased, February 2012). Co-author of *The Last Lecture* and of *Gabby: A Story of Courage and Hope.* Columnist for the Wall Street Journal.

Foreword II

It is with great honor and pleasure that I have the privilege of writing a Foreword for *Fathers and Divorce*, Dr. Florence Kaslow's latest tome. I am proud to have had the opportunity to be a contributor to a few of her previous books, and I recognize the passion, dedication, and careful research she invests in each of her volumes.

Dr. Kaslow's incredible professional career includes her having developed acknowledged expertise in many clinical domains such as individual, marital, family, divorce, and sex therapies as well as treatment of military families, in consultation to family businesses and professional practices; and executive, life transition, and relationship coaching. Additionally, she is an inspiring teacher, speaker, and prolific writer often forging new frontiers as is evident in the topic of this new book.

After a fascinating opening chapter on the history of thinking about child custody in the United States, and the changing views of women and men's roles and competencies as parents, the book portrays 13 illustrative and heart-wrenching case studies of divorced men. Also included are four chapters that elaborate and analyze many of the issues depicted in the case studies that should prove informative to professionals as well as divorcing/divorced moms and dads. The focus of this book is a unique and often neglected view of divorce. The dads who are "good dads" who suffer deep hurt and loss due to the process of their divorces and the ensuing grief over the diminished and sometimes truncated relationship with their children have all too often been relegated to the status of not very important people and their needs and value to the children disregarded or downplayed. This book valiantly attempts to redress this disparity in the law, the judicial system and in the conceptualization and treatment by some therapists, as well as the interventions of some mediators and others involved in the divorce process.

As Dr. Kaslow so clearly highlights, there is a large body of work on the plight of the divorced moms with a scathing literature on the "deadbeat dads," abusive dads, or dads that abandon their families. Yet, there is a dearth of literature on the good husbands and dedicated dads. These men may not have precipitated the divorces. Or, they may have been in such destructive relationships that their survival was contingent on "getting out" of their unhealthy relationships when their wife suggested a divorce. Many men who chose to leave unhappy relationships seem not to have been really aware of the losses and consequences of their decisions until after they had experienced the fracture of the family.

Chapter 15 summarizes the material culled about the 13 respondents and illuminated by the wisdom Dr. Kaslow has accrued during her study of and career in the fields of marital, individual, and divorce therapy as well as divorce mediation. Even though the subject pool contains men of diverse religious and ethnic backgrounds, the majority of the men are well educated and "successful" in their careers. Included in Chapter 15 is an excellent Typology of Divorced Dads which Dr. Kaslow has expanded from the extant literature by adding a number of neglected types who are frequently encountered in the divorce arena. This chapter also proffers an expansion of the concepts Eric Berne delineated of the emotional games people play. She has adapted this concept to games divorcing or divorced couples may play which sadly impact tremendously on each other and on the children. These games often cause alienation, loyalty conflicts, and brainwashing of the children and may entail out and out blackmail and manipulation by spouses.

Chapter 16 encompasses the potential value of various kinds of professional help which, if utilized, could lead to far healthier outcomes in divorce. These include Divorce Therapy, Divorce Mediation and Collaborative Divorce. A perspective on choosing the kind of lawyer who is more inclined to facilitate a cooperative, fair, and equitable divorce settlement is provided by Benson, a matrimonial lawyer. A comprehensive review of the value of Family Evaluations, in divorce in aiding the family, the judges, and other individuals involved in the process, written by Benjamin, provides a detailed explanation of the process of Family Evaluations, the value of the procedure and its potential for minimizing unbridled litigation, and future visits to the courts. In her commentary section, Carter discusses the role of the Parenting Coordinator in helping families find more productive and healing ways to deal with co-parenting, residential issues, and the ongoing challenges of fractured families. The final part of this chapter is written by Schwartz, who focuses on the role of the Child Advocate. Professionals in each of these roles can play a critical part in the facilitation of a more manageable and kinder process during an extremely painful, often contentious time in a family's life, for all those involved: the divorcing couple, the children, and the extended family and friends.

Chapter 17 is noteworthy in its focus on the impact of the described personality disorders of some of the women on their spouses and children. Individuals with personality disorders generally have an exacerbation of their symptomology during stressful periods. The chapter highlights the characteristics that initially enticed these men but then often became the very ones that tore the men and children to pieces as the marriage and subsequent divorce proceeded.

The final chapter (Chapter 18) is a treasure trove of advice to those in each profession and the numerous individuals who become involved in the divorce process. These include divorce therapists, divorce mediators, child custody and family evaluators, ex-wives and ex-husbands, children of divorce, matrimonial attorneys, and family court judges. It also challenges legislators and courts to review the biases and traditions surrounding divorce and work toward bringing about any additional changes in legislation and the content of legal decisions that are warranted.

Overall, this book seeks to invoke changes in thinking about divorce in terms of advocating not only an awareness of "good dads" but also a challenge to all professionals and families involved to seek less adversarial divorces and improve postdivorce healing and well-being. Given that over 50 % of marriages today in many countries of the world end in divorce, the hope engendered in this book is to help families survive and thrive as best as possible within the context of a very difficult life process. This book evokes thoughtful considerations for all parties involved in divorce.

Dr. Kaslow has again succeeded in writing a readable, informative and thought-provoking book that challenges some of the current thinking in the field and entreats the professionals, as well as husbands and wives; to go "about the business of divorce" in a more compassionate and healing manner – what she has called *divorce with integrity*.

Wilhelmina S. Koedam, Ph.D.
Licensed Psychologist
Divorce and Family Mediator
Custody Evaluator
Hollywood, Florida
July 2012

Preface

Deadbeat dads? (Boumil & Friedman, 1996; Braver, 1998). Percentage wise, very few. And contrary to popular opinion, many, if not most, divorced dads have not been alcoholics, nor drug addicts. Nor have they been physically or sexually abusive. Why then have they, as a group, been given such a "bum rap"? Why have their stories not been told, or if told, not heard? This book will provide answers to these questions and other serious issues concerning divorced dads and their children, *from the dad's point of view*, in order to fill this enormous gap. Much has already been published, broadcast, televised, and communicated in other forums about what happens to moms and to children during and postdivorce, *but the dad's story has either been neglected or overly sensationalized*, especially when it has been one of abandonment, neglect, or nonpayment of mandated child support.

The myriad "good guy" dad stories have been shoved asunder as if insignificant and unimportant. It is urgent that a representative sample of "good dad'" stories be told – on their behalf – to illuminate a more comprehensive and realistic kaleidoscopic overview for the various professionals in the legal, judicial and mental health systems engaged in working with those embroiled in painful, disturbing divorces; other men (and their families) who have felt alone in their rejection and isolation from *their children and grandchildren*; children of divorce; couples contemplating divorce; and others who want and need to know more about this large and growing segment of men the world over.

A quote from one dad interviewed sets the stage for some of the real-life dramas that unfold in the 13 case stories that appear in this book.

It's Father's Day and although I'm a dad, I won't see my children. My ex-wife has always come up with some way to keep me apart from them – like intercepting my birthday and holiday cards and gifts to them and returning them, and then berating me to the children – saying I was too unconcerned (or cheap) to send a gift and thereby driving a wedge of resentment between us. Sometimes when it was supposed to be my turn to have the children she would say they were sick or had plans with friends, etc. Father's Day is always an especially sad day as I always wanted to be a dad and loved being one – before I was told to leave. Now I'm a childless dad and it hurts.

Thousands of dads have a similar lament because it seems to them that "no one hears and no one cares." This book focuses attention on why and seeks to lead the way to rectifying this egregious oversight. It is critical to highlight the fact that although marriage may end legally, it is never fully over if there are children. They are the ties that bind the original biological parent couple together – "'til death do them part." And the judicial system and all of the professionals involved in the process of divorce *should* unite to make this experience less cumbersome, traumatic, debilitating, punitive, and stressful.

Most of the literature on postdivorce focuses on two parts of the prior family – the wife/mother with the emphasis centering on *her legal rights and emotional needs* and *those of the children*. These are critical aspects of the divorce scenario which merit and have received much attention, *and they are not being minimized here*. However, little has been written about the postdivorce emotional needs for contact with and involvement of those *fathers* who have been dedicated and deeply attached to *their* children in their lives before the breakup. This book seeks to fill this gap for all of the professionals who are charged with "helping" them and for the fathers and mothers who may choose to read it. Given that 50 % of all marriages in the USA (and some other countries) end in divorce, this is a critical problem *right now*, and the sooner it is addressed on both the microcosmic and macrocosmic levels, the better for our entire society.

The marital settlement sessions and the legal arguments presented in court and the marital settlement agreements (MSA) handed down by the judges usually focus on issues confronted by the ex-wife/mother (Wallerstein, 1986) and on the custody and visitation plan. Yet few consider what it will be like for the children to live both in Mom's house and Dad's house (Ricci, 1980; Wallerstein & Kelly, 1980). The relationships with two sets of grandparents (Kaslow, 2007) usually receive scant attention in the deliberations and final agreement. Nonetheless, these are issues that surface quickly and ultimately need to be handled with a wide-angle lens that considers *everyone's needs and feelings*. What is it like for children to shuttle back and forth, often finding they left something they need at the other household, and resenting that parents wanted the divorce but they are the ones forced to live with these unsettling consequences? Where will the children really spend the holidays and vacations; what a *fair* rotation is from *both parents* and the *children's point of view*; decision making in specific realms of the children's lives; and *how continuing parental discord will be resolved may not be addressed (specifically enough) in mediation, settlement sessions, or in court*. In fact, sometimes the party's respective attorneys have whipped up the areas of disagreement and exacerbated the schism to make their arguments more convincing and the issues at stake less resolvable. Eventually the areas of conflict must be worked through, or they will continue to distress one or both adults and the children for many years to come and color the divorced dad's future dating relationships and willingness to marry again. Children are not the "property" of either parent – they are people with their own hearts and thoughts – and their best interests should be paramount. But what best interests and as determined by whom? That is the question! This book will address these salient issues.

First, a history of factors influencing child custody decisions over the past century is presented to provide a backdrop against which to understand the current emotional climate and expectations, the legal and judicial machinations, and the postdivorce difficulties experienced by various members of the immediate and extended family. Next, 13 individual case stories of divorce, as told to the author in personal interviews with 13 divorced dads based on a questionnaire administered to each (See Appendix 1) in person, are chronicled. Many are heart wrenching as the pain, loss, hurt, and anguish of not living with their children on a daily basis as part of their nuclear family often linger for years and become intensified if the children have been alienated from them and their fathers do not see them. This is not what occurred in all of the cases, and the two types of outcomes emanate from different sets of partner dynamics and personality types of the individuals involved in the specific divorces.

In Chapter 15, an analysis of the themes in the cases as an aggregate is presented, and Games Divorcing and Divorced People Play are analyzed and made more easily recognizable. Chapter 16 offers responsive commentaries on the cases by experts in the field of divorce, and they each discuss how the outcomes might have been more positive for all members of the families if different services/interventions had been utilized and provided by well-trained professionals with a systemic perspective capable of considering the gestalt of the best interests of all members of the family. Subdivided into five parts, the vantage points of the divorce therapist, divorce mediator, and collaborative divorce specialist are the first three separate specialties covered in Part I. Part II delves into the domain of the matrimonial lawyer. Part III ventures into the relatively new arena of family evaluation – which includes and goes well beyond child custody evaluation. Parenting coordination, another fairly new specialty in the widening array of services available to divorcing couples, receives attention in Part IV. And the spotlight shines on the role of the child advocate in Part V. So many more services are available now than when many of the men interviewed were divorced that we can only ponder whether they and their wives had been willing to use them if, in reality, they would have made a positive difference.

Chapter 17 looks at why some people can share their children reasonably amicably, and others cannot. It ponders the variable of the personality of each parent as a key ingredient in determining the outcome of the divorce process and aftermath (Baum & Schnit, 2005).

The specific common factors or *personality patterns* that emerged in the former couples, based on the ex-husband's reports, that seem to have contributed to their difficult divorces and to much of the postdivorce continuing poor communication and antipathy and often loss of or infrequent contact with one's children are identified. The stages of the divorce process as they are relevant to the issues and dilemmas being discussed are highlighted and summarized in Appendix 2.

In Chapter 18, suggestions made by the divorced dads, others formulated from my years of clinical practice as a psychologist doing couple, family, divorce therapy and divorce mediation, and a summation of the best ideas culled from the contributing authors and the literature meant for professionals dealing with divorcing and divorced families – be they lawyers, therapists, mediators, child custody evaluators, parenting coordinators, or family court judges – are contained.

"Tips" are provided on how to improve the situation, even many years later, to both former partners and the "*children of all ages, if they are amenable to trying to heal, improve, and/or reconcile relationships*" (Gold, 1992). The idea of utilizing a *divorce ceremony*, even many years after the legal divorce, is introduced as another technique for shifting relationships into a more positive direction. A ceremony I have utilized in the past (that has been published previously) is alluded to illustratively, in the tips portion of this chapter, and included as Appendix 3 (Kaslow, 2010). There is also a discussion of forgiveness and its many facets as they may be applicable (Bonach, 2007; Freedman, 1998).

It is hoped that this book may have wide reverberations by making an impact on legislators who can change the laws regarding divorce to make them more equitable in today's world where many dads help raise the children and moms work full or part time; where more judges will give greater amounts of time and thought to the decisions they render and use mechanisms to insure adherence to them; where all family and child custody evaluators will be adequately trained and function objectively; where matrimonial lawyers will continue to represent their clients well *and* try to persuade them to negotiate with honesty, integrity, and a sense of fairness; and the entire system and all of the structures that revolve around "divorce" will be more humane, beneficent, logical, coherent, and truly in the best interest of the children – with their being protected from abuse, exploitation, and alienation from either or both parents (and extended family members). If some of these recommendations are utilized by the respective professionals, and the laws governing divorce are changed nationally and/or in some of the states to be more humanistic and equitable, and if those decrees that already have been enacted are enforced, then the drama and trauma of marital breakup should become less painful and destructive for many experiencing it. And the prodigious effort invested in this volume will have been well worth it.

Florence W. Kaslow, Ph.D.
Palm Beach Gardens, FL, USA

References

American Psychological Association. (2010). Guidelines for child custody evaluations in family law proceedings. *American Psychologist, 65*(9), 863–867.

Baum, N., & Schnit, D. (2005). Self differentiation and narcissism in divorced parents' co-parental relationships and functioning. *Journal of Divorce and Remarriage, 42*(3/4), 33–60.

Bonach, K. (2007). Forgiveness intervention model: Application to co-parenting postdivorce. *Journal of Divorce and Remarriage, 48*(1–2), 105–123.

Boumil, M. M., & Friedman, J. (1996). *Deadbeat dads.* Westport, CN: Praeger.

Braver, S. L., & (with O'Connell, D). (1998). *Divorced dads.* New York: Jeremy P. Tarcher/Putman.

Freedman, S. (1998). Forgiveness and reconciliation: The importance of understanding how they differ. *Counseling and Values, 42*(3), 200–216.

Gold, L. (1992). *Between love and hate: A guide to civilized divorce*. New York: Plenum.

Kaslow, F. W. (2007). Post divorce relatedness between parents, their divorced sons, and their grandchildren: A pilot study. In C. A. Everett & R. E. Lee (Eds.), *When marriages fail: Systemic family therapy interventions and issues* (pp. 141–156). New York: Haworth Press.

Kaslow, F. W. (2010, Appendix III). Ceremony prepared in the 1980's for use with patients and at workshops and revised numerous times. *The divorce ceremony: A healing strategy.*

Ricci, I. (1980). *Mom's house, dad's house: Making shared custody work*. New York: Macmillan.

Tesler, P. H., & Thompson, P. (2006). *Collaborative divorce: The revolutionary new way to restructure your family, resolve legal issues, and move on with your life*. New York: Harper Collins.

Wallerstein, J. S., & Kelly, J. B. (1980). *Surviving the breakup: How children and parents cope with divorce*. New York: Basic Books.

Contributing Authors

Benjamin, G. Andrew H., J.D., Ph.D., ABPP (Board Certified Couple and Family Psychology). Affiliate Professor of Law and Affiliate Professor of Psychology, University of Washington, Seattle, Washington. Author of numerous articles in psychology journals and law reviews, principal author of *Family Evaluations in Custody Litigations: Reducing Risks of Ethical Infractions* and co-author of several other relevant books. gahb54@u.washington.edu

Benson, Sally S., J.D. Practicing Law in Palm Beach Gardens, FL., specializing in Family Law. President of "One Day at a Time," a 501(c)(3) which assists families and juveniles who are dealing with alcohol and drug addiction. Member of Akron Law Achievement Council and appointed by the Dean to assist University with decisions regarding the Law school.

Carter, Debra Kaye, Ph.D. Clinical and Forensic psychologist, licensed in Florida, certified as a Family Law Mediator and a Qualified Parenting Coordinator by Florida Supreme Court. Co-founder and Chief Clinical Officer of the National Cooperative Parenting Center (TheNCPC.com). Dr. Carter offers, and supervises, a wide spectrum of services to the Mental Health and Legal Communities and to families and children struggling with divorce-related issues. dkc@carterpsych.com

Kaslow, Florence W., Ph.D., ABPP (Board Certified, Clinical, Forensic, Couple and Family Psychology), Director, Kaslow Associates, a Family Business and Professional Practice Consulting Firm; Executive, Relational and Life Transition Coaching; Marital, family and divorce therapist and mediator. Distinguished Visiting Professor of Psychology, Florida Institute of Technology, Melbourne, Florida. Author or editor of 30 books including *The Dynamics of Divorce: A Life Cycle Perspective* with Dr. Lita L. Schwartz and over 180 articles in the professional literature. drfkaslow@bellsouth.net

Schwartz, Lita Linzer, Ph.D., APBB (Board Certified, Forensic Psychology), Distinguished Professor Emerita at Pennsylvania State University. In her independent practice, the focus was on parenting and child custody in divorce and adoption cases. She is a co-author with Dr. F. Kaslow of *Painful Partings: Divorce and Its Aftermath* and author of numerous other relevant books and articles. lls2@psu.edu

Acknowledgements

Without the 13 dads who participated as respondents, this book could not have happened. The same holds true for the myriad other male friends, colleagues, and clients over many years who have trusted me enough to confide many of the details of the stories of their stressful divorces and the long-term sequelae. To all of them, I want to express my deepest gratitude.

To my patient and understanding husband of many decades, Sol Kaslow, my thanks for just being there and encouraging me to write this book about a subject that he knows I believed so deeply needed to be covered. Honey, being married to you has been a wonderful experience, and it is important for the readers of this book to know that the contents did not emanate from any personal bitterness experienced in my own marriage to the great dad of my own children.

To my empathic, brilliant daughter, Dr. Nadine Kaslow, thanks for helping me broaden my sample of questionnaire respondents.

To my secretary, Lauren Kellar, who has diligently typed and retyped the pages of this manuscript for me. Without your help, it would not have ever gotten to the publisher!

To my outstanding editor at springer, Sharon Panulla, your collaboration and guidance, are ever so much appreciated.

And, to those who wrote the commentary sections, thank for your valuable contributions and the collegial manner in which you worked with me.

Florence W. Kaslow, Ph.D., ABPP
Palm Beach Gardens, FL
June 2012

Contents

1   **Evolution of Thought About Custody Decisions:**
     The Past 100 Years 1

2   **Case 1 Dr. Blue Eyes: Dreams That Turned into Nightmares** 17

3   **Case 2 Mr. Bob Straight: I Promised Myself I Would**
     Be a Good Dad 25

4   **Case 3 Dr. Jorge Garcia: Promises Made, Promises Kept,**
     Until Forever Is Too Long 31

5   **Case 4 Mr. Reuben Guy: The Nastiness Never Stopped** 37

6   **Case 5 Dr. Ron Dedicated: Why Can't Judges Also Be**
     Trained to "Do No Harm"? 45

7   **Case 6 Mr. Bill Brogan: Feeling Trapped, Escaping,**
     and "The Big Lie" 53

8   **Case 7 Mr. Terry Kelly's Saga of Betrayal** 61

9   **Case 8 Mr. Gene Goodman: My Life Revolves Around**
     My Kids Now 69

10 **Case 9 Dr. Ari Regis: The Relentless Demands**
     and Criticisms Never Cease 79

11 **Case 10 Mr. Arturo Miguel: Some Courts Deprive Dads**
     and Their Children of Each Other's Companionship/Love 89

12 **Case 11 Mr. Hy Hopes: The Fallout of Crazy in Love** 97

13 **Case 12 Dr. Zack Determined: It Is a Strange**
     World After All 105

14 Case Unlucky 13: My Greatest Loss 115

15 Case Analysis and Games Divorcing/Divorced People Play............... 125

**16 Commentaries on Cases: How Outcomes Might
      Have Been Different if Other Services
      or Professionals Had Been Utilized** 137
      Part I: Divorce Therapy, Divorce Mediation,
      and Collaborative Divorce 137
          Florence W. Kaslow, Ph.D., ABPP
      Part II: A Different Lawyer: A Different Result...................................... 148
          Sally S. Benson, J.D.
      Part III: Family Evaluation in Custody Litigation:
      Reducing Risks of Devastating Relationships 160
          G. Andrew H. Benjamin, J.D., Ph.D., ABPP
      Part IV: Parenting Coordination... 171
          Debra K. Carter, Ph.D.
      Part V: The Role of the Child Advocate 183
          Lita Linzer Schwartz, Ph.D., ABPP

**17 Why Can Some Individuals Share Their Children,
      While Others Cannot, or Will Not? Is Personality
      a Major Key?** 189

**18 Harken All Professionals Involved in the Tragedy
      of Divorce! The Urgency of Humanizing the Legal,
      Judicial, and Psychological Aspects of Divorce**.................................... 197

Appendix 1 Questionnaire Divorced Dads.. 213

Appendix 2 Model of Stages in the Divorce Process 225

Appendix 3 The Divorce Ceremony: A Healing Strategy 231

Author Index... 235

Subject Index... 239

Chapter 1
Evolution of Thought About Custody Decisions: The Past 100 Years

The Impact of the Industrial Revolution

In the United States, the advent of the strong legal and social preference for mother custody coincided with the beginnings of the industrial revolution when many fathers no longer spent most of their time being in or near the family homestead – working on the farm or somewhere in a nearby village. Our predominantly agrarian culture decreased markedly in size. Instead, he now left home early in the morning and often returned late in the evening after a long shift in a factory, mine, shop, corporate, or professional office. Mothers were often home alone with the children for long hours, and sometimes, this was true six days a week. The kinship or extended family structure which had prevailed in many families for centuries was replaced by the nuclear or conjugal family as many younger couples and their children moved from rural to urban, suburban, or metropolitan areas. This trend toward urbanization continued for many decades and decreased the closeness with and reliance on the extended family in many families.

Children now spent most of their time in the care of women – mothers, nannies, baby-sitters, neighbors, and schoolteachers (the vast majority of who are female). Over time in this and other countries in the Western world, children seemed to be the property of women – financially supported by a father they did not know very well.

In many families, the fathers' other key role besides that of financial provider was to be the disciplinarian – with many children being told when they misbehaved – "wait until your father gets home." For decades, many hardworking dads no longer shared countless hours on the farm working with their children. Instead, they had precious few hours to help their children with homework, play games with them, guide their Scout troops, coach their teams, or just "hang out" with them. When these dads finally got home from work, they were exhausted. And on weekends, their role was frequently to be Mr. Fixit for the long "honey do" list that had accumulated during the week. Many people who grew up during the pre-World War II era report that they rarely had a conversation or activity time alone with their dad and that they did not know him as a person. Mothers were at the hub of the family's interactions and communications.

F.W. Kaslow, *Divorced Fathers and Their Families: Legal, Economic, and Emotional Dilemmas*, DOI 10.1007/978-1-4614-5535-6_1,

These sweeping economic and societal developments of the first half of the twentieth century coincided with the spread of psychoanalytic thinking (the psychiatric deluge) from Germany and Austria to the United States and other Western countries (Freud, 1923, 1933). Great emphasis was and still is placed on the importance of the infant and young child forming a strong bond with the mother or "mothering one" (Sullivan, 1953). Conversely, little emphasis was placed on the centrality of the fathers' role as a parent or supportive partner to his wife. In some of the literature, he almost seemed to be relegated to being a bystander at best. Think of the movies you have seen of childbirth where only women were allowed in the birthing area, with the exception of course of the male doctor, if there were not a midwife performing the delivery.

This began to change in the late 1930s and 1940s and during World War II when many women entered the workforce replacing men who were in the Armed Services. Other women became WACS and WAVES and nurses serving in military hospitals (both in the United States and overseas) and were not on the home front; it was seen as their patriotic duty. Home and children were no longer the epicenter of their universe. When the war ended, many women did not return to being full-time moms and homemakers. They enjoyed the stimulation of the workaday world and relished earning a paycheck. The dynamics changed in many family constellations as married women began to forge a separate, personal identity in addition to being Mrs. Somebody or somebody's mommy. Their roles, status, and choices in the world expanded.

The Feminist Revolution

This period of rapid change was followed by the emergence of the feminist revolution, and the writings of women like Betty Friedan, whose book, *The Feminine Mystique,* appeared in 1963. Women were urged to be assertive and independent and to fulfill their potential in all aspects of life (Friedan, 1963). *Ms. Magazine,* an American liberal feminist magazine, was cofounded in 1971 by feminist activist Gloria Steinem (Steinem, 1983) and Letty Cottin Pogrebin, its first editor, and several others and has continued to be published into the second decade of the twenty-first century – under the helm of different editors and publishers – sometimes stirring up great controversies about issues such as day-care sexual abuse, Satanic ritual abuse, and the "We Had Abortions" petitions featured which over 5,000 women signed revealing their unashamed decisions to have an abortion. Motherhood ceased being the only pathway to fulfillment or the totality of many women's lives (Greer, 1984). Some women wanted it all – career, family, and income they personally earned plus status built on their achievements and separate identity, not just based on who their husband was and what he did. More women attended college, graduate, and professional schools and entered professions that had previously been considered "masculine." Their sense of their own power and competence grew (Steinem, 1983). Bella Abzug, an attorney, became a member of the United States House of Representatives from New York in 1971 and joined with other leading feminists including Friedan and Steinem to found the National Women's Political Caucus. For married women to be able to have it all, they wanted and needed their husbands to assume a more significant and central role in their family's life in terms of being available emotionally and conversationally to them, participating in their children's activities, chauffeuring, childcaring, and helping with homework – being a real co-parent as well as the woman's best friend, lover, confidante, playmate, and contributor to the family's daily life as a wage earner (McGoldrick, Anderson, & Walsh, 1989). This development happened concurrently with several others, and each impacted on the others. For example, labor laws had been passed that shortened the workday. These were exciting and heady times for women.

And as the wives/mothers wanted more time and energy to work outside of the home and family and to earn salaries on their own, some fathers/husbands were working less hours and became more involved with their children and family activities. An increasing number of dads also began not only to cook at family barbecues and picnics but also to prepare and serve some family meals in the home.

Natural Childbirth

Backtracking a little, another development which began in Great Britain in the 1940s had a spin-off effect on fathers' involvement in child rearing. Dr. G.D. Reid's book *Childbirth without Fear* (Reid, 1944/1953) heralded the advantages of *natural childbirth*, that is, childbirth without the woman receiving any anesthesia. This method entails months of preparation during pregnancy for the actual event of childbirth – reframing the experience of contractions from pain to the belief that the contractions are to be considered welcome signs that the baby will soon arrive. Women are taught breathing and relaxation exercises in classes to help them feel more comfortable during pregnancy, so they can stay awake and be able to cooperate with the physician by bearing down during the birthing process. Husbands attend the classes, learning to truly "be with" their wives through supportive and encouraging comments, holding her hand, and rubbing her back or tummy during the delivery. He is prepared to be present in the delivery room and thus truly involved with and bonded to mother and baby from conception onward. A dramatic vignette illuminates this approach and its beneficial consequences:

> A client of mine, after reading Dr. Reid's book, decided to have natural childbirth in the 1950s. There were few obstetricians in such cities as Philadelphia, where she lived, who were trained and willing to do "natural childbirth" deliveries at that time. The involvement of her husband was so meaningful to her and laid the foundation for his strong attachment to their children and vice versa. In this approach husbands are not banished from what is considered the world of women and babies – their role is seen as vital, collaborative, and highly valued. Like the mother, the father becomes a closely attached parent when the newborn's life begins. When their first born, a daughter, arrived, she did not cry. The delivery room filled up immediately and the on-call pediatrician's first question to the husband was "did your wife have any anesthesia?" When he said "no", that she had natural childbirth, he told them, "then there is a chance the baby will live", which she did, despite needing weeks

in the hospital in an isolet. She recounts that without her husband's comforting presence it would have been an even more horrible ordeal for her. Both knew the problem was not caused by a medical error.

If after having children the parents are divorced, fathers like the one described in the foregoing vignette who have been so integrally involved in their children's lives, by choice, are likely to be loath to relinquish daily contact, participation in school and sporting events, celebrating birthdays and holidays together, knowing their child's friends, reading together at bedtime, and sharing family vacations. They may fight very hard to prevent such an extrusion or cut off from happening.

History of Sociolegal Custody Decisions

From biblical times forward to the first third of the twentieth century, in many countries, women and children were considered and treated as "possessions" of the husband/father and his biological family or clan. If the mother died or there was a separation or divorce, the children automatically remained with the father's family, according to prevailing customs and mores. In agrarian societies comprised mostly of extended, kinship families, there was always a grandmother or aunts and older cousins to help the father with the childcare and child-rearing activities in the event of a mother's absence. The family in a sense constituted its own village.

By the 1940s, as indicated earlier, belief systems, values, as well as family form, structure, and dynamics were undergoing prodigious modifications, and these were leading to legislative changes about divorce and child custody – a trend that continues to this day. From a tradition of a presumption of father custody, which still prevails almost exclusively in some non-Western countries of the world, the United States shifted to a presumption for mother custody – especially during the "tender years" (Hodges, 1991; Stuart & Abt, 1981) which led to jurists ordering children until they were age 7 or double 7–14 years to remain with their mothers. Roughly, 90–95% of court custody awards specified for the next six decades that the primary custodial or primary residential parent should be the mother, unless she was found to be "unfit." This de facto doctrine appears to have influenced several of the cases included in this volume. Unfit usually means seriously mentally ill, mentally challenged, abusive, a prostitute, or an addict. Such allegations need to be substantiated and that can be complicated to do.

The vast majority of decisions, as part of the marital settlement agreement (MSA), including the property settlement or division of assets, award the marital home, child support, and spousal support to the woman. Within the last decade, many of the states have shifted to a presumption for joint custody. Yet recent orders from actual cases obtained from professionals across the country engaged in the divorce process indicate that in point of fact, many of the judges still defer to the long prevailing doctrine of maternal preference, especially during the children's tender years.

Losses and More Losses

Many of the divorcing and divorced dads I have counseled, coached, or interviewed for this book recounted the number of *gigantic losses* they experienced concurrently or sequentially just before, during, and after the legal divorce was finalized. Not only has contact and access to children been curtailed, but existing relationships have been impacted by the conflict between the parents. Losses often include close relationships to some members of the former in-law family whom they cared about who believed keeping in touch with "him" would be interpreted as betrayal or disloyalty by the ex-wife. Sometimes his family, particularly his parents, may have seemed to favor his ex-wife because she apparently was perceived as the conduit they would have to go through to maintain closeness to their grandchildren and influential as to what the children's "opinions" of the paternal grandparents would be over time. Many men bemoan the loss of couple friends who often feel caught in the tug of war, but since the women customarily make the social arrangements, they find the wife gets "custody" of the friends. It may take many months before he realizes he will have to take the initiative to reconnect with former couple friends. There are exceptions to this of course, especially when friends are eager to have a newly available bachelor buddy to introduce to other female friends or if the ex-wife has done something they consider reprehensible, like having an affair or getting involved in the substance abuse or gambling scene.

Most of the literature on divorce portrays the husband as being the one who has the affair, but not all men who cheat do so with single women. Many prefer a married woman as their "lover" as she is less likely to demand time together on weekends and holidays, and like him, she is also concerned about "getting caught" and upsetting her marriage and family, so she is apt to be more circumspect – unless they jointly decide to go for their divorces. Many married women admit to having had affairs, and some even gossip about it to their friends. Many men who are cuckolded decide to seek a divorce when they initially learn of their wife's clandestine affair. More than half of the divorced dads interviewed for the case studies in this book (seven to be exact) had become aware of their wife's infidelity; only two of the men indicated that they had engaged in extramarital sexual activity.

Since the man is generally the one pressured to move out of the marital home, no matter if it is the woman who seeks or precipitated the breakup, he may forgo whatever contact he had previously with neighbor friends. And family pets usually remain in the family home which was awarded to the wife, especially when she has primary custody of the children. The cumulative total of these losses, the dislocation he experiences, and the change of lifestyle from daily living as part of his family of creation to living alone much of the time with his shattered dreams of marriage and his family can leave him not only angry, bewildered, resentful, and broke but also feeling lonely, forgotten, and adrift. Often men whose wives were the ones who wanted and pushed for the divorce, report as do women when the situation is reversed, that they feel rejected, discarded, and unwanted and that their sense of self-worth and self-confidence have taken a severe bruising. It is within the context of this larger picture that he tries to find living quarters where the children, when in residence with him, can have their own or a bedroom to share with a sibling, can have adequate indoor and outdoor play space, and live close enough to their school to get there easily if and when they sleep at dad's house and to their friends – so they won't feel isolated when they are with him – if he can afford it on what remains out of his paycheck for his own use. (Many of the dads in this study who were told precipitously that they had to leave or came home to find themselves locked out initially moved in with a friend – until they could pull themselves together emotionally or financially. None went home to their parents, as some women do in similar circumstances.) Although the court may have awarded him X number of days and nights per month of access, it tends to be done more according to a formula (called guidelines) than by individualized planning tailored around the specific needs and personalities of each unique postdivorce family. And these families vary enormously – one custody plan does not fit all!

Best Interest of the Child: As Determined by Whom?

The doctrine of "the best interest of the child" (Stuart & Abt, 1981), first articulated by Supreme Court Justice Louis Brandeis in 1925, remains a key legal and psychological premise which supposedly undergirds custody decisions. The crucial factor therefore should be *who determines the "best interest of these particular children" and what their training is in child development and family dynamics*. Is it the presiding judge, the lawyer who presents the strongest case, or a mediator who is trained in mediation as well as law – but not in complex family relationship systems? Or is it the more dominant parent or a court appointed custody evaluator? (see commentary on child custody by Benjamin in this book). Hopefully, if the latter, the person is a well-trained psychologist who has conducted an objective psychological battery on each member of the family, interviewed each parent alone and with the children, observed the child interacting (preferably in their own home environment) with each parent, gathered information from objective collateral sources like the child's teachers, and has followed the child custody evaluation guidelines of the American Psychological Association (APA, 2010). After the report is tendered to the court based on a comprehensive set of findings, the *judge* or other decision-maker can generate a well-deliberated, informed plan for the parents and for the children. If the couple have completed a mediation with a behavioral science trained mediator, who is an expert in family dynamics and conflict resolution (Folberg, Milne, & Salem, 2004), or gone through a collaborative divorce (Tesler & Thompson, 2006), hopefully both parties will have had maximum input into any plan for the future care and well-being of *both of their children* and not have let the decision-making fall to people who barely know their children and probably will never see them again after the divorce decree is finalized. The two parents conceived or adopted their children and are the adults responsible for their ongoing care, which should include *decision-making based on their love and concern for their children's well-being* above all. And there should be a proviso for reconsidering the plan every two to three years as the developmental needs of the children and the time, health, personality, and availabilities of the parents change. Strange indeed how some of the most crucial divorce decisions impacting families and their futures are made by relative strangers and are inflexibly etched in stone! (Schwartz & Kaslow, 1997).

In the post-separation and postdivorce family, the two parents remain or become co-parents, who live in separate residences. In actuality, there are two postdivorce families – his and hers – and many children will spend some time in mom's house and some time in dad's. The reality is that the children now have two homes, and almost always, the responsibility of going back and forth falls to them (Blau, 1993). Since the word "custody" implies ownership, many professionals prefer the term and concept– residential parent to custodial parent – with the parent with whom they are residing on any given day having the major responsibility. Being a visiting parent or the children visiting one parent occasionally is a plan best reserved for situations with extenuating circumstances, such as when one parent is in the military; the parent has a job that entails much travel and the parent cannot make a commitment to a regular schedule; has had to relocate and so the "typical" schedule is not feasible; the child has "special needs," physically, intellectually, or emotionally and alternating between homes with any frequency would be too difficult; or the parent is physically impaired or mentally or emotionally too limited to handle solo parenting responsibilities. Otherwise, if both parents are committed to the parenting role and responsibilities and are deemed "fit," why should they not have shared and relatively equal custody?

"No Fault": Really?

Many states have shifted from fault to "no fault" laws, and decision-making is no longer predicated on seeking to determine blame for what has gone awry in the marriage. Often those divorcing very much want to project the blame for all that has gone wrong on their soon to be ex-spouse and are infuriated when the law does not sanction this. One may have "committed adultery" once or many times, and been negligent or uninvolved with their children, cheated on their income tax or in business, been in different kinds of rehabilitation programs repeatedly, but their behavioral history may not be deemed relevant. Proving one to be "unfit" is difficult. In many states, as long as one is deemed "fit," they are usually awarded some amount of parenting time, even if initially it is under the supervision of the court. This is most apt to occur if a parent has been accused of being negligent, abusive, or inept. However, if he or she has been involved with another person while still married, courts in many states close their eyes to this behavior and do not consider what it conveys to children about "the sanctity of the family" or the importance of concepts of loyalty, integrity, and "fidelity." Adultery is no longer "grounds" for divorce or for losing of access to one's children. In states where one can only get a "no fault divorce," adultery, or coming out of the closet, may still be used as reasons for the divorce, but this charge alone is not the sole determinant of who gets primary custody.

It is believed by most mental health professionals and substantiated by much research that *children need ongoing access to both parents, preferably who have a stable co-parenting relationship* (Ahrons, 1994; Schwartz & Kaslow, 1997; Roberson, Sabo, & Wickel, 2011) so they continue to feel loved, valued, and important to both and know that although their parents are divorced from each other, they are "not divorced from the children." Often the thought is expressed that children in intact families live with less than perfect parents and that a higher standard should not be set for divorced parents. Yet how do we factor in the reality that the bilateral postdivorce family usually has a much more difficult task of child rearing than married co-parents do and may indeed need to be more skilled, empathic, and compassionate, and not embroiled in continuing battles of one parent attacking or stonewalling the other?

Additional Recent Trends

Kramer vs. Kramer

Let us return to some of the historical trends that have brought us to the current prevailing practices in the child custody/residence vista. In 1979, the emotional picture *Kramer vs. Kramer* (1979) caused quite a sensation and won the Academy Award for Best Picture of the Year. Top-notch dramatic actors Dustin Hoffman and Meryl Streep played the lead roles of Ted and Joanna Kramer, the divorced couple. Streep's character, Joanna, left their son, Billy, to be raised by Ted. Joanna did not want custody of their son, then about four years old, because she wanted to be free to "find herself," like other liberated women were doing. The boy went to live with his dad, who had to quickly figure out how to be "Mr. Mom." He soon taught himself how to fulfill this role well, and he and his son soon began to enjoy their new relationship. But dad lost his job because he had to take time off from work to go to his son's school, something the business world was not prepared for; there was no flextime for dads.

Billy found it difficult to understand why his Mom did not want him. When the mother returned about 18 months later and wanted to resume primary custody, more conflict ensued. Just as dads cannot "abandon" children for a while and then expect to resume their former relationship with the child and ex-spouse and want everyone to *act as if* their vacation from parenting never occurred or to be happy for them because they "did their own thing," moms who take a leave of absence from parenting also experience consequences, often long term, based on the child's own reactions and interpretation, and not predicated on what the other parent might have told the child in a disparaging or blaming manner. Initially, in response to her situation, the court returned Billy to her as primary custodial parent, but she soon realized that by then, her young son had built up too much resentment toward her and wanted to be back with his dad. They all concurred mom would be the parent he would visit.

Some men who saw this film realized they too could become and enjoy being the primary residential parent or at least having the child(ren) with them 1/3–1/2 of the time and thus still remain active and very involved in their children's lives. Many dads also became aware of what being a very involved single parent entailed and of the toll it could take on their workaday and personal life.

The Men's Movement

Meanwhile, another movement was slowly evolving. The men's movement provided impetus to the importance of men being verbally and physically expressive fathers who demonstrate their love and affection in words, gestures, and behaviors (Levant & Kopecky, 1995). Central to the birth of the movement was Robert Bly, an award winning poet and student of mythology and Jungian psychology. Bly offered an analysis of the deep confusion and alienation experienced by modern-day men tracing it back to the start of the industrial revolution alluded to earlier in this chapter. As dads were often out of the home all day and into the evening because of work demands, physically and emotionally, they became less connected to their families. Those most affected were young boys, who lost not only the emotional security of having their fathers around but also the presence and participation of other, older men in their lives, according to those in the mythopoetic men's movement. Men lost touch with what Bly called "the male mode of feeling," something that provides a son with a certain confidence and awareness of what it is to be male.

Because mothers continued to stay home with the children, they did not experience a similar type of loss of contact with their children. Girls stay close to their mother throughout childhood and adolescence and receive from her, what Bly called, the "spiritual food" of her presence that demonstrates how to be a woman. He predicted, however, that as women increasingly joined the work force out of their homes, similar damage would happen to girls and women that had come to typify boy's and men's emotional inner life.

Bly posited that boys have experienced this mass exodus of the men from their day-to-day lives as a great wounding. They felt longing, grief, and anger at this loss, and it was buried deep within the "psyche." The consequences of this wounding led men to distrust older men and to require too much from the women in their lives. Men learned to detach themselves from their emotions and to seek fulfillment through work and the rewards their careers bring.

During the 1960s and 1970s, a "new" male model emerged that was, in certain ways, a positive move away from the military and corporate "warrior ideal" of previous generations. Bly noted that these men learned to be receptive, but it was not enough to sustain their marriages. In every relationship, something fierce is needed occasionally by both the man and the woman. Some men became able to say, "I can feel your pain, and I consider your life as important as mine." But many men still could not articulate what they wanted (Levant & Pollack, 1995).

In men's meetings, Bly discussed how a woman can do a good job bringing up a baby boy through adolescence but that she cannot initiate her son into manhood without sacrificing her femininity. In his opinion, this is a task only the older men can accomplish, be it a father or another closely involved man. He believed boys are forced to turn to each other for rites of passage into manhood, increasing the allure of gangs, fraternities, etc. Or, as they get older, they turn to the women in their lives. But while many men learned nurturing qualities and vulnerability from…women, those feelings are never fully internalized until men see them exhibited by a respected older man. Older males can uniquely empathize with and nurture the younger boy. The adult male can never fully do that in adulthood for his wife or his children, unless it has been modeled for him [by a man].

Bly observed three types of men who came to his workshops: the first group had experienced severe pain or grief in their lives, often through physical or sexual abuse, and were seeking some understanding of these emotions in order to heal themselves. The second group was unable to get in touch with their life force and spontaneity; they were incapable of expressing anger (i.e., were emotionally frozen) and felt closed off from "the fire within." The third group he called "terminal adolescents," who needed to learn to let go of their fears of manhood and of responsibility.

In Bly's *men's-only* workshops and retreats, he and his co-facilitators used story, shamanic work, drumming, dance, music, and discussion to explore men's unique approach to emotional experience. Participants were often astonished to discover feelings they did not know they possessed. Some found they could let go of much of the posturing that they normally did when women were present. They reported a sense of homecoming and familiarity, a welcome breakdown of feelings of isolation and loneliness.

The reaction of feminists and pro-feminist men to the *awakening of men's consciousness* at its most balanced was simply to caution men not to forget or reject their mother's or women's contributions to their lives in their excited explorations into their male psyches. Other feminist commentators appeared to reject any possibility that men can gather together by themselves and not turn into "good old boys," capable of doing nothing more than talking sports, business, and women-bashing. They accepted the idea that it is beneficial for women to gather without men, but they wanted to deny that right to men, protesting that whether the men meant it or not, they were glorifying the essential blood-thirsting tradition of the warrior. Conversely, in point of fact, the men's movement taught many men how to feel and communicate their feelings and how to bond emotionally *and not to glorify the warrior persona*.

The type of gender role socialization influenced by traditional masculine ideology that Bly highlighted, which is believed to force boys to suppress or repress their natural emotionality, often leads to development of mild to moderate of alexithymia, that is, lack of words and of the ability to identify and describe feelings (Sifneos, 1967; Levant, 1998). In the 1980s and 1990s, many male mental health professionals became active in the men's movement to get in touch with their own feelings so as to become more expressive to their partners and children and to be able to help male clients do so also (Levant, 2006).

The women's movement enabled women to break away from outdated and negative stereotypes and patterns. The emergence of "Goddess Consciousness" enabled many women to rejoice in their femininity in its myriad forms. It enabled them to come into their relationships with the world and with men strengthened, renewed, and more confident.

Several decades later, men began finding their way to also break away from rigid stereotypical patterns. Thus, in some ways, the men's movement (Levant & Pollack, 1995, 2009; Philpot, Brooks, Lusterman, & Nutt, 1997; Pollack, 1995), which has continued beyond Bly's innovative and startling activities and *gone through various modifications,* has paralleled the mammoth importance and life trajectory changing impact of the feminist movement. A field of study designated "The Psychology of Men and Masculinity" has evolved that investigates such issues and concerns as traditional and changing male ideologies, the male gender role strain paradigm, gender role socialization, normative male alexithymia, and the implication of all of these factors in men's relationships and in their treatment (Brooks & Silverstein, 1995; Levant & Williams, 2009). These patterns and processes also affect their choices, feelings, and behaviors in marriage and divorce.

In sum, as women sought more satisfaction and recognition outside of the home and family in the worlds of work, philanthropic activity, sports, and organization life, many men who had participated in or read about the men's movement and/or who felt something lacking in their emotional lives opted to become more engaged with their families of origin (parental family) and families of creation (partner and children). Subsequently, men who have divorced or are divorcing have tended to be more integrally involved with their children and loathe to settle for a residence (custody) and visitation plan that allows them only every other weekend, plus maybe one weekday or weekend night for dinner, one or two vacation weeks a year, and having to negotiate additional time to see their children with their ex-partner. They not only believe they have or should have a *legal* right to be much more integrally involved in their children's lives in terms of time together but have an *emotionally* compelling need to have almost daily access and contact – beyond text messages, e-mailing, and phone calls – that is critical to their well-being and their child's. Alexithymia does not characterize all men, and many men are quite capable of expressing and demonstrating a wide range of emotions and parenting skills.

Alternative Routes to Divorce

Until the 1970s, the primary route to getting a divorce was an adversarial one in which one partner hired an attorney who served their partner with divorce papers – sometimes much to their surprise and consternation. In many states, they had to allege "fault" and prove it. After undergoing his own very painful divorce, attorney Jim Coogler, (1978) proclaimed "there must be a better way." Many others, like John Haynes, agreed and moved to the forefront of the mediation movement (Haynes, 1981). Thus, using an alternative dispute resolution (ADR) strategy became a separate subspecialty within marital and family psychology/therapy, and many couples turned to divorce therapists to help them decide if breaking up their marriage was really what they wanted to do and if so, what might be the least detrimental option for doing this. In the 1990s, collaborative divorce was born and entered the mainstream as another alternative dispute resolution strategy (Tesler & Thompson, 2006). These are discussed in Chapter 16, section "Divorce Therapy, Divorce Mediation, and Collaborative Divorce."

Other Major Contemporary Developments

Despite the availability of alternative dispute resolution strategies for divorce, many acrimonious divorces continue to occur entailing bitter battles over what has traditionally been called custody or primary resident, visitation, or access, so well as about the financial issues of child and spousal support (alimony), and the distribution of property and other marital assets. Unfortunately, some embittered spouses have drawn their children into the fray, and they have become children caught in the middle with deeply divided loyalties or worse yet subjected to what has been called brainwashing (Clawar & Rivlin, 1991) and parental alienation (Baker, 2007; Bernet, 2010). Although many have debated the existence of this syndrome, more and more professional articles and books are appearing that describe and document the behavior and its impact on the children and the target (or lost) parent (Baker & Ben-Ami, 2011; Vassiliou, 1998). First-person stories by targeted parents are also on the market (Hudson, 2011).

In 2006, the National Organization for Women (NOW) denounced parental alienation as a marketed legal strategy that had caused much harm to victims of abuse, especially women and children, and called it "junk science." They posited the term was proposed by abusive ex-husbands. But the past few years have witnessed some marked changes in their attitudes. Currently, many women are petitioning NOW to reverse its stand saying "alienation does exist…it devastates families." They attest that women as well as men sometimes are the targeted parent and point out that even when it is the man, the women on his side of the family are negatively affected by the alienation process. They emphasize that alienation, no matter how it is perpetrated, constitutes emotional abuse of children and that the stance is a misinformed position (Women's Rights Petition to NOW, 2012).

As indicated earlier, some states have rewritten their divorce laws to favor shared parental responsibility or joint custody. Within the past decade, the Florida Legislature dropped the words "custody" and "visitation" and instead mandated "time-sharing" of the children. Now, "primary residence" is only a designation to be used so schools know where to send records. The concept of "rehabilitation alimony" introduced in the 1980s as an alternative to permanent alimony when the recipient party is employable with additional training/education has been replaced with "durational" (time-limited) alimony. Thus, for example, someone married three years is no longer entitled to permanent alimony (unless there are serious extenuating circumstances), and the payer party is not encumbered with a lifelong dependent.

Mother's, Father's, and Children's Rights and Needs

Much has been written in the professional and popular literature about the legal, economic, and emotional rights of mothers (Weitzman, 1985) during and postdivorce. Similarly, many books and articles have been published about the needs and best interests of children of divorce (Ahrons, 1994; Hakvoort, Bos, Van Balen, & Hermanns, 2011; Hodges, 1991). Father's rights groups have addressed and advocated for the legal rights of fathers, sometimes in a very hostile and combative manner. But little has been written from the devoted, loving dads' point of view in terms of his emotional needs, rights, and quality of life during and postdivorce. This book is written to fill that gap by providing a forum for a representative group of such voices. It seemed the best way to do this was to invite various men, divorced between four and 40 years, to tell their stories. And they have – poignantly, honestly, and engagingly. In reading about them, it is important to be aware that many of their divorces occurred before the more recent changes discussed above.

The Case Studies

Thus as author, I constructed a questionnaire and interviewed 13 divorced men, some of whom I knew personally and others who were recommended to me by friends, clients, and colleagues. I interviewed all of them in person, driving cross state to interview one person and flying to another city to conduct three of the interviews to encompass more diversity in the sample. All responded to the same questionnaire to maximize consistency in the focus and information being sought. To my knowledge, none of the respondents are or have ever been "deadbeat dads"; all have paid the requisite alimony and child support in a timely way and gone beyond that in absorbing many additional expenses. None have been physically or sexually abusive of their children or ex-wives; one had a history of alcohol abuse and has been sober for the past 18 years, and another had a brief excursion into drugs after his divorce to assuage the pain of divorce and loss of his children until he became the full-time "Mr. Mom" and wanted to exemplify good behavior to his children. They all fall into a category I call "*devoted dads.*"

The identities of the men kind enough to share their stories have been carefully disguised to protect their and their families' privacy and confidentiality. This has been done in a manner that does not interfere with the essence and substance of the narratives, which I have written up in the form of case stories for each chapter.

Prior to finalizing the questionnaire, I sent it to two psychology (professors) colleagues, who are divorced dads who have spoken to me about their trials and tribulations with their children over a period of many years. They were part of the inspiration for this book. I asked them to review the questionnaire and see if they thought it needed any modifications or additions. I also hoped they would agree to participate. Both were helpful in making comments but refused to be respondents.

I asked and got permission to use parts of one of their responses (paraphrased slightly) as it illustrates poignantly the long-term sadness and painful impact of divorce on many father–child relationships (see below). This is not the kind of hurt one can just "let go of." It lingers and reoccurs. These passages also carry some self-recriminations – in which he conveys his sense of responsibility for what happened. His daughter, the elder of the two children, has refused to see or communicate with him for years. He has worked hard to rebuild a reasonably good relationship with his son and now daughter-in-law and teenage grandson who have chosen to live nearby his and his wife's home:

> I have pored over your questionnaire and generally admire its thoroughness and incisive probing. My only substantive reaction is that you might make use of questions concerning relationships with in-laws and grandparents. A divorce, as you know, may cause in-laws to experience a deep sense of rejection and abandonment. I think their hurt and loss merit more attention as well as their sense of helplessness in the face of what is happening to their child and their child's spouse…in-laws can also prosecute and condemn in everyday talk. What are children to think and feel?
>
> I have also noticed gender issues in divorce. Divorced mothers tend to bind their daughters to them and may allow their sons to continue to pursue a relationship with the father. Thus, the mother may require the daughter to join her in believing that the divorced father abandoned them and emotionally rejected them. The son, however, may not accept this way of thinking. He may work out a new relationship with the divorced father and enjoy new freedom from maternal control.
>
> Thank you for accepting my opting out of being one of your divorced dads. Revisiting these issues is hard for me. I am never far from lingering feelings of sadness and loss. In all candor, my divorce from my children's mother is my greatest failure in life. I feel guilty, embarrassed, and deeply sad for my children. I should have done better. I did not do better because I was immature, self-centered, and insufficiently guided by good foundational values and high-road motivations. Whatever mistakes others made, these were my mistakes, and they are sufficient to occupy my thoughts of (self) blame. The one thing I had right, after the breakup, was to keep my children out of the middle by not asking them anything about what was being said, not appealing to them or pleading any case to them, saying nothing bad about their mother and not trying to divide their loyalty. I offered no defense and mounted no offense.

I fully understood his declination, especially knowing that no matter what gentle and generous overtures he has made, he has not heard from his daughter in years. His letter encapsulates the pervasive pathos of divorce that so many experienced and that this book, perhaps with a degree of grandiosity, hopes it may play a role in diminishing.

There can be no doubt that wherever possible, protracted *Wars of the Roses* (1989) should be avoided, as they are detrimental to all.

References

Ahrons, C. R. (1994). *The good divorce: Keeping your family together when your marriage comes apart*. New York: Harper Collins.

American Psychological Association. (2010). Guidelines for child custody evaluations in family law proceedings. *American Psychologist, 65*(9), 863–867.

Baker, A. L. (2007). *Adult children of parental alienation syndrome: Breaking the ties that bind.* New York: Norton.

Baker, A. L., & Ben-Ami, N. (2011). To turn a child against a parent is to turn and child against himself: The direct and indirect effect of exposure to parental alienation strategies on self-esteem and well being. *Journal of Divorce and Remarriage, 52*(5), 472–489.

Bernet, W. (Ed.). (2010). *Parental alienation, DSM-5 and ICD-11.* Springfield, IL: Charles C. Thomas.

Blau, M. (1993). *Families apart: Ten keys to successful co-parenting.* New York: G.P. Putnam & Sons.

Brooks, G. R., & Silverstein, L. S. (1995). Understanding the dark side of masculinity: An interactive systems model. In R. F. Levant & W. S. Pollack (Eds.), *A new psychology of men* (pp. 280–333). New York: Basic Books.

Clawar, S. S., & Rivlin, B. V. (1991). *Children held hostages: Dealing with programmed and brainwashed children.* Chicago: American Bar Association Section of Family Law.

Coogler, O. J. (1978). *Structured mediation in divorce settlement.* Lexington, MA: D.C. Heath.

Folberg, J., Milne, A. L., & Salem, P. (2004). *Divorce and family mediation.* New York: Guilford.

Freud, S. (1923). *The ego and the Id.* (Standard ed., Vol. 19). London: Hogarth Press.

Freud, S. (1933). *New introductory lectures on psychoanalysis.* (J. Strachey, Ed., & J. Strachey, Trans.) New York: W.W.Norton.

Friedan, B. (1963). *The feminine mystique.* New York: Dell Publishing.

Greer, G. (1984). *Sex and destiny: The politics of human fertility.* London: Pan Books.

Hakvoort, E. M., Bos, H. M., Van Balen, F., & Hermanns, J. M. (2011). Post divorce relationships in families and children's psychosocial adjustment. *Journal of Divorce & Remarriage, 52*(1–4), 125–146.

Haynes, J. M. (1981). *Divorce mediation.* New York: Springer.

Hodges, W. F. (1991). *Interventions for children of divorce: Custody, access and psychotherapy* (2nd ed.). Hoboken: Wiley.

Hudson, B. (2011). *Two versions: The other side of fame and family.* Bellevue, WA: Dailey Swan.

Levant, R. F. (1998). Desperately seeking language: Understanding, assessing and treating normative male alexithymia. In W. S. Pollock & R. F. Levant (Eds.): New Psychotherapy for Men Hoboken, (pp. 35–56) NJ: Wiley.

Levant, R. F. (2006). *Effective psychotherapy with men.* (DVD & Viewer's guide). San Francisco: Psychotherapy.net.

Levant, R. F., & Kopecky, G. (1995). *Masculinity reconstructed.* New York: Dutton.

Levant, R. F., & Pollack, W. S. (1995). A new psychology of men: Where have we been? Where are we doing? In R. F. Levant & W. S. Pollack (Eds.), *A new psychology of men* (pp. 384–387). New York: Basic Books.

Levant, R. F., & Pollack, W. S. (2009). A new psychology of men and masculinity. In R. F. Levant & C. F. Williams (Eds.), *The Wiley-Blackwell handbook of family psychology* (pp. 588–599). Malden, MA: Wiley.

Levant, R. F., & Williams, C. F. (2009). The psychology of men and masculinity. In R. F. Levant & C. F. Williams (Eds.), *The Wiley-Blackwell handbook of family psychology* (pp. 588–599). Malden, MA: Wiley.

McGoldrick, M., Anderson, C. M., & Walsh, F. (Eds.). (1989). *Women in families: A framework for family therapy.* New York: W.W.Norton.

Philpot, D. L., Brooks, G. R., Lusterman, D. D., & Nutt, R. L. (1997). *Bridging separate gender worlds.* Washington, DC: American Psychological Association.

Pollack, W. S. (1995). No man is an island. Toward a new psychoanalytic psychology of men. In W. S. Pollack & R. F. Levant (Eds.), *A new psychology of men* (pp. 33–67). New York: Basic Books.

Reid, G. D. (1944/1953). *Childbirth without fear: The principles & practice of natural childbirth.* New York: Harper Brothers.

Roberson, P. E., Sabo, M., & Wickel, K. (2011). Internal working models of attachment and postdivorce coparent relationships. *Journal of Divorce and Remarriage, 52*(1), 187–201.

Schwartz, L. L., & Kaslow, F. W. (1997). *Painful partings: Divorce and its aftermath*. New York: Wiley.

Sifneos, P. E. (1967). Clinical observations on some patients suffering from a variety of psychosomatic diseases. *Proceedings of the 17th European Conference on Psychosomatic Research*. Basil, Switzerland: Kargel.

Steinem, G. (1983). *Outrageous acts and everyday rebellions*. New York: Henry Holt.

Stuart, I. R., & Abt, L. E. (1981). *Children of separation and divorce: Management and treatment*. New York: Van Nostrand Reinhold.

Sullivan, H. S. (1953). *The interpersonal theory of psychiatry*. New York: Norton.

Tesler, P. H., & Thompson, P. (2006). *Collaborative divorce: The revolutionary new way to reconstruct your family, resolve legal issues, and move on with your life*. New York: Harper Collins.

Vassiliou, D. (1998). *Parental alienation syndrome: The lost parent's perspective*. Master thesis, McGill University, Department of Educational Psychology, Montreal, QE.

Weitzman, L. J. (1985). *The divorce revolution: The unexpected social and economic consequences for women and children in America*. New York: Free Press.

Women's Rights Petition to NOW. (2012). www.change.org/petitions/women-want-now-to-change-their-position. Retrieved from www.change.org.

Films

Benton, R. (Writer), & Benton, R. (Director). (1979). *Kramer vs. Kramer* [Motion picture]. Columbia pictures.

Leeson, M. (Writer), & Divito, D. (Director). (1989). *The war of the roses* [Motion picture]. Twentieth Century Fox & Gracie Films.

Chapter 2
Case 1 Dr. Blue Eyes: Dreams That Turned into Nightmares

Brief Personal History

A tall, neatly groomed man of 68 years, Dr. BE, has a degree in a medical specialty plus he has taken some graduate courses. He was born, raised, and educated in a large, east coast metropolitan city and now maintains a solo practice on the west coast of Florida and is on staff at several local hospitals.

His dad was a prominent and charismatic physician who was also a composer and an artist. Dr. BE plays an instrument and finds pleasure and relaxation now in playing alone or with a small group of friends. He described his parent's marriage as highly conflicted and attributed some of this to his dad's self-involvement. He was the youngest child and very close to his mom, captured in his statement "I loved her dearly." He resented his dad's lack of time for the family and never made peace with him before he died. His dad showed a clear preference for his sister as "perfect" and had told Dr. BE and his brother that they would both grow up to be "failures." (It is hard to forgive and make peace given that kind of parental prophecy.) He still rues the fact that he never saw displays of affection between his parents. To this day, he wonders if his dad had a long-term affair with his secretary, with whom he often worked (supposedly) until 9:00 p.m. at the office. [The affair theme resurfaced twice later in his personal life but in reverse – that is, it was his wife who cheated (Brown, 1991)].

First Marriage, First Child, First Divorce

Dr. BE married his first wife, Diane, when he was 26 years of age. Both are Caucasian, born in America, Jewish, and came from similar family backgrounds. He very much wanted children. However, she did not – apparently an issue they had not discussed before they got married. (Many couples assume they both want the

---

Areas in () in the following case studies are author interpretations and notes to reader

F.W. Kaslow, *Divorced Fathers and Their Families: Legal, Economic, and Emotional Dilemmas,* DOI 10.1007/978-1-4614-5535-6_2, © Springer Science+Business Media New York 2013

same things and do not verify with one another that these assumptions are correct.) When Diane got pregnant, he went to La Maze classes with her in preparation for the delivery, and they had a daughter. Diane "froze" emotionally and did little for the child, for him, or for and in their house. He described her as "cold, controlling, and angry," frequently embroiled in arguments with those close to her, and as someone who never smiled (i.e., chronically unhappy).

After 10 years of marriage, he "couldn't stand her anymore" and left. A two-year separation ensued, prior to the divorce – for which Diane did the filing. During the separation period, the still married Mrs. Blue Eyes had an affair and an abortion, which Dr. BE paid for. When the divorce was final, Dr. BE felt enormous relief mingled with a continuation of his longtime sadness that the wife he had selected was such a controlling person and so resentful for having become pregnant and having a child. Nonetheless, she was awarded primary custody/residence of their daughter (Florida law terminology at that time).

Second Marriage, a Stepdaughter, and a Son

Happily for him, or so he thought at the time, he met an attractive woman who traveled in the same social group that he did, shortly after the divorce was concluded. It did not take them long to decide to marry. He was then almost 40 years old. She was a few years younger, also divorced, and with a daughter one year senior to Dr. BE's daughter. They fell very much in love, and for the first few years, it was the kind of passionate and highly sexual relationship he wanted and she enjoyed. The trouble in their marital paradise seemed to stem from the fact that her daughter, Katrina, from her first marriage, lived with them almost full time, and when his daughter, Sally, came to visit, she felt Katrina was favored. Dr. BE thought his ex-wife wanted Sally to "spy" on him and his new family, and this caused much tension. As the girls got older, Katrina was much "faster" than Sally, which Dr. BE was not pleased about. He acknowledged that his sexy second wife, Jamie, tried to be a "good stepmom," but his daughter resented her now being dad's partner. Dr. BE and Jamie had a son together, who is seven years younger than his daughter and lived with the new couple full time. This further complicated the family relationship system and contributed to Sally feeling like an outsider.

He coached his son's sports teams and went to many of his games. Sadly, his son, whose ADHD caused him to have difficulty concentrating and studying, did not finish high school. His mom was glad to have him at home to keep her company, so she did not insist he complete his education. Later, Dr. BE persuaded him to go back and complete his GED.

Dr. BE became close with Jamie's daughter, who was six when they married, and felt bonded to her for as long as they were together. After the divorce, he had little contact with her because her mother objected to his staying in touch with her and as a stepparent; he had no *legal* right to do so. He knows that when she was 18 years old, she moved from her mother's house and allegedly maintains little contact with her mother also.

Addictions Eroded the Marital Bliss

When other, more troublesome behaviors on Jamie's part surfaced, they did seek good professional marital therapy. At the beginning of treatment, he realized that Jamie was abusing drugs and alcohol and had a very serious problem with both. He had known her dad had been a heavy drinker, and her mom had taken Miltown (an early tranquilizer) daily but had disregarded the likelihood that Jamie would follow the same path. Much animosity and anger were exchanged between them, and Jamie finally went into a revolving door pattern of drug and alcohol inpatient and outpatient rehabilitation treatments (Bepko with Kreston, 1985). He was told and ultimately recognized he had tried many times to "rescue her" and was "codependent." He attended Al-Anon groups where he learned to "keep the focus on himself." Although they had separated at one point and she had primary custody of their son, at the urging of the drug counselor, he returned to Jamie for another five rocky, unhappy years. Her bouts with addiction were intermittent even though she trained to become a drug counselor and briefly served as one (Leesa & Scanlon, 2006). Her heavy smoking and overeating continued, and she was no longer attractive to him. Personality-wise, she was morbid, negative, critical, and depressed. After 14 years, he once again felt "I have to get out." He could not stand being trapped any longer. The trigger event that made it possible for him to extricate himself was coming home from work and finding a prophylactic in the toilet. On a tape the "other man" left behind, which Dr. BE heard, she and her lover were talking about their feelings for each other. This was how he learned Jamie was having an affair with his best friend's brother – who they both knew was a substance abuser and alcoholic. Frustrated and enraged, he left and was and is proud of his courage to do so and not be inveigled and guilted into being a lifelong caretaker.

The Postdivorce Years: To Whom Do the Children "Belong"?

During subsequent years, Jamie was caught taking and using her son's, Don's, prescription for Ritalin (he has ADHD). The police were frequently called to her house by neighbors because of her disruptive behavior – like running outside naked when stoned and trying to break into their son's bedroom. There had been calls to Child Protective Services (CPS), and they did come out to the house to check on Don. But given that he was protective of his mother and would not reveal all that went on in the house and that there were no visible signs of physical abuse, no formal charges were filed by the CPS investigator against Jamie. [*Unfortunately, all too often children of divorce become "parentified" by one parent, that is, are thrust into the role of taking care of a parent who is physically challenged, emotionally disturbed, and/or has some kind of addiction. They are assigned the adult role and become the protector (Sauber, L'Abate, Weeks, & Buchanan, 1993). They have no one in the home concerned about their well-being and about their developmental needs being met.*]

As part of the interview, I queried Dr. BE as to why he had not petitioned the court for custody of his son when he realized how Jamie's condition had deteriorated and the untenable emotional climate in which Don was living at his mother's house, where he resided the majority of the time. He answered that he saw Don as often as Jamie would allow, that he knew the court in his jurisdiction continued to give preference to mothers who wanted primary custody, and that his petition would not have been granted. He continued to help support his son beyond age 18 and paid for his post-high school vocational training. When he was free to make his own choice and was no longer under court jurisdiction, his son moved in with him of his own accord. Now 10 years later, his son and daughter-in-law and their child live with him, and he is a very attached and doting grandfather – thrilled to have them all under his roof and to be part of a real family – every day.

When he first left Jamie, he went to live with a buddy temporarily (as many men do until they sort out what want they to do), so he would not feel totally alone and until he could find and afford a suitable apartment. At that time, he thought the children had responded to living in two households and going back and forth easily and well.

Although his relationship with his own daughter has improved somewhat in recent years and she now works in his office part time, he believes she still sides with her mother, is still angry at him for leaving, and shows him little warmth. She too is married and has a child. She indicates she thinks he prefers her half brother's child over hers just as she felt he preferred her stepsister and half brother when they were growing up and as Dr. BE's father had preferred his sister over him and his brother. [Often relational patterns of rivalry and competition are transmitted and repeated down through the generations as seems to have happened here (Bowen, 1988)].

Finances

Dr. BE paid child support and alimony after both divorces. He paid his first ex-wife a total of $190,000 combined child support and alimony from the time they separated, and Sally was only three years old until she was 18 years old, a total of 15 years. He paid his second wife $164,000 in total over eight years plus he underwrote all the costs of his son's summer camp and medical and dental expenses. He now provides free-living quarters for his son and his family and is supplementing Don's income while he is looking for a better job – something he has done periodically for many years. Although at the peak of his career Dr. BE's gross earnings fell in the $101,000–150,000 range, since the economic downturn of the last five years and the severe cut back in insurance reimbursement for medical services, his gross income is under $100,000. Despite his hard work and middle-class income, after paying so many years of alimony and child support and supplementing both by covering many additional expenses for the children, he always was strapped financially. He finally bought an inexpensive house and has a little money for dating and vacations. The other two households he was supporting had first claim on his income most of his adult life.

Experience of Divorce: Then and Now

The *most painful aspect* of the divorce (Schwartz & Kaslow, 1997) was "the loss of the kids" and not being able to be part of their everyday life. Despite knowing to survive and retain any semblance of sanity he "had to leave," he still had felt guilty each time he finally said "I'm out of here." Over the years, he has come to understand why he chose each of his wives and to take responsibility for his part in the breakup of his marriages. Even though his daughter is cold and seemingly judgmental of him, he sees her several times a week at the office, and this pleases him. However, she is curt and tends to "talk back" to him. She comes to visit him at home with her son. He is happiest when children and grandchildren are at the house and finally feels he has the "family" he always wanted. The prospect of taking his two grandchildren to Disney World soon thrills him.

Postdivorce Interactions with Ex-Spouse and Her Family

He was unable to discuss concerns about his daughter and son with their mothers. There was little communication across the separate households. His first wife continued to make his having a relationship with his daughter difficult by undermining his authority, criticizing his behavior, making negative remarks about him, and claiming he never sent enough money. Jamie was also very critical, accusing him of deserting them. She tried to play on his guilt about abandoning a "sick" wife.

In the early postdivorce years, he had no contact with his first in-law family. Neither he nor they wanted it. Years later, his ex-mother-in-law called to say she had gotten to know her daughter better and realized how difficult it must have been for him to live with her, and he had her sympathy. Subsequently, she decided she would like to become his patient as she held him in high regard and knew he was a good doctor.

Most Important Contributions to His Children's Lives

Dr. BE sees himself as always "being there" as a *stable* and available father, being a role model of consistency in their lives and in his career/work, trying to guide his children to have solid values, and helping both children – when possible – to find good jobs. Currently, he contributes all he can to keeping his son, daughter, their partners, and children close as a family in the here and now.

Feeling Stymied, Left Out, Unable to Be as Much a Part of Children's Lives as He Wanted to Be

His first wife's constant negativity and failure to imbue their daughter with warmth and softness thwarted his efforts to be close to Sally and to try to make joint decisions with her regarding their daughter. She exercised "mind control" over Sally, and the impact of this modus operandi during her childhood is still potent (Bernet, 2010). Sally thinks whatever her mother dictates she is obliged to do. With second wife Jamie, her serious addictions (American Psychiatric Association [APA], 1994) and frequent relapses continued to widen the schism between them and exacerbate the differences in their approach to child rearing. (It made dealing with her akin to a roller-coaster ride.)

Retrospective

Among Dr. BE's worst times and memories were making the decision to leave each wife, the process of leaving, and the actual day of moving out. Yet he knew he was dying inside and could not survive if he remained, particularly in his second marriage. He stated, "fortunately a therapist gave me permission to set myself free and go out and live, but it was all so painful while it was happening and for many years afterwards."

His dreams and plans for marriage and being a dad had been "until death do us part," raising children together with their mother and building a close-knit family. He never anticipated he would be divorced, yet his dreams were shattered twice. Now he is thoroughly enjoying being a "dad" to his two grown children and grandfather to his grandchildren – it is the most important aspect of his life. He dates and has occasionally had a long-term relationship but in the past has been too hurt and disillusioned to seriously contemplate making another permanent commitment. (This is often the sequelae of such painful partings which entail betrayal, the violation of trust, and questioning of one's own judgment.) For recreation, he enjoys being with friends, playing an instrument, and going to jam sessions and concerts.

References

American Psychiatric Association. (1994). *Diagnostic and Statistical Manual of Mental Disorders IV*. Washington, DC: American Psychiatric Association.

Bepko, C., & Kreston, J. A. (1985). *The responsibility trap*. New York: Free Press.

Bernet, W. (Ed). (2010). *Parental Alienation, DSM-5 and ICD-11*. Springfield, Ill: Charles C. Thomas Publishers, Ltd.

Bowen, M. (1988-Second Edition). *Family Therapy in Clinical Practice*. Northvale, NJ: Jason Aronson.

Leesa, N. R., & Scanlon, W. F. (2006). Substance use disorders. In *Wiley concise guides to mental health*. Hoboken: Wiley.

Sauber, S. R., L'Abate, L., Weeks, G. R. & Buchanan, W. L. (Eds) (1993). *The Dictionary of Family Psychology and Family Therapy*. (Second edition). Newbury Park, CA: Sage.

Schwartz, L. L., & Kaslow, F. W. (1997). *Painful partings: Divorce and its aftermath*. New York: Wiley.

Chapter 3
Case 2 Mr. Bob Straight: I Promised Myself I Would Be a Good Dad

Brief Personal History

Bob Straight was born in 1950 and raised in a southern state. His African American parents separated when he was three years old. His dad moved to another state, and he did not see nor hear from him during his growing up years. His dad finally called him "once or twice" when Bob was in his late 30s and his dad's health was failing. His father "passed" before Bob turned 40 years of age; he had never seen him again after he abandoned him when he was still a toddler. Somewhere during his adolescent or early adulthood years, he vowed to himself that if he were lucky enough to become a dad, he would be a "great dad" and would never, ever desert his child or children.

His parents were Methodist but did not go to church. He had very little religious upbringing. He was raised by his single mom who worked hard to see that he finished high school and went on to complete two years of data processing training in a technical school. He still lives and works in one of the major metropolitan areas of Georgia.

This 60-year-old man is of medium height and stature, was polite and thoughtful during the interview, and was kind enough to come to a session with me on a weekend day as that was when I was able to fly into his city to meet with him.

First Marriage, Son, and Legal Divorce

When Bob was 27 years of age, he married Julia. She was also African American with a Protestant family background; however, hers was Episcopalian. This difference was never a problem for them.

Their son, Kenny, was born when they had been married for three years. Mr. S was delighted to have a son. But, he and Julia did not get along well, and they argued a great deal. Three years after Kenny was born, Julia said she wanted a divorce.

F.W. Kaslow, *Divorced Fathers and Their Families: Legal, Economic, and Emotional Dilemmas*, DOI 10.1007/978-1-4614-5535-6_3, © Springer Science+Business Media New York 2013

By then, both were 34 years of age and knew what they were doing. As it was clear that she did not want to be with him any longer, he did not contest her decision, and despite not wanting to leave his son, he moved out at J's insistence.

Mr. Straight suspects that his wife was having an affair. He had to be away for his work sometimes, and she seemed preoccupied with something beyond him and their son, their life together, and her normal activities. Often, she would seem to cover up whom her phone calls were to and from. (This was in the era before caller ID or there were cell phones.) He felt hurt, angry, and very disappointed that they had been unable to resolve their differences and improve their marriage for the sake of their son. (Mr. S appeared to be a dignified, soft spoken, somewhat reticent man who did not wish to be highly critical of his son's mother in the interview.)

Finances

Mr. S paid $165 per month child support for 15 years or 180 months. In addition, he covered all of the medical and dental expenses for Kenny through his employment health insurance plan. His ex-wife was not awarded alimony as she was working at the time of the divorce. However, he left with nothing except his car, stereo set, and his clothes. He felt and thought he had gotten a "raw deal." Years later when Kenny went to college, Bob gave him money directly to cover room and board. He received a scholarship to cover his tuition. Mr. S is still working as an engineering technician doing analyses of ingredients in a large food processing plant. He currently earns under $100,000 per year. He seems comfortable with his current life and lifestyle.

Early Postdivorce Period

Leaving his son and his home by moving out caused a big upheaval and adjustment for him. But he was "told to leave" and did not see any other option, although Julia was the one who initiated the idea of divorce and filed for it. It meant "beginning all over again." He could not help wondering and worrying about what was going on in his little son's mind about his dad not living with him anymore. The fact that in some ways history was repeating itself in that Bob's dad had moved out when he was three years old as he was doing to his son at the same age had troubled him enormously. He never considered filing for primary custody. It just was not granted to fathers in the state where they resided. "Traditionally kids belonged with their mom," and dads had no chance to be named the primary custodial parent (Myers, 1989).

The MSA specified that he was to have Kenny during the summer (he was vague on the amount of time) and every other weekend. Generally, Julia was good about sharing their son and not making the transitions between homes difficult; although if she knew or sensed Mr. S had his own plans when a weekend visit was to be over, she often came to pick him up late (see Games Divorcing and Divorced People Play in Chapter 15).

Bob and Julia were basically in agreement about and supportive of one another regarding child rearing. This was true in all of the areas he was queried about, namely, limit setting, school, sports, and other activities. Ken did not get involved with doing drugs nor with heavy drinking.

For the first six months after Bob moved out, he lived with a friend and split the rent. He needed time to pull his thoughts together and decide what to do next. He had never contemplated getting divorced, so this had all come as a shock to him, and he had to decide just how he wanted to "start all over again." After six months, he found and rented his own apartment and then remained there for five or six years. During this first six-month period, his little boy did not stay overnight with him. Once Mr. S had his own place to live again and fixed up a room for Kenny, he was glad that there could be overnight visits. Julia actually allowed him more time with Kenny than had been legally decreed as she wanted more time for her own activities. She was happy to have Bob see their son more often, particularly to take him to his teams' practices and to sporting events. This worked out well for everyone. She shared Kenny easily and made sure transitions went smoothly.

Kenny did not display much "hurt" about his parents separating and divorce. Yet occasionally, his actions showed he wanted them back together (this is a typical reaction and a long-term fantasy of children of divorce, that is, that parents will reunite) (Kaslow & Schwartz, 1987). For example, when Bob would go to pick him up, Kenny would say "won't you come in," which Bob did not do. Kenny did not display any difficulty moving back and forth between mom's house and dad's house (Ricci, 1980).

Julia never remarried, but she did have live-in boyfriends. One spanked Kenny. The (seemingly) mild-mannered Mr. S, who does not like to make waves, told J "make sure it never happens again"! It did not! But Kenny did not ask to move in with Dad, and Bob did not request a change of custody, as he had been led to believe that Georgia courts would not grant this. Bob was often skeptical about J's choice of baby-sitters but recognized he could not control this.

Postdivorce Interactions with In-Law Family and His Family

The Straights had never seen much of Julia's family as they did not live in the same city nor nearby, so not seeing them postdivorce was not a loss to him. His family was attached to Kenny, and they continued to see their grandson postdivorce as he was often with Bob (Kaslow, 2007).

The Later Postdivorce Years

After the initial period of getting accustomed to the idea of "having to start all over again," Bob decided he would "learn how to date all over again" and "get back into the game." (For many men, like Bob, who married "'til death do us part" and who were faithful husbands, dating initially is an alien concept and takes a while to feel acceptable and comfortable – contrary to popular opinion). He knew he did not want to get hurt again or to be tied down, so he decided he would "avoid falling in love" and that he was in "no hurry to get married again." Apparently, he was candid in telling this to any woman he dated more than a few times.

After a while, he began seeing Melinda, a woman who had been a friend through work, prior to his divorce. They remained "just friends" for several years. Their friendship turned into a romance, and six years after his separation, he and Melinda were married. They have two children together, and Kenny visits often. He gets along well with his half-siblings. They care a great deal about one another, and Kenny and his stepmom are fond of one another. She has been very good and kind to him. Melinda is described as a caring person who has given Kenny a great deal of encouragement and guidance when it has been sought.

During the years of their marriage, Melinda has gotten her Ph.D. in a mental health field. She teaches at a local medical school and sees patients privately. She has been a wonderful role model for all of the children, and together Bob and Melinda have instilled a value system that emphasizes the importance of family loyalty and of education. Ken has chosen to work at the same hospital where his stepmom is employed (which seems like quite a tribute to her).

Bob stated, with much conviction, that he has made a much stronger commitment to his second marriage and family than he did the first time around. His vow to himself was and is "whatever it takes." This marriage has lasted 25 years, and he is quite content with and proud of his family.

Experience of Divorce and Relationship to Son

The most painful aspect of his divorce (Schwartz & Kaslow, 1997) was and still remains not having been able to be a "traditional live-in father" for Kenny. He has done all that he could to be a present and available father and to include him in his second family.

Some of the highlights in his relationship to Kenny have been watching him play sports (mentioned by many of the dads interviewed regarding sons and daughters), attending his high school and college graduation, getting him his first car, and spending Thanksgiving with him. Sadly for Mr. S, Kenny was always supposed to spend Christmas with his mom, and Bob deeply missed being with his boy on Christmas mornings. Aside from that, he recollects having participated in almost all aspects of his son's life and that his most enduring contributions are that Kenny was and still is "always sure of my love," that "I am there for him," and that we spent a great deal of time together.

Retrospective

Mr. Straight described his ex-wife as "nice, considerate, not mean, nasty, or disturbed." He appreciates that they really did put Kenny's best interest front and center and made his life in two homes transitioning back and forth as easy as possible. He harbors "no animosity" and feels that a person can "get over divorce" and that the "pain doesn't have to last forever." His major lingering regret and how his life evolved differently than his original dream was that he could not remain a live-in dad for Kenny. [Mr. S. has certainly been a very present and active father and husband in his second marriage and has included Kenny in his family to the extent possible. In this case, we have a clear example of a couple who choose not to stay married but truly acted in accordance with the doctrine of the "best interest of the child," and *both* appear to have reasonably "healthy" personalities, which is not true in many of the other cases. Their divorce and its aftermath have been quite civil (Gold, 1992)].

References

Gold, L. (1992). *Between love and hate: A guide to civilized divorce*. New York: Plenum.

Kaslow, F. W. (2007). Post divorce relatedness between parents, their divorced sons, and their grandchildren: A pilot study. In C. A. Everett & R. E. Lee (Eds.), *When marriages fail: Systemic family therapy interventions and issues* (pp. 141–156). New York: Haworth Press.

Kaslow, F. W., & Schwartz, L. L. (1987). *Dynamics of divorce: A life cycle perspective*. New York: Brunner/Mazel.

Myers, M. F. (1989). *Men and divorce*. New York: Guilford Press.

Ricci, I. (1980). *Mom's house, dad's house: Making shared custody work*. New York: Macmillan.

Schwartz, L. L., & Kaslow, F. W. (1997). *Painful partings: Divorce and its aftermath*. New York: Wiley.

Chapter 4
Case 3 Dr. Jorge Garcia: Promises Made, Promises Kept, Until Forever Is Too Long

Brief Personal History

Dr. G was born in 1944 and raised in Cuba during the 1940s and 1950s in a Hispanic, Catholic family. He had a strict upbringing that stressed loyalty to the family, adherence to the principles of the church, and the importance of a good education. He attended Catholic schools in his home country. He met his future wife, Carmina, a girl from a similar background, while he was still a teenager living in Havana, and they became boyfriend and girlfriend for a year. He left Cuba during the early Castro years because he disagreed with the direction in which his country was heading and because he wanted to go to medical school in the United States (USA). Initially, Carmina wanted to remain in Cuba, but she soon changed her mind and decided she too wanted to leave and join her boyfriend in the USA. Jorge, partially at her family's insistence, committed to helping her leave, which meant participating in getting the paperwork done (Bernal & Shapiro, 1996).

Today Dr. G is an attractive, articulate, 67-year-old man who carries himself well. He is active in the local, state, and national professional community in his field.

Early Marriage and Family

After he made that guarantee, her family would not let Carmina leave for the USA unless she and Jorge were married – it was unthinkable for them to allow it any other way within their religious and cultural belief and value system. So, Jorge and Carmina were married by proxy (through the mail) so she could join him here. He never intended to consummate the marriage. But, once she arrived, he felt pushed into a proper, traditional wedding. He felt duty bound to do "the right thing."

All of this took over a year to expedite, and during that period, he had had a year of freedom here in the much more liberal southern USA. He had enjoyed socializing with his new friends and not living in his previous restrictive environment. However,

F.W. Kaslow, *Divorced Fathers and Their Families: Legal, Economic, and Emotional Dilemmas*, DOI 10.1007/978-1-4614-5535-6_4, © Springer Science+Business Media New York 2013

he was honor bound to live the life of a married man – although by then he was only 20 years of age, and so he did.

The marriage was "never great from the beginning." They separated once before any children were conceived but decided to reconcile. Then, she became pregnant. Once the children started coming into their lives, he decided to stay with Carmina and "make the best of it." Their first son, Pedro, was born three years after they married; their daughter, Maria, came along two years later; and the second son, Juan (now Jon), was born eight years after Jorge and Carmina were wed. They remained married for 23 years. Jorge liked being a father and has a generally positive outlook on life, so although the marriage was not terrific, he was reasonably content.

During the first decade of his marriage, he was also busy doing his residency in psychiatry in one of the best medical schools in the southeast. Because of his studies, he lived away from his wife and children for long periods of time. (It is not clear why they did not relocate with him each time he had to move – but this is not unusual when one spouse is attending graduate or professional school and/or doing an internship or residency.) Carmina was concerned that he often acted "like he was single" and her suspicions were justified. He did have an affair. She was angry and disappointed. Dr. G does not think the children were ever apprised of his dalliance.

The Actual Divorce

At the time that his wife decided to file for divorce, the family was living together in a southeastern state. Carmina moved out, and the three children, by then ages 20, 18, and 15 years of age, went with their mom. She moved to the southwest and Dr. G only saw them infrequently on holidays for a number of years. The children came to visit him, or he went out to see them. Although he felt free to go on with his life, he did not like the circumstances of having the children living so far away. His ambivalence also partially emanated from the fact that divorce goes against his religion and his religious beliefs. (He never fully accepted Carmina's decision to move far away, which prevented him from being a major positive influence in the children's lives during their adolescence and early adulthood, and he did not have the option to relocate too; it was counterindicated professionally.)

Despite his priest's insistence that they have their marriage annulled, they never did. To have the marriage declared null and void would have invalidated something that had been very real and meaningful in the marriage to both Carmina and him and would have negated the children's legitimacy in the eyes of the church.

They did not have a fixed custody agreement and actually shared the children easily. No limitations were imposed – they worked out arrangements as they went along. He told the children that nothing had changed between him and them; no great drama unfolded when they moved out (but that in and of itself and relocating to a new state was a big change). Their two sons seemed accepting of the separation and divorce, but their daughter was very angry with him.

Finances

Dr. G was the payer of alimony and child support and Carmina was the recipient. In addition, he covered all of the three children's travel expenses back and forth for visitation over the years, even though it was Carmina's decision to move rather far away to another region of the country. He also paid for their cars, their college educations, and all medical and related expenses.

In order to be able to afford this and his own expenses, he worked very hard to earn sufficient money during his residency years. A resident's salary 25 years ago was quite limited, so he had to take on an extra part-time job as well as take out loans. Financially, he really struggled to manage and to provide well for everyone for about four years.

He still "helps out" 25 years later whenever his grown children need assistance. At this time, each has his or her own apartment or home, and he has provided money toward down payments on homes. He and his second wife take the children on long family cruises to different parts of the world and frequently give them very substantial gifts.

Postdivorce Period

Toward the end of his residency in the mid-1980s, Dr. G met a female Cuban resident, Dr. M, whom he found interesting and attractive. Three years after his divorce, they were married. She was also divorced and had a daughter from her first marriage who was then 12 years old and who lived with them, almost totally.

His sons seemed to accept his remarriage and showed little animosity toward his new wife or their young stepsister. They continued to visit their dad and his new family, alternately spending holidays with him and with their mother. At first his daughter showed some jealousy of his relationship to his new wife and exhibited some rivalry with her stepsister. She evolved a love/hate relationship with her. With Dr. G and Dr. M's loving, accepting, skilled, and welcoming handling of all, the two families were able to meld into one. They now all vacation at Dr. G's cottage in the south and often take vacations together.

Most Painful Aspects of Divorce

Dr. G experienced no post divorce illnesses or stress-related problems – only sadness. He was disappointed that his marriage had failed, although he never personally felt like a failure. He was distressed by the loss of daily contact and involvement with his children, of his ability to "set limits" on what they were permitted to do, and on his "loss of control" over what was happening in their daily lives. He maintained frequent and open communication with them and always tried to maximize his influence on their upbringing and thinking (as he knew he had so much love to share and of value to offer them).

Postdivorce Interactions with Ex-Spouse and Her Family/His Family

Dr. G and Carmina retained a helpful and cooperative attitude toward one another and consulted with each other when any problems concerning the children arose. They were mutually supportive and collaborative regarding child rearing despite the physical distance which separated their respective households. Carmina was neither critical nor deprecating of him to the children nor did he demean or say negative things to them about their mother. It really sounds like they geared their interactions and transactions around promoting the "best interests of their children" and that this was not a bitter, contentious "War of the Roses" (much to the benefit of all involved). Like Dr. G, Carmina sounds like she was an emotionally healthy person with an optimistic outlook on life and about herself. His practical and accepting disposition contributed to postdivorce harmony (Ahrons, 1994).

Carmina was an only child, and she sometimes took the children back to Cuba to visit her family there. He had left Cuba before he had had a chance to be close to them, but he did continue to have a pleasant relationship with her extended family postdivorce by phone and mail. He never felt ostracized or excluded by them.

Dr. G's dad had passed away by the time he got divorced. His mom was unhappy about the ending of his marriage. She relocated to the USA following his divorce and seeing her grandchildren became an important part of her life.

His Important Contributions to the Children's Lives and Activities Participated in Postdivorce/Poignant Memories

To the extent possible, Dr. G gladly stayed involved in every aspect of the children's lives in which he could be, without being intrusive or overbearing. He tried to be a good role model and teach by example. His actions exemplified hard work, loyalty to family, and a strong moral and ethical code as well as clear religious values. This continues to be true in his relationships with them in the here and now.

Whenever he could, he attended (and attends) the important events in the children's lives and spends holidays and vacations with them, and they attend many family gatherings together.

He is delighted that all of his children have graduated from college and are self-sufficient. His daughter, Maria, has become a successful consultant in the health-care industry. His eldest son is a television director. His younger son has settled nearby his dad and stepmom. As adult children, they all maintain frequent contact with their dad and each other. But his dream was that at least one of them would become a physician "like dad," and none of them have chosen to follow that part of the model he set.

Differences Based on Children's Gender in Terms of Loyalty to Their Mother

Maria was initially concerned that if she became attached to and allowed herself to care about her stepmom, she would be "betraying her loyalty to her own mom." Drs. G and M were able to help her understand that she could love and like them both, differently, and that Dr. M was not trying to replace her mom or squeeze her out of the family constellation. Eventually, this resolved itself. His oldest son, Pedro, came to live with them for a while, and his youngest, Jon, often "buddied up with his stepsister" (Pryor, 2008).

Some of the Worst Memories

Having the children move out of this home was an unwelcome and grueling event, but it was handled as well as possible by all.

The truly worst memory surrounds the death of his ex-wife several years ago. At that time, she was living with his daughter in a large city in a mid-Atlantic state. The family knew she had a medical condition, but it was supposedly under control and she was not ill. One day when Maria returned home from work, she was horrified to find her mother sitting motionless at the desk, not breathing. When the ambulance came, the paramedics said she had had a massive coronary and was already dead. Maria called Dr. G immediately after calling 911, and he flew up to be with her and to help her deal with the horrendous and shocking tragedy and to arrange for the funeral and all that goes along with it and was there to mourn his ex-wife's passing with the children and to comfort them. In his recounting this part of his story, one hears empathy and compassion for the children and for their mother, for whom he once cared deeply and whom he continued to like and respect. [Some experts in the field of family dynamics and treatment believe (as does the current book's author) that when a couple have been married and had children, they can never be completely divorced. They remain connected through the children and therefore should behave admirably well, even heroically in such circumstances, as Dr. G seems to have done, in order not to make the situation even more painful for their children.]

Retrospective

Dr. G is a wise and gentle man who places a high value on the institution of the family and on family loyalty. He did not permit "the failure of his first marriage" to undercut his self-esteem but retained this. He has gone on to build a happy second marriage to which he is totally committed. He and Carmina were able to avoid "locking horns" and did not become adversaries, which made it easy to share the children and be supportive of each other's parenting. It also laid the groundwork for his children's acceptance of his remarriage, their stepmother, and stepsister. He views marriage as a "sacred covenant," and he lives according to this precept in his second marriage. They enjoy their beautiful, spacious home, where they frequently entertain; he has built an excellent and satisfying career and does not ruminate over having made a "mistake" or "having failed," nor is he bitter or resentful. He is a contented person who takes problems in stride, works to resolve issues and conflicts, and seems to count his blessing. As he is comfortable in who and what he is, and in his own being, he is comfortable to interview and be with. (His story presents quite a contrast to some of the other stories told in this volume, and the key differences are elaborated in Chapter 17 on Personality.)

References

Ahrons, C. R. (1994). *The good divorce: Keeping your family together when your marriage comes apart*. New York: Harper Collins.

Bernal, G., & Shapiro, E. (1996). Cuban families. In M. McGoldrick, J. Giordano, & J. K. Pearce (Eds.), *Ethnicity and family therapy* (pp. 155–168). New York: Guilford Press.

Pryor, J. (2008). *The international handbook of stepfamilies: Policy and practice in legal, research and clinical environments*. Hoboken, NJ: Wiley.

Chapter 5
Case 4 Mr. Reuben Guy: The Nastiness Never Stopped

Brief Personal History

Mr. Guy is a soft spoken, nice looking, pleasant, successful 77-year-old attorney, who is and has also practiced as an engineer. He is still engaged in an active law practice. He was raised by Caucasian, Jewish parents in the northeast section of the USA. He was inculcated with a strong sense of the importance of family and family loyalty, of acquiring and valuing a fine education in a professional field, and of hard work. He was a good student and obtained his J.D. degree from a law school when he was 28 years old.

First Marriage, Children, and the Legal Divorce

When Reuben was 22 years of age, he married Estelle, who was then only 18 years old. They had four children together. For the first 18 years of their marriage, his wife stayed home and took care of the children and the house. At that time, he thought she was content, like he was, with their life together and as a family.

In the early years of their marriage, Mr. Guy went to both law school and engineering school at night and was awarded degrees in both of these fields. He worked during the day and kept a very full and busy schedule. (This was not atypical for many ambitious young people of that era.) Estelle only had completed one year of college and then turned her attention to homemaking and mothering. He felt his wife "idolized" him during the first 18 years of their marriage, and he was emotionally unprepared for the upheaval that then occurred.

When the children were all passed their preadolescent years, Estelle decided to become a travel agent. She became quite aggressive as she became more and more successful, and she thoroughly enjoyed earning her own independent, separate income. She decided to have plastic surgery so she would look younger and more attractive and began to go to social events without her husband. He was not pleased with the change in

F.W. Kaslow, *Divorced Fathers and Their Families: Legal, Economic,*
and Emotional Dilemmas, DOI 10.1007/978-1-4614-5535-6_5,
© Springer Science+Business Media New York 2013

the status quo and the disequilibrium her new attitude and behaviors caused in the family. He saw his pleasant wife evolve into a "bitter, nasty, and mean person." When she decided to accept an invitation to a New Year's Eve party and did not ask him to accompany her, he felt spurned. Soon after that she asked him to leave. The marriage was no longer the compatible relationship he had had and still wanted, and their mounting incompatibilities took them beyond compromise. He went to talk to a counselor at a family service agency, tried talking to his Rabbi, and to family and friends, but could find no help wherever he went. Estelle refused flat out to go for marital therapy. The entire situation left him feeling devastated. He agreed to move out of the marital home because he saw the marriage as irretrievably fractured. The lack of any expression of affection for a prolonged period of time clearly conveyed her lack of love for and emotional attachment to him. There was no alternative for him but to file for divorce.

Mr. Guy does not think his ex-wife ever had an affair, nor had he. This was not a reason for the breakup.

At the time of the separation, the Guy's four children ranged in age from 13 to 19 years of age. Initially, they all remained in the family home with their mother. Apparently a rule (unwritten mandate) was imposed that they were all "forbidden" to discuss anything about their mother with their father, and they have abided by this dictum for the most part, for the past 35 years.

Finances and Other Provisos of the MSA

The divorce agreement mandated that Mr. Guy gives his wife the house and all the furnishings. He left with very little except a few pieces of china and glassware, barely enough kitchenware to set up in a small place he rented to live on his own. She refused to allow him to see the children unless he returned everything. (Using the threat of withholding access to the children if the husband does not comply with what the wife dictates is unfortunately not an infrequent type of blackmail (see Chapter 15 – Games Divorcing and Divorced People Play.) Many of the men caught in this bind do not want to enter the revolving door of the courthouse to contest violation of their agreement; all too often they report finding the judges are so biased in favor of the mothers that they do not enforce the court orders they have handed down so it is to no avail to enter an appeal, and these returns to court are expensive and time consuming.)

He was ordered to pay $200 a month per child until each one turned 18 years of age, which amounted to five years of paying child support. In addition, he paid college tuition and some of the other college expenses for all four of his sons. His eldest son, Greg, paid for his own graduate school. Given that Mr. Guy's wife had her own substantial income by the time the divorce hearing took place, he did not have to pay any alimony. He was granted the right to retain his own pension. When he tried to reach Estelle to discuss finalizing how they were going to pay taxes for their last year together, she refused to talk to him. Nevertheless, she was willing to encounter him later when she petitioned the court to have him pay for her tuition to return to college. This was not granted.

Estelle has not talked to him since he moved out of their home 35 years ago – even when they have both been in the same room for the same event. (Such behavior usually causes much consternation for children and grandchildren and is rarely in the "best interest of the children." Carrying such a grudge for so long usually does damage to the bearer of the grudge who harbors it. One wonders what purpose it serves several decades later and how the benefits can possibly outweigh the continuing harm it perpetuates.)

Postdivorce Changes in the Family

Shortly after Mr. Guy moved out and was no longer a living-in part of the family who could buffer the children from their mother's wrath, she "threw one son (Jerry) out of the house." When Reuben realized this fracas was more than a temporary ousting, he deducted the child support due for the one child. This son has a chronic illness, and though it is not fully debilitating, he has never worked steadily. Mr. G indicated that this son had quit college, is hard to get along with, and has never married. Because of his sporadic work history, Mr. G still helps support Jerry. He does not live in the same state in which either his mother or father reside. Mr. Guy does not see this son very frequently.

Mr. G moved into an apartment about 10 minutes from the marital home. Estelle had primary custody; they had no formal visitation plan as the four teenagers all had busy schedules and wanted to evolve visitation times spontaneously with their father. It seems he never questioned this type of arrangement nor pushed for anything more formal; this sufficed for a number of years.

He has never discussed their mother with them nor asked any questions about her and her life. But through innuendoes made by them, comments by friends, and remarks he heard from others through the grapevine, he is aware that she is viewed by others as he perceived her to be, as lacking compassion, as bitter and mean, having a bad temper and often "flying off the handle" at the kids. This did not surprise him as she had told him on more than one occasion, "I do not know why I ever had kids."

After a few months of mainly working, seeing his children sporadically, and just getting by, Mr. Guy took a trip to one of the islands with a buddy and had a fun time. He realized other people enjoyed his company and really gravitated toward him. His ego, so badly bruised by Estelle, rebounded. He decided it was time to find a new life for himself and so began to reach out socially. He began to see himself as attractive and desirable, as he made good friends and became popular in the older singles scene. As his confidence grew, he was better able to cope with Estelle's rejection, being evicted from the home he had helped build physically as well as financially, and the loss of living with his children.

Ultimately, Estelle chose to move to a different state and pursue her Ph.D. in the research end of a finance field. Here, too, she accomplished her objective (apparently her nastiness was not vented in professional situations, and she became quite successful).

Most Painful Aspects of the Divorce/Greatest Losses
(Everett & Lee, 2006; Schwartz & Kaslow, 1997)

The most searing event occurred on the New Year's Eve when Estelle left to go to a party without him, never having invited him to go along. He was stunned and felt abandoned. All of the coldness he had been experiencing enveloped him in a stinging blanket akin to porcupine quills. Next, her telling him to leave her, the children, their marriage, and their home was almost too much rejection and being "castoff" to bear. Having his attempts to save the marriage scoffed and added the proverbial insult to injury. Her lifelong unwillingness to ever converse with him again has mystified him and made it hard for him to savor whatever was good in the relationship they once had – out of which they created a family of four children that they once shared. He felt it ended bitterly and tragically for all.

The greatest loss was the dream of family togetherness and of the many accumulated wonderful shared experiences that were short circuited. He very much valued a strong family milieu in which the several generations were committed to being connected to each other and sharing the various holidays with each other, and this stopped being possible when the children were teenagers.

Estelle's disparaging behavior did not culminate when the legal divorce was over. To illustrate, she made very disturbing and destructive remarks to the children about their dad, one of which was repeated to him by friends who overheard it. "I wish he were dead." (One wonders what motivates one parent to say something like this about the other parent to *their* children. It not only denigrates the person that parent supposedly loved for many years and had chosen as a partner, calling into question his or her own judgment, but conveys malevolence of spirit and cannot make the parent uttering so much hatred seem like a loving person to their kids. And in what way is such a verbalization in "the best interest of the children"? It appears to be the exact opposite – to be in their "worst interest.")

When he learned she was outspoken in telling the children "I do not want you to go to his wedding" several years after the divorce and at another time, that she called his new wife a "fat, ugly person" – (I've seen her, and most would consider her quite attractive and well built) according to reports from friends, he was displeased, but no longer shocked. The children did go to his wedding as by this time they were all adults; she did not like their defiance of her wishes. (It is important to emphasize again – once a couple has children, they can never be fully divorced. They remain linked, positively or negatively, through their offspring – "til death do them part").

The Wonders of Remarriage

Once Reuben started to like and respect himself again, his social life shifted into high gear. He met a peppy, bright, versatile, funny woman who is also Jewish and shares much of his heritage and values, and they really clicked. They enjoyed many of the same activities – including going dancing, going to the theater, golf, tennis, and traveling. Two years after his divorce, he and Ileana, who was also divorced, decided to get married, and now some 33 years later, both are glad they did.

His second child, son Aaron, lived with them for a year or two after they got married. Then he went abroad for awhile and returned to live with them again for a short time until he went back to college at the age of 21. This was all *his* choice. Her daughter, Beth, also lived with them for a year after she graduated college. The children and grandchildren have always been welcome in their lovely home in a beautiful community in a southeastern state (Ganong & Coleman, 2004). Both Rueben and Ileana are still working and lead a full and interesting life.

He has remained close to Aaron, who is in a technology field and lives in New York. He is married and has three children, and they all have a good relationship. He also feels very connected with his youngest son, Hank, who lives on the west coast of the USA with his wife and two children, and they go there to visit him periodically.

Among his best times since the divorce are the spontaneous phone calls from their grandchildren and the various family celebrations they attend, although they dislike having to see "her." He does his best to be indifferent to Estelle at these events and not let her presence upset him, but when she creates a scene, it is difficult to ignore.

Postdivorce Relationship with Ex-In-Law Family/His Family

When Mr. G happens to see Estelle's sister and other relatives, they are all quite friendly. However, he has been totally excluded from all of her family of origin/extended family functions. Her rantings and ravings against him cast him in a negative frame. Likewise, his family does not invite her. His dad, who was a man of few words, simply said she was "crazy," and his sister, who was very supportive of him, said "get a life for yourself." He remains close to his siblings and their families.

Important Contributions to Children's Lives/Their Events He Participated In

During their growing up years when Mr. Guy lived with his children (until they were 13–18 years old), he provided a nice home for them – including building the playroom for them in the basement and the patio in the rear of the house. He stressed the importance of secular education and of religious education and often drove the children to and from religious school. He provided them with music lessons and was involved with their Boy Scout activities (as committee chairman). He took them to sporting events, such as wrestling matches, and enjoyed being a hands-on dad who spent as much time as he could with his boys.

He has fond memories of attending all of their graduations but rues the fact that he had little one on one time with any of them postdivorce while they still lived with their mom. In the present when they come to him to help support their favorite charities, he does. (He appears to be considerate, generous, and affable and wants to be liked – especially by his children – so he does all he can to keep his relationship with each one of them as warm, peaceful, and harmonious as possible.)

Long-Term Divorce Sequelae

Estelle was furious that he was invited to Greg's wedding (son #1). She refused to allow his current wife to walk down the aisle as part of the procession, although she had been invited to do so. (Research shows it is not unusual for a parent to object to stepparent being part of the bridal party.) There was a shortage of seats up front designated for family members, and when Reuben's brother- and sister-in-laws attempted to take the only remaining seats, which were next to her (Estelle), she screamed at him in front of everyone. Eruptive scenes like this turn many a family event into a disaster (Millon, 2011).

Retrospective and Prospective

In reviewing his story during the interview, Mr. Guy realized that part of the reason he kept so busy with his college studies and work during the early years of his first marriage was to escape from his wife as she became increasingly bitter, nasty, angry, jealous, punitive, impulsive, and selfish. The other part was his drive to be successful and set a good example for his sons and to be able to provide a comfortable life for his family. He knows there was nothing he could have done to have made Estelle into a more compassionate, less destructive person. Today he can more freely see the irony and treachery of her choosing one of his friends to be her attorney in the divorce action and of his friend agreeing to do so. (In some states, this would be considered a conflict of interest – but it was permitted where they resided.)

He still has moments of sadness that he could not have been present as a live-in father throughout the years his sons were home, that they were told so many untrue, bad things about him (Bernet, 2010), and that to this day most family events that should be celebrations and happy times are fraught with tension and sometimes marred by one of Estelle's outbursts.

He hopes that Jerry (son #3) will come into his own and be able to earn a decent living. He treasures his (and his wife's) good relationship with Aaron (son #2) and Hank (son #4).

Like many divorced moms, it sounds like Estelle drew their eldest son, Greg, closest to her and cast him into a partial parental or caretaker role. Today she lives in an assisted living facility almost next door to her son- and daughter-in-laws.

Mr. G describes Greg's wife as a terrific person who has found a way to get along with Estelle.

Mr. Guy hopes that his happy and contented noncontentious second marriage, now of 33 years duration, will continue for many years to come and that he and his wife can find more ways and times to see their children and grandchildren when Estelle and her intrusive, chaotic actions are not part of the scenario.

References

Bernet, W. (Ed.). (2010). *Parental alienation, DSM-5 and ICD-11*. Springfield, IL: Charles C. Thomas.

Everett, C. A., & Lee, R. E. (Eds.). (2006). *When marriages fail: Systemic interventions and issues*. New York: Haworth Press (now Taylor & Francis).

Ganong, L. H., & Coleman, M. (2004). *Stepfamily relationships: Development, dynamics and interventions*. New York: Kluwer.

Millon, T. (2011). *Disorders of personality: Introducing a DSM/ICD spectrum from normal to abnormal* (3rd ed.). Hoboken, NJ: Wiley.

Schwartz, L. L., & Kaslow, F. W. (1997). *Painful partings: Divorce and its aftermath*. New York: Wiley.

Chapter 6
Case 5 Dr. Ron Dedicated: Why Can't Judges Also Be Trained to "Do No Harm"?

Brief Personal History

Dr. Dedicated, who is now 58 years of age, apparently realized when he was quite young (as many future physicians do) that he wanted to devote his life to ministering to the health and well-being of others. In the interview, he appeared to be extremely bright (probably in the superior, brilliant category), very energetic, and as the kind of compassionate, knowledgeable, and caring physician in private practice every patient longs to have.

He comes from a Caucasian Jewish family. He was born and raised in a northeastern state. His parents had a long-term marriage, and there was no history of divorce on either side of his family of origin. His parents always encouraged him and were very proud of the kind of person and son he was and of his ambitions and achievements.

First Marriage, Children, and Legal Divorce

RD was 21 years old when he got married in 1975 to Belinda. He made his career intentions clear to his fiancé before their marriage. His fiancé came from a similar Jewish Caucasian family and had been raised in a metropolitan area in the northeast. Their first child, a daughter, was born when they had been married for four years – during which time he was going to college and working. Their son was born two years later. They all accompanied him to Western Europe when he went to medical school there after getting his Ph.D. here in the United States. Next he did a four-year residency at one of the most acclaimed hospitals affiliated with a medical school back in the northeast and finished the fourth year of residency as chief resident – usually a testament to the high esteem in which someone is held by faculty and fellow residents alike for their skill and competence.

F.W. Kaslow, *Divorced Fathers and Their Families: Legal, Economic, and Emotional Dilemmas*, DOI 10.1007/978-1-4614-5535-6_6,
© Springer Science+Business Media New York 2013

Several decades later, he still seems to "love and enjoy" his profession and remains committed to it. By contrast, his wife, Belinda, called him a "bad father" and criticized him for "never being around" because he was "studying or working all of the time." She did not work outside of the home as she had chosen to be a full-time mother and home-maker, both of which she did well. She was an extremely bright woman who resented that their lives seemed to be centered around his career needs and goals. They had moved from their native Canada to England for him to go to medical school, then back to Canada, and then on to the United States for him to do his residency. (However, she did not articulate her discontent nor try to contextualize the situation as a problem they should both try to resolve, and he was unaware of her resentment.) She did not commu-nicate that she wanted something more out of life for herself nor does it seem she did much to make it happen in their years together – that came later. For example, Belinda did not get a job nor become active in philanthropic endeavors once both children were in school. And that was the only place she did become involved.

The children constituted the "totality of her life," but apparently she felt unfulfilled (and projected the blame onto him). This included the fact that she usually slept two nights a week with their daughter in the child's bedroom, leaving him alone in their bedroom. He remembers how neglected he felt, but this was not a discussable issue for Belinda. He knew this arrangement was not healthy for his daughter, but he felt "helpless" to stop it.

One day, he came home from the hospital and found the locks to the doors on the house had been changed and saw his clothes outside. Despite her recent complaints that "only your career is important," she had never told him she was unhappy. Nor had she indicated that she was starting on the pathway to divorce when they had purchased and moved into a new home costing about $500,000 a few months earlier. She had contrib-uted over $200,000 to the purchase from her inheritance, and ostensibly both had seen this *and* his contribution as an investment in their joint future. Belinda apparently rel-ished the fruits of his labor, and at the same time she criticized the very work that made supporting their lifestyle possible. He naively thought they had "a good marriage" and was shocked and bewildered to find he was being thrown out of his home and family.

During the next two years, he tried repeatedly to reconcile. Throughout this period, she made it impossible for him to see the children (Clawar & Rivlin, 1991). They had a few sessions of marital counseling in which Belinda used the time to criticize him. She had become a controlling and unreasonable person (like her mother). Nonetheless, he wanted to reconcile so he could go back to living with the children and being part of his family and in his home.

After he was literally "thrown out" of his house, he looked for a hotel room in which to stay temporarily. He soon learned Belinda had overdrawn their bank account, taking out $40,000 and emptying it. He also learned that, unbeknownst to him, for the three months prior to evicting him, she had been depositing his checks in a separate bank account, set up in her name only. He was devastated and flabbergasted. Evicting him had obviously been planned for a long time; it was not an impulsive act. (Such chicanery was beyond his ability to grasp for a long time.)

The marital settlement agreement stipulated that they were to have joint and equal custody, but she interpreted this, nonetheless, to mean she was the primary custodial parent. She insisted on making all of the decisions on her own. He took their case back to court twice, and the judge merely admonished her to "act like an adult" and implement the actual agreement. She did neither, and *the judge did nothing by way of enforcing the MSA*. Finally, disillusioned and discouraged, *he gave up fighting*. (Judges obviously were not trained to "do no harm"; the children's isolation from him was harmful to him and to them).

Like many of the other dads interviewed for this book, Dr. Dedicated rues the fact that she also kept the children from seeing his parents. The children were never able to spend any of the Jewish holidays with their paternal grandparents. Yet, Belinda knew the holidays were very important to them (Rosen & Weltman, 1996). His parents felt deeply hurt and experienced this as a great wound and loss (Kaslow, 2007).

Finances

Although Belinda summarily evicted her husband and was the one who initiated the idea of divorce, she was awarded the new home and all its contents plus combined child support and alimony of $9,000 per month or $108,000 per year. This was payable in weekly installments that served as a constant nagging painful reminder of his ongoing obligation and tie to her. Out of this, she was directed to pay the mortgage on the house, which was still substantial. (He, like other husbands, came to understand why she had refused to work once the children started school; she knew she would be awarded much more in alimony and child support if she had no work history. See Chapter 15 – section on Games Divorcing People Play.) Belinda began cohabitating two to three years after she evicted him. She and her new partner bought a country house together, but the alimony did not stop as apparently the MSA did not contain a clause which terminated it in the event of cohabitation. Twelve years after the divorce, she told Dr. D she would be willing to get remarried to said partner, which would end the need for alimony (by then both children were over 18 years of age, but apparently this was a combined figure, and the child support had not been phased out) if he bought himself out for a sum close to $50,000. Their agreement contained "no termination clause," so to do so would have meant returning to court, which he had been loathe to do. After having paid $1,296,000 in alimony, while receiving just about nothing in return from Belinda for 12 years, he was relieved to finally have a way to get this burden off his back and out of his heart and made the lump sum payment. (One wonders, is such an arrangement really just, especially once cohabitation has begun and the children are beyond the age that child support is customarily provided?)

Postdivorce Period and Relationship to Children

Eventually Dr. Dedicated bought himself a much smaller home in the same city where he was practicing medicine and his wife and children lived. The children each had their own bedrooms in this house.

Since Dr. D prefers to avoid conflict, he shies away from confrontation. Therefore, he has never talked to the children, not even since they became adults, about what transpired for him when he was evicted and when they were not made available to visit with him. He has always taken good care of them financially, long after court adjudicated responsibility ended. He paid for college for both and for postgraduate professional school for his daughter.

He has often taken the children on trips here and abroad, just with him, and also with his second wife and their child, since he remarried 16 years ago.

Dr. Dedicated realized during the conflicted, unhappy separation period that the marriage had never really worked well as he was always "low man on the totem pole." Several times during the interview, he connected the facts that "he never says no," is "not a fighter," and "does not like to discuss problems" in order to avoid calling attention to a conflict, with why nothing ever got (or gets) resolved. He tends to see issues as either black or white, and that too makes them "non-discussable."

Children's Reactions and Aftermath

He believes their separation and divorce were very difficult for the children, but they never raised any questions about it with him nor made any comments – not even about the event that precipitated his moving out. They too choose not to initiate any discussion of the topic then or now – although both are in their 30s. (Important issues that are never broached often fester and become barriers to improving relationships over time. They also tend to seem more insurmountable because they were "too hot to handle earlier." Dealing with an issue can lead to resolution and decrease the fear of what might happen.)

Both children were always good students and achieved well academically. Each is already a successful young career person in their field. His daughter received many awards as she went through professional school, and as he talks about her, it is apparent that he is very proud of her.

Now that they are grown, he talks with them by phone weekly. He sees his son as very responsible and has made him trustee of his estate.

Experience of Divorce

There were several very painful aspects of this unexpected and initially unwanted experience (Kaslow & Schwartz, 1987). First was "getting thrown out of his home," the home he had provided for Belinda and the children – with no discussion and no warning. It just happened suddenly – *he was irrevocably "locked out" when the locks were surreptitiously changed.* He resented her taking total control over the children's lives and not involving him at all in decisions about rearing the children.

The second long-lasting painful aspect was paying so much money for alimony and child support for so long without having the pleasure of living with his children and being there to help raise them nor of residing in the expensive home that was planned and bought as their family home. In his thoughts, that included him. *It felt like a lifelong sentence.* (It meant 12 more years of continuing total financial responsibility for a 14-year marriage during which she had been unwilling to work and had been very well supported.)

His attempts to get the provisions of the MSA enforced fell on deaf ears when he twice returned to court to enforce his joint custody status and his access to his children on an every other weekend basis. He became embittered and still is (which is true of those other dads in this study who seem to have been treated most unfairly). Again the "do no harm" caveat taught to doctors comes to mind; such "servitude" is dangerous to the physical and emotional health of the father.

His ex-wife did not permit the children to visit him for two years following the separation and apparently continued during that time to be highly critical of him to them. She intercepted all of his attempts not only to see the children but to communicate with them (Baker, 2007). He had been dismissed and extruded from their lives, except that *his weekly checks were always welcomed.* She took total control of the children's lives; he had no input or voice in their rearing, about their schooling, or extracurricular activities.

Postdivorce Interaction with Ex-In-Law Family/His Family's Reactions

Although Dr. D had had a close relationship to his father-in-law during the years of his marriage, that was completely severed when he was sent away by his wife. This puzzled him, but he was unable to approach him about it. He had never particularly liked his mother-in-law, who he had found to be very bossy. When he did go back to get the remainder of his clothes, they threatened him if he "ever put a hand on their daughter," although there had been no history of any abuse to warrant such a threat. (I have known Dr. D in various ways for about 10 years; it is hard to fathom him being violent – even if severely provoked.) He was no longer included in his in-law family's functions and learned that their comments to the children about him, like his ex-wife's, were critical and derogatory (Clawar & Rivlin, 1991).

His family was devastated. The loss of contact with their grandchildren violated his parents' sense of family loyalty and continuity. This was the first divorce in either side of his family of origin, and everyone was displeased and dismayed by it. But they remained sympathetic to Dr. D and sorry for the tragedy that had befallen him. Nonetheless, his parents tried to maintain a relationship with Belinda with phone calls several times a year. Still she would rarely let the children visit their paternal grandparent when she and they were back in Canada for other reasons.

Life Events He Participated in with Children Postdivorce/Poignant Memories

After the initial two years of almost "no contact" with the children, Belinda decided to comply with the court order because of changes in her personal life and allowed him some visitation and involvement. Dr. D then attended as many of the children's sports activities as he could and went to their high school and college graduations and their campus May Day celebrations. He was not invited to see them prior to their various proms and clearly recalls how left out he felt.

His best and most poignant memories include sharing their college and professional school graduations and the trips he has taken alone with them. Fortunately his second wife is not "jealous" and does not become upset when he wants to travel just with his two children from his prior marriage.

Among his most important contributions to the children's lives has been his continuing financial support – well into their adulthood – and letting them know by his behavior that he is "always there for them." It continues to disconcert him that he rarely sees them as they live in one of the mid-Atlantic states, and he lives in the southeast. They rarely come to his home to visit with him and his second family.

Postdivorce Stress, Turmoil, Illnesses, and Scars

For Dr. D, *the separation was like a death*; he found it inconceivable to not be allowed into his own home. This turned his life upside down. Belinda had totally betrayed his trust, and he was thoroughly befuddled. For a year, he was depressed; work was his only salvation. He was completely unwilling to socialize.

Despite still seeing his ex-wife as controlling, cranky, critical, nasty, manipulative, argumentative, inflexible, and as someone who believes it is "my way or the highway," he grudgingly states "she is a good mother even if she is overly enmeshed with the kids." (It is hard to juxtapose his descriptive adjectives of Belinda with the phrase "good mother" – good mothers are not "overly enmeshed" with kids – but seeing her this way may be necessary so he can have a modicum of peace of mind.)

The current saga is that his very accomplished daughter, who earns a salary into the six-figure category several times over, is planning her wedding. Belinda asked him what he was willing to contribute. In anticipation of such a call from her, he had talked to several of his buddies who told him to have a figure in mind of what he was willing to spend and not to deviate from it, which he did. (This is sound advice once children are over 18 years of age and healthy.) He did so but he felt guilty about setting any limits. (Many divorced dads have excessive trouble with this. They fear they will lose whatever love the child feels for them or will be seen as the ogre their mother described.) He decided after setting this limit not to make any issues but to just be cooperative and asked to be told what else was requested of him. He wants the wedding plans to go smoothly and the wedding to be a happy occasion.

Belinda became a professional career woman after the divorce and took her BS and an advanced degree at a prestigious northeast university. She has since developed a solid career and become quite independent.

Remarriage

Dr. D remarried eight years after the heart-wrenching separation. His current wife, Janine, has a profession and works for a well-respected firm. They have a 10-year-old child. When his older children call, his wife is polite and cordial, but she does not initiate contact with them. Nor does she do anything to neither interfere with his relationship with them nor discourage his contributing to them financially or taking them on vacations. There is ample income for all. Both Dr. D and Janine were pleasantly surprised recently when his daughter invited their child to be in the bridal party. This should make the wedding an easier event for them as that signifies a true gesture to them of "we really want you there."

Retrospective

Although Dr. D is happily remarried, has a thriving practice, has fared well financially, and is well respected in his local community, he misses his former university hospital and academic community world. He states that he is still very angry and bitter and believes he was terribly taken advantage of and with the court's permission. He has been extremely generous to her and the children. He savors the closeness he had to his parents and his sisters and remains upset that his parents were punished by Belinda who did not let the children visit them. He regrets not having been able to cultivate a similar closeness with his son and daughter from his first marriage.

In addition to all of the other tangible losses suffered from the divorce, the smashing of the dream of "happily ever after" and "being there with and for the kids as a live-in dad" are the hardest facts to integrate into his self-concept and personal world view. He is trying in every possible way to make sure it does not happen again. He believes when one has children, one makes a commitment to parenting actively until they are grown and resents he was not allowed to fulfill his commitment and "hang in during the rough spots." He still seeks a more complete rapprochement with them and their love and respect and to be able to relate to them directly and not through someone else. And in his own life he follows the Hippocratic Oath of DO NO HARM and wishes the judges would also do this by not allowing one parent to banish the other from *their* children's lives, especially when they are in violation of the MSA.

References

Baker, A. L. (2007). *Adult children of parental alienation syndrome: Breaking the ties that bind.* New York: Norton.

Clawar, S. S., & Rivlin, B. V. (1991). *Children held hostage: Dealing with programmed and brainwashed children.* Chicago: American Bar Association Section of Family Law.

Kaslow, F. W. (2007). Post divorce relatedness between parents, their divorced sons, and their grandchildren: A pilot study. In C. A. Everett & R. E. Lee (Eds.), *When marriages fail: Systemic family therapy interventions and issues* (pp. 141–156). New York: Haworth Press.

Kaslow, F. W., & Schwartz, L. L. (1987). *Dynamics of Divorce: A life cycle perspective.* New York: Brunner/Mazel.

Rosen, E. J., & Weltman, S. F. (1996). Jewish families: An overview. In M. McGoldrick, J. Giardino, & J. K. Pearce (Eds.), *Ethnicity and family therapy* (2nd ed., pp. 611–630). New York: Guildford.

Chapter 7
Case 6 Mr. Bill Brogan: Feeling Trapped, Escaping, and "The Big Lie"

Brief Personal History

Mr. Brogan is a big, strapping, attractive Caucasian man, 69 years young at the time of the interview. He was born, grew up, and married in the Midwest. He was raised in the Lutheran church; his ancestry is a mixture of Norwegian, Danish, Irish, and Welsh. He received his B.S. from a Big Ten Midwestern University and took one year of postgraduate work before embarking on a career as an engineer. He has remained close to his family of origin and is a devoted son; he sees his mother and sister for several long visits each year, even though he now resides in a southeastern state. His dad died a number of years ago, and he still misses him.

First Marriage, Children, and the Legal Divorce

When Bill was 22 years of age, in 1964, he married Cynthia, a Methodist woman of Swedish and Austrian descent from a similar Midwestern town and background. Thus, cultural, religious, and ethnic differences were not a factor in what led up to their marital problems and ultimately their divorce 26 years later, in 1990. They had two daughters and a son together. Their married life seemed fairly typical. Mr. B reported that when the children were growing up, his job had been contingent upon his being able to travel, and he had often been away from home during the week. In his leisure time, Bill enjoyed, and still enjoys, boating. Therefore, when he received a sum of money for selling his share of a business, they decided to sell their home and buy a boat and the family of five, which included three teenagers, took off for a six-month sailing trip which entailed living in very close quarters. Being together constantly was new for all of them. It turned out to be a "trip from hell."

Over the years, he and Cynthia had lost "their loving feeling" for each other. One evening when they were ashore at a party at a friend's house, he saw Cynthia cuddled up with another guest. During the preceding few years, his wife had

F.W. Kaslow, *Divorced Fathers and Their Families: Legal, Economic, and Emotional Dilemmas*, DOI 10.1007/978-1-4614-5535-6_7,
© Springer Science+Business Media New York 2013

distanced herself from him, and he knew their relationship was "over emotionally," but he had "hung in for the kids." However, witnessing her behavior that evening was the trigger that pushed him to admit to himself that "he could not stand her anymore."

He volunteered that during the last few years of their marriage, he had two or three sexualized relationships that meant little to him. In fact, one brief encounter had been with a friend of Cynthia's who had "approached" him. He was flattered and succumbed. This too had signaled him that he was no longer emotionally committed to his wife. However, it was seeing her flirting and snuggling with another man that aroused his indignation and made him realize it was time to take action to dissolve the marriage. Despite her overt display of affection that evening, he does not think she ever actually had an affair.

When he decided divorce was inevitable from his point of view, Bill continued to live on the boat and found an apartment for Cynthia. He told her to "get out." He was the one who filed for the divorce. By then, their oldest daughter, Patty, was 23 years old and in college. Their middle child, Jessica, was 21 and spent most of her time traveling for her job. Their youngest, a son, Brad, was 19 years of age and chose to move out too so he could live with his mom. Apparently, he had some learning disabilities, an average I.Q., did not go to college, and was more attached to his mom than to his dad.

Initially, Cynthia had sought the services of a reasonable attorney who was geared to negotiating an equitable settlement, and everything got off to a "good start" from Bill's perspective. However, someone convinced her to change lawyers, and she then hired a "barracuda." Overnight, there was a noticeable shift in the tone of their interactions.

When the Brogans had sold their house and gone to live on the boat, their furniture had been stored at several different relatives' homes. One day after the separation, Cynthia collected and took all of these items out of storage, without notifying Bill, and then sold his belongings, including such personal items as his underwear, at a garage sale, while he was out of town. When his father learned about the sale, he knew Bill would be dismayed over losing some of his possessions and in such a surreptitious manner, so he went to the sale and bought back some of the items that had previously been stored in his garage.

Mr. Brogan then realized "my nice-guy lawyer is not what I need; I'll have to engage an even fiercer barracuda," which he did. It turned into a dreadful divorce battle. Finally, under the settlement agreement, he got to keep his boat, on which he was living, and she was granted all remaining household items.

Finances

Since both lawyers had fought hard for their respective clients, the costs added up to being very expensive; they both had charged top fees for that geographic locale. Mr. B ended up having to pay all of the legal fees to both attorneys, and they tallied over

$40,000, leaving him "flat broke." By then, the children were all over 18 years of age, so no child support was levied. He was to pay Cynthia $500 a month alimony or $6,000 a year for three years. However, at her request, he borrowed money and gave her a lump sum of $10,000, which left him free and clear of lingering indebtedness to her.

Early Postdivorce Period

Her behavior increased Mr. B's sense of bitterness. Although he was irate over what he considered her "theft" of his items from storage, he decided not to file charges because *he felt so guilty* about breaking up the family. But soon, the guilt was purged by the fury. It was a hellish period for him which followed their very nasty divorce.

His eldest daughter came to visit him occasionally during the early postdivorce period, but his other two children did not for a two-year time interval. He is still not sure why they spurned him for so long.

He does conjecture now that it might have been because they saw their mother as helpless and dependent and felt that by divorcing her, "Bill" was basically abandoning a child. In hindsight, he also realized that they felt he abandoned them, too, because he had no money to support them and no home to offer them, other than the boat they, at that time, hated. Never mind that two of the children were already independent and the youngest was supposed to be living with his mother. Cynthia moved out of state shortly after the divorce and left Brad on his own. He was angry with Bill for getting a divorce and would not accept help from him, so he spent a few horrible years scrounging off friends. He was old enough to be on his own and working, but with only a high school education, he did not earn enough money to be self-supporting. He blamed his miserable life on Bill for breaking up the marriage (Divorce is not only the death of a marriage but also children realize it marks the breakup of the existing family as they know it, and it usually disrupts the children's sense of security, safety, continuity, and predictability. In their own thoughts and feelings, they may believe their "heart connection" to the departing parent has been severed – that he or she is divorcing them also – and they are likely to place all of the blame for the demise of the marriage on one parent while seeing the other as the injured party who did nothing to contribute to the problems and dissension. Sometimes one parent is portrayed and then perceived as all good, the other as all bad. This is rarely the case, but the process of brainwashing may have been begun, and the children simply do not realize what is happening as they desperately cling to one parent for reassurance and stability. It sounds like this is what occurred in the Brogan family.) (Clawar & Rivlin, 1991).

Everyone's emotions were raw. Cynthia and the children all nursed their grudges against him. Disillusioned and disheartened, Bill worked part time doing odd jobs on boats, even serving as a licensed ferryboat captain. He seems to have lost much of his motivation to work hard postdivorce after several decades of being his family's major "breadwinner" and after working 50–56 hours per week for several decades.

Most Painful Aspects of Divorce

Bill continues to be baffled by Cynthia's poisoning of the children against him and by the false allegations she made against him to the children and to their friends (Bernet, 2010). To this day, over 20 years later, old friends still mention that she denigrates him to them.

About 10 years after the divorce, his eldest daughter, Patty, abruptly stopped talking to him. He had no idea why. She had been the only one of his three children who initially had expressed any empathy to the fact that she recognized he needed something different in his life and who had kept in contact with him. Only recently, he found out why she had totally cut him out of her life. In a letter she sent him, Patty accused him of having sexually abused her when she was 18 months old, which shocked him, as this had never occurred. When he called her about this, she said that she would only discuss it with him if he would come with her to see her therapist. To her surprise, he went back to their home community and did just that. She insisted he meet her at the therapist's office, refusing to actually go with him.

Since his second wife is a prominent doctoral level therapist and author of psychotherapy books, some of which focus on gender issues and couple and family relationships, they had sometimes discussed such issues. Therefore, he was reasonably conversant with this arena of therapy and how family dynamics are likely to play out and be handled by a skilled therapist. He went to the session with an optimistic attitude as to what could be accomplished to clear up Patty's misconception so they could reconnect. To his dismay, the therapist she was seeing was not doctoral level (i.e., she was neither a psychologist nor a psychiatrist). In introducing herself, she stressed she herself was a "survivor of incest" and that 80% of her clients were incest survivors – so she "knew how to deal with this." She had used age regression therapy to bring back this memory from very early childhood. (This is not a widely accepted therapeutic technique and at times has led to false memory syndrome.)

The therapist was not willing to give any credence to his denial that this had never occurred; she dismissed it by saying something akin to "most men deny such awful behavior." In the session, Patty disclosed that she had heard that he had had his first sexual experience when he was 14 years old with a 30-year-old woman – whom she even named accurately. Since his ex-wife was the only one who knew this, it was clear where she got this information and that Cynthia had crossed a generational barrier line (Minuchin, 1984) to malign him to their daughter. Patty used this as further proof of his sexual depravity and worthlessness (author's interpretation). He left the session alone, as he had come, his high hopes for a positive outcome destroyed by the therapist's subjective, unprofessional stance and his daughter's hostility and unwillingness to hear what he had to say. He was dismayed and distraught knowing he had been unjustly accused, and yet, there was no way to explain or defend himself. (*What a terrible quagmire in which to be caught as all too many dads falsely accused of child sexual abuse are. About 75% of such allegations actually turn out to be unfounded and false.*) Now two years later, he still hears through the various "grapevines" about the rumors Cynthia, who is already on her third marriage, and Patty, who has married and had children, spread about him. He tries to toss these off but is saddened by the fact that he cannot be a father to Patty when she needs one nor a grandfather to her children. (What a loss for all.)

Postdivorce Interactions with Ex-In-Law Family and His Own Family

Mr. B's relationship to his former father-in-law had never been good; Cynthia's father was a blue-collar worker, and TB was a "college guy" – something he abhorred. Her mother was agoraphobic, and the paternal grandfather was an alcoholic, so there were numerous problems transmitted in her family. He found them to be a "rigid Swedish/Austrian family," and he did not find it a good fit for him. During their marriage, Cynthia and the children were closer to his family of origin than to hers. He learned that after their divorce, Cynthia's father had cut her out of his will – but he did not know why.

Cynthia totally alienated his dad when she took BB's belongings from his house and sold them. His sister never liked her so the divorce did not perturb her. However, to this day, his mother maintains contact with Cynthia, with whom she had had a good relationship, partially because she wanted to continue to have access to her grandchildren and great-grandchildren (Kaslow, 2007).

The Later Postdivorce Years

Mr. B met, fell in love with, actively pursued, and married Dr. Vibrant within a year of his divorce. He was quickly smitten by her upbeat, fun-loving personality, her intellectual brightness and curiosity, and her academic achievements and ambition. A very attractive woman, he instantly admired her well-balanced ability to juggle her own family and home responsibilities (three grown children and grandchildren), her high profile career, and her busy social life. He found being in her company made life much more worth living. As an added bonus, she shared his love of boating and golfing. When they got married, only Patty and Dr. Vibrant's three children attended the wedding. His other two children were still boycotting him, which wounded him deeply.

He views himself as being a much more cooperative husband and partner the second time around. In the early years of this marriage, when Dr. Vibrant was still working and earning substantially more than TB was, he often took care of their home and made many of the meals. He also built some of their furniture, which he does with great skill. Now that she is retired, they share these responsibilities. Their sailing, driving, and golfing trips have been fun adventures. They have a huge circle of friends. Each is more content in their second marriage than they were in their first (continuing after the initial novelty and excitement of marriage had dissipated).

Much to BB's pleasure, his son, Brad, has chosen in recent years to move to the same city in the southeast where his dad and Dr. V reside. He does not approve of his mom's choice of men and dislikes her current boyfriend. Mr. B is glad to have him nearby, and sometimes, they just "hang out together." His son's employment record continues to be somewhat marginal. Like his dad, he is skilled with his hands and is good at construction tasks and electrical work.

His middle child, Jessica, lives about an hour away, and they see her occasionally and have a good relationship. Both she and Brad get along well with Dr. V. Like Brad, she has never married, but she has a successful career.

Mr. B slowly developed a reasonable relationship with Dr. V's children. They are all still close to their dad. Dr. V's divorce was an amicable one year before she met BB, so there is no spill over animosity, and they can all be together at holidays and other occasions that warrant it. Her ex-husband is also comfortably remarried. Since both sets of children were adults when they met and married, none of the children lived with them, and they did not assume active stepparenting roles for each other's children.

Experience of Divorce: Then and Now

Whenever possible, BB participated in important events in his children's lives. Sometimes he was purposely excluded, much to his sorrow, as when he was deliberately not invited to his son's high school graduation. By the time Patty was graduating from college, he had moved far from his daughter's college and could not afford to fly back for the ceremony. He felt overwhelmed in both instances by the sense of loss over the realization of what he was missing.

He continues to resent their mother's false accusations against him to their children, to their friends, and to *his* mother. Cynthia's attempts to bind their loyalty to her first and foremost have also contributed to alienating them from him. He believes she coddled Brad too much which contributed to making him timid, fearful, and lacking in confidence and courage. He sees his son as capable in various building skills. He also noted that he has a fine singing voice but will neither volunteer to do karaoke nor to audition for local theatricals. He is still trying to encourage, motivate, and reassure his grown son of his value and talents.

Most Important Contributions to Children's Lives

Mr. Brogan, who wanted children and liked being a father, believes Patty acquired much of her "can-do" attitude, her courage, and her resiliency from him as these are assets he too possesses. Jessica, also, is characterized by a confident, "can-do" approach to life and exhibits logical thought processes similar to her dad in his scientific, engineering mind-set. Brad too is endowed with a logical way of viewing things. BB provided his three children with the best he could and encouraged them when it came to schoolwork and education in general – something he highly values.

Best and Most Poignant Memories with Children

Even though the children originally claimed to have "hated" the family six-month boat trip, in recent years, they have talked about it with fond reminiscences. For him, there were many good times aboard ship, and it was the last time they all did something together as a family. He thoroughly enjoyed attending their sporting activities when he was in town – including Patty's swim meets, Jessica's cheerleading, and Brad's T-ball. Sharing these aspects of their lives gives him a real sense of fulfillment.

Retrospective

When Mr. B embarked on his first marriage, he expected to remain married "until death do us part," as his parents had. Unfortunately, good intentions were not sufficient to overcome the lack of compatibility, the differences in values and lifestyle preferences, and so much more. When he told Cynthia he wanted a divorce, he did not anticipate that it would turn into such a tempestuous one from which he would emerge "flat broke," disillusioned, and disheartened. Nor would he have believed Cynthia would have purposely sought to alienate all three children from him.

Bill thinks that Patty believes as she does because she is a victim of *false memory syndrome* (Schneider, 1994) probably induced by her therapist. Cynthia has not tried to correct this misconception, to his knowledge, even though she knows that he is unlikely to have done such a thing. Nor to his knowledge had she ever made an effort to share her doubts with Patty. The unanticipated consequences of losing contact with each of the children for long periods of time have caused him much grieving and sadness.

He also regrets that two of the children have not married and wonders if this is partially attributable to their growing up with their own parents' marriage as an unhappy and poor model of what marriage is like. He had hoped for more grandchildren.

Subsequent to our interview, Mr. B decided to write a concise, heartfelt letter to his children clarifying the facts regarding the alleged abuse of Patty, which he posits never occurred. He candidly expressed his continuing love and regard for the children and the fact that he still wants them all to be an active part of his life and vice versa. (Such behavior, aimed at reconciliation, is included in the tips section of Chapter 16. I can verify that this was done as I saw a copy of the letter).

BB's second wife is a peppy, full of fun, adventurous, and loving person. He appreciates the wisdom of his choice and that he is able to fulfill many of his personal dreams in this relationship. He is ever hopeful that Patty will accept "the truth," that the "relational damage" can be repaired (Miller, 2010), and that ultimately she will reestablish a positive relationship with herself and with him (Baker & Ben-Ami, 2011).

References

Baker, A. L., & Ben-Ami, N. (2011). To turn a child against a parent is to turn a child against himself: The direct and indirect effect of exposure to parental alienation strategies on self-esteem and well being. *Journal of Divorce and Remarriage, 52*(5), 472–489.

Bernet, W. (Ed.). (2010). *Parental alienation, DSM-5 and ICD-11*. Springfield, IL: Charles C. Thomas.

Clawar, S. S., & Rivlin, B. V. (1991). *Children held hostage: Dealing with programmed and brainwashed children*. Chicago: American Bar Association Section of Family Law.

Kaslow, F. W. (2007). Post divorce relatedness between parents, their divorced sons, and their grandchildren: A pilot study. In C. A. Everett & R. E. Lee (Eds.), *When marriages fail: Systemic family therapy interventions and issues* (pp. 141–156). New York: Haworth Press.

Miller, A. (2010). Young adult daughter's accounts of relationships with nonresidential fathers: Relational damage, repair and maintenance. *Journal of Divorce and Remarriage, 51*(5), 293–309.

Minuchin, S. (1984). *Family kaleidoscope*. Cambridge: Harvard University Press.

Schneider, J. G. (1994). Legal issues involving "repressed memory" of childhood sexual abuse. In *Psychology psychologists legal update* (No. 5). Washington, DC: National Register of Health Service Providers.

Chapter 8
Case 7 Mr. Terry Kelly's Saga of Betrayal

Brief Personal History

Mr. Kelly was a clean-cut boyish-looking young man of 38 years of age at the time of the interview. Casually dressed on a weekend day, he carried himself in a poised, confident, open, and accessible manner. He was friendly, articulate, and quite willing to participate in this project and tell his story as he believes this book is much needed and can ultimately provide useful information to many people who are involved in the divorce process, either personally and/or professionally.

Initially raised in the Catholic religion, he switched to being Methodist during his childhood when his parents changed their faith and church. He has remained in the Methodist church, and religion is important to him. His family has Scotch and Irish roots.

His original college degree is a B.A. in history from a well-ranked university in the southeast United States, and his law degree (J.D.) is from one of the most prestigious law schools in the northeast. He clerked with a federal judge and then worked for a law firm in the southwest for a while. He is quite familiar with divorce and divorce law and the havoc this whole process can wreak on the family.

First Marriage, a Child, and the Legal Divorce

Terry and Ellen were married in 1999 when he was 26 years old. She is also of Methodist persuasion and had a rather similar background, so that part of their marriage was an easy fit. Ellen was also an attorney, so they had much in common, professionally as well as personally, or so it seemed. Terry joined a consultation firm soon after they got married, and his new position involved traveling, sometimes out of the country. He was usually away from home Monday through Thursday, working hard to build his practice and his salary. Ellen was also very "career focused." Two years after they were married, she decided to leave the firm she was with and start her own practice.

F.W. Kaslow, *Divorced Fathers and Their Families: Legal, Economic, and Emotional Dilemmas*, DOI 10.1007/978-1-4614-5535-6_8,
© Springer Science+Business Media New York 2013

A short while later Terry became "suspicious" that she might be having an affair. He confronted her, and at first, she denied it. But eventually she admitted to being involved with another attorney. The man's wife also found out about their clandestine relationship and was infuriated. Terry told his wife to leave, which she did for a short while. But when Ellen pleaded to come back, stating she wanted to try again and promising to be faithful, Terry, who had married "till death do us part," capitulated and committed himself again to attempting to make the marriage work. Together they went for marital counseling, and in addition, he went for individual therapy. Shortly after their reconciliation, they went together to a dinner party at a neighbor's house and probably had a little too much to drink. When they came home, they "had sex"; this was the first intimate encounter in a very long time. Ellen became pregnant that night. It was not a planned pregnancy.

The time of her pregnancy was (for him at least) probably the best year they had spent together. Their daughter, Adriana, was born late in 2003, and he was overjoyed. He looked forward to having more children. But from the first, Ellen did not like being a parent. She returned to work two weeks after the baby was born. She called their daughter "a nuisance" and passed her care off to a nanny and to her own mother, who Terry described as a very kind person.

Shortly thereafter, Ellen also took on a directorship of a nonprofit law group. He described her as "narcissistic and aggressive," wanting to be in the limelight and at the center of attention. She liked the excitement and glitter of the entertainment field and had ambitions about becoming a star on a national television show, for which she went so far as to audition. The world outside the home was much more enticing to Ellen than being an active mom who combined motherhood and career. So she did not let her daughter "interfere" with her other ambitions and activities.

During Adriana's infancy period, Terry decided to take a job which involved less traveling so he could be home more with his family and enjoy his darling daughter. He wanted to achieve a good balance between his personal/family life and professional/career life. He placed a high value on a close-knit family and wanted to help offer his little girl consistency and continuity of parenting. Ellen was annoyed about his impending job change as she liked his having a huge salary and the lifestyle that this combined with her income permitted them to enjoy.

He became suspicious about his wife's behavior once again and decided to go home early from an out-of-town business trip and surprise her and see if his suspicions were validated. And surprise her he did. He walked in after a red-eye flight back from the west coast to find another man there with her. Great actress that she is, she tried histrionically to lie her way out of it, but the evidence was right there in front of him (Glass & Wright, 1996).

He was finally completely convinced that the marriage had to end. They had widely discrepant ideas about fidelity, loyalty, integrity, parental responsibility, and preferred lifestyle. He was going to bring the ongoing struggle between them to an end (at least the being married aspect). Subsequently he filed for the divorce, and Ellen was the one who moved out of the marital home.

Early Post-separation/Divorce Period

Terry experienced a great sense of relief after they separated, and he was much happier. With his change of jobs, he was away from home much less so he could spend more time with Adriana. His life felt more balanced and less erratic, even though he experienced some anxiety about being divorced – a status that had never been part of his life plan or dream. He loved being a dad; it is a defining aspect of his identity.

Their MSA stipulated that they were to have true joint and equal custody. Adriana spends alternating weeks with each parent. (Thus, each parent is involved in the emotional, physical, legal, and financial aspects of parenting, and Adriana does not have to move back and forth several times a week.) At one point, Adriana lived with her dad 100% of the time for eight months because of mutual agreement (reason not clarified) (Braver, 1998).

He was basically dissatisfied with the custody and visitation plan the court decreed as he would have much preferred to have been awarded primary and almost full custody. If this desire had been realized, he would have moved back to his original home state so he could have lived near his family of origin and raised his daughter in a healthier, more wholesome, loving extended family milieu. But since this was not to be, he was determined to make Adriana's transitioning back and forth from mom's house to dad's house (Ricci, 1980) as easy as possible and to never disparage Ellen or sabotage what she was "trying to do with and for *our* daughter."

Shortly after their divorce, Ellen became pregnant again. She married the baby's father, who, incidentally, was the lover Terry had caught her within their home. Her two affairs were unconscionable within his belief system of meaning and value (Lusterman, 1998). Terry was concerned that Ellen's behavior would have a negative influence on Adriana, and *he is struggling with how to protect his daughter from this without maligning her mother*. He describes her now, as he sees her even more clearly several years postdivorce, as very charming (superficially and when she wants to be), manipulative, intelligent, a liar who often believes her own lies, and someone who easily makes and then destroys relationships. For example, she has trouble keeping nannies, which has meant rapid turnover of Adriana's main caregiver at mom's house, and this worries Terry. (This rarely leads to stability and consistency of nurturance and handling in a young child's life – so his concern is rooted in well-documented facts.) All of this plus her prior lying directly to him has led him to distrust her and to questioning the veracity of much that Ellen says to him.

Child's Reaction to Divorce

Adriana was only one and a half years old when her parents decided to split up and turned two about the time of the divorce. Because her parents have been cooperative about making her transitions to and fro easy (rather than stressful) and have not "badmouthed" one another, she has handled living in both mom's and dad's house well. (It is what she has known since she was a toddler, so this is her normal way of life.)

During the past five years when Adriana is at her mom's house, she has had four different caregivers in the course of each week, her maternal grandmother, a nanny, the housekeeper, and mom. Both the nanny and housekeeper tend to turn over often. Terry does not agree with this plan because it is haphazard and inconsistent, but he has no choice as to how Ellen handles child care arrangements in her home. At his home, he has provided most of the parenting with the help of a nanny, who has stayed with him and Adriana for an extended period of time.

Finances

Although Terry has joint an equal custody with Adriana in residence with him half the time, he has paid Ellen $30,000 per year in child support for the past five years. The judge dismissed Ellen's claim for alimony because of her infidelity. Terry also pays totally for Adriana's medical and dental care costs, her extracurricular activities, and her private school, although the MSA specified that Ellen is to pay half of the private school fees. He would rather pay and avoid hassling then to go back to court for a court order mandating she pay her half. Currently, Terry's income is in the $250,000 range and so is Ellen's and her husband's combined income. (How does one define *fair* in such circumstances? What role does and should the one who is the "cuckold" play? What does it take for a dad to put his child's needs first when he has been and continues to be exploited? Virtue, valor, and unselfishness are no doubt all qualities that count a great deal.) Ultimately, he will have paid child support for 16 years by the time Adriana reaches 18 years of age totaling $540,000 *plus* all of the additional expenses for medical, dental, insurance costs, etc., and what he covers when his daughter is with him half of her life. (Clearly the expense of a divorce goes on and on and on.)

In addition, Ellen's income has been supplemented by her parents, who have bought her a car, bought another car for the nanny in her household, and pay for many things she wants. He sees Ellen as very proficient at "guilt induction" and her parents, who are good and kind people, as very susceptible to her manipulations.

Most Painful Aspects of Divorce

Terry was disillusioned by Ellen's betrayals, her infidelities, and her lying to cover them up. He was dismayed that he had so misjudged the woman he asked to become his bride. He was and still is worried about the impact of her roller-coaster behavior, style, and mood swings on Adriana – she can be charming and sweet one minute and so nasty, self-centered, inconsiderate, and mean a few minutes later. She also knows how to "push a button" to make Adriana "feel sorry for Mommy" (Kernberg, 1975). Ellen became increasingly critical of him when she learned that he was planning to get married again, even though he had waited five years to do so while she had remarried quickly because she had gotten pregnant.

He is distressed that Ellen cannot function on a more even keel (Millon, 2011). When Adriana is at Ellen's home, she spends very little time with her, but he finds she is unwilling to discuss principles and practices of child rearing with him. They do not talk very often or much; like many divorced couples today, they communicate by e-mail and text messaging – keeping everything brief and to the point. If he includes any suggestions or commentary, his words are interpreted as an attack. She has become highly critical of Terry and screams at him in front of Adriana, curses him out, and threatens to take him back to court. Adriana has pleaded with her mommy, "don't send daddy to jail." (How frightening for a child to witness such histrionic, angry parental outbursts. Many child experts would consider Ellen's behavior emotionally abusive behavior.) Terry frets about the impact of such scenes on their daughter and does what he can to keep Ellen pacified, short of losing his own self-respect, and demonstrating that the only way to live around Ellen is to give into all her demands. [He has not yet figured out how to help his daughter cope with her mother's egocentricity and volatility. He cannot nor have her parents. People with the personality constellation Ellen reportedly exhibits are among the most difficult for close family members to deal with unless they pander to all of their whims and provide frequent flattery (Millon & Everly, 1985)]. In sum, they have different ideas about child rearing and are not supportive of each other's styles, ideas, and plans. One example of this is that Terry would like Adriana to have more religious education and attend Sunday school every week. Ellen's husband is either an agnostic or an atheist so when Adriana is at her mom and stepdad's house, she does not go to Sunday school. The church looks askance at such an every other week pattern of attendance, as does Terry, and their disparate values and expectations seem to be very confusing to their little girl.

Changes in Relationship to In-Law Family/His Family Postdivorce

Sadly, Terry's mother had died in an accident when he was very young. He had bonded well with his in-laws and stayed closed with them during the separation and after the divorce. He loved them as people and had a personal relationship with them apart from the one that Ellen had. They are the only grandparents Adriana has, and he wants to continue to nurture the special and close grandparent/grandchild attachment. His mother-in-law and he had enjoyed good rapport and a mutual liking to the extent that she even stayed with his pets at his house when he had to be out of town for business. But, this lovely attachment began to be challenged by Ellen when Terry got married to Sally in 2010. Ellen became enraged at him, and there was a terrible "blowup" in front of Adriana the week before he got married.

She does not like Sally, nor does she want Adriana to like her. Ellen harps on the fact that Sally, who has not been married before and has no children, is not and cannot be her mom. Terry has tried to emphasize that their daughter now has two sets of parents who love her and this is a bonus, but Ellen won't listen. The transitions, which until he remarried went smoothly, are now much more tense as Ellen does not like her going to Terry's house because his new wife is there. [And she apparently fears the competition and is very jealous of Sally's evolving role in her daughter's life (Kaslow, 2006)].

Adriana is the only girl in his family – his parents had two sons. She is also the only *grand*daughter. She is truly the "princess" in his family, and everyone adores her.

His Important Contributions to His Daughter's Life

Terry believes he has imparted a strong value base for living to Adriana that includes respect for self and others as well as the importance of being a good, kind, and thoughtful person. He has offered a consistent, stable, and comfortable home environment and much love and support. He coaches Adriana's soccer team and tries to set a good example for her in how he lives. He emphasizes the importance of cultivating inner as well as outer beauty and not developing excessive vanity.

He took Adriana and Sally to France for a month last year, and his former in-laws joined them there for one week. They had a marvelous time together. He relishes when Adriana is at her mom's house, and she calls just to talk to him and now Sally also.

Other Divorce Sequelae

Although Terry has adjusted to the reality of his divorce in a reasonably healthy manner, he lost 10 lb during the separation and in the months afterward. His dream of being married "till death do us part" was irrevocably crushed. Having Adriana with him only half time left a terrible emptiness in his life when she was not with him. And each time she left to return to her mom's house, he felt sad and frustrated. He does appreciate that although Ellen promotes the importance of women being strong and independent, she does not do so at the expense of denigrating men.

Retrospective and Prospective

Over the past decade, Terry has realized that being a very good and involved father is a core part of his identity and an aspect of his life that he thoroughly enjoys. It took him about five years to recuperate sufficiently from Ellen's double betrayal and his disillusionment over the demise of his marriage to be ready to embark on a second marital journey. From his description of Sally, he has chosen a woman with a very different kind of personality. She sounds warm, generous of spirit, compassionate, and desirous of partnering and being partnered. She was fully cognizant of his situation and willingly transitioned into the stepmom role, knowing Ellen might try to disrupt her blossoming relationship with Adriana and Ellen's parents, who have remained important to Terry. She is also involved in a high-level career in the field of human behavior but seems to approach her professional life in a manner that facilitates a happy work – family life balance (Pryor, 2008). They are eager to have children together.

Despite Ellen's irascible, volatile nature and unpredictable outbursts, Terry remains determined to continue to co-parent with Ellen and her husband as best he can and not to make issues over small matters. But he will take a strong stand when need be to protect his daughter when her mom's narcissistic needs, actions, and demands go over the top and she becomes irrational. In his heart, mind, and spirit, he sincerely seems to have Adriana's "best interest" as his paramount concern, and his behavior seems to match his words. He is cautious and circumspect regarding Ellen, but has not become embittered, and is optimistic about his personal and professional present and future.

References

Braver, S. L. with O'Connell, D. (1998). *Divorced dads*. New York: Jeremy P. Tarcher/Putman.

Glass, S., & Wright, T. (1996). Reconstructing marriages after the trauma of infidelity. In W. Halford & H. Markman (Eds.), *Clinical handbook of marriage and couples interventions* (pp. 471–507). Hoboken: Wiley.

Kaslow, F. W. (2006). Familias que han experimentado un divorcio (Families undergoing divorce: A multicultural and international phenomenon). In A. Roizblatt (Ed.), *Terapia familiar y de pareja* (pp. 617–639). Santiago, Chile: Mediterraneo (In Spanish).

Kernberg, O. (1975). *Borderline conditions and pathological narcissism*. New York: Jason Aronson.

Lusterman, D. D. (1998). *Infidelity: A survival guide*. Oakland, CA: New Harbinger.

Millon, T., & Everly, G. S. (1985). *Personality and its Disorders*. Hoboken, NJ: John Wiley & Sons.

Millon, T. (2011). *Disorders of personality: Introducing a DSM/ICF spectrum from normal to abnormal* (3rd ed.). Hoboken, NJ: Wiley.

Pryor, J. (2008). *The international handbook of stepfamilies: Policy and practice in legal, research and clinical environments*. Hoboken, NJ: Wiley.

Ricci, I. (1980). *Mom's house, dad's house: Making shared custody work*. New York: Macmillan.

Chapter 9
Case 8 Mr. Gene Goodman: My Life Revolves Around My Kids Now

Brief Personal History

Gene, now age 51, was born and raised by Jewish Caucasian parents in a middle Atlantic state. His mother was an immigrant to the United States from the Ukraine/Russian border area. His dad was born in Poland and during World War II had been involved in helping to smuggle other Jews out of this country to escape the Nazi holocaust. He is deservedly proud of his dad, who received a medal of honor for his valiant work on behalf of the Jewish people from the Israeli government (Rosen & Weltman, 1996). A good education was highly valued and encouraged in his family, and Gene went to a college in his home state where he obtained a B.A. in communications. He took some course work in a master's degree program in counseling but did not complete the requirements leading to the second degree. Despite his parents' Jewish heritage, he was raised to be an agnostic. His own adult belief system incorporates many Buddhist as well as Jewish values.

When Gene was only 32 years old, he was sued by the federal government for a staggering sum in the multimillion-dollar category for committing fraud! He was indicted but never convicted and was later fully exonerated from all of the charges. He was represented in the lawsuit by a health-care law firm, and one of the attorneys recommended that he get married, as this would help with protection of his assets. He stated in our interview that he had done nothing wrong and that since then he has been super cautious about his business and other transactions, making sure they are all quite legal and ethical.

When Gene was 34 years old (in 1994), he met Marlena, a US-born Caucasian woman whose father was Jewish and whose mother had been born Protestant. He found her to be exciting, charming, and carefree. Nine months after they met, they eloped.

Marlena's mother had converted to Judaism when she got married and then converted back to being Lutheran after she and Marlena's dad were divorced. Marlena was raised in the Midwest in a family of mixed English and Irish heritage. There were numerous marked differences in Gene and Marlena's respective family of

F.W. Kaslow, *Divorced Fathers and Their Families: Legal, Economic, and Emotional Dilemmas*, DOI 10.1007/978-1-4614-5535-6_9,
© Springer Science+Business Media New York 2013

origin's lifestyle and systems of meaning and value. Gene initially found these differences interesting and did not think they would later loom large and pose a huge problem.

Marriage, Children, and Divorce

Initially, Gene and Marlena had loads of fun together and were able to afford living high and often splurging. He had not gotten to know her family well and was unaware that one brother was a heroin addict, another had been charged with driving while under the influence of drugs, and her mother was a heavy drinker. She had been raised in an unstable environment, but he seemed to have been unaware of how this could affect their marriage (and what the deeper level of his wife's personality was because he was so smitten by her that he choose to ignore warning signs that emotional difficulties may well lie ahead).

Their first child, a daughter, Leona, was born in 1997 and was four years old when they separated in 2001. Their son, Kyle, was a mere 8 months old when Marlena moved out of their marital home. She had been having an affair and often did not come home to sleep. They tried a few sessions of marital counseling (with a non-doctoral level counselor). In counseling sessions, she often "told lies" and referred to him as a "worthless piece of s---." When he spoke to relatives of his who are Ph.D. psychologists and described her behavior and personality, they told him she seemed to meet the criteria for the diagnosis of a "borderline personality," and if this was accurate, it is a condition that is extremely difficult to treat and change (Solomon, 1996). Nonetheless, since Marlena was the spouse who wanted the divorce and was being erratic in her parenting and because he still wanted to make the marriage work, Gene would not move out of the house. Marlena did and they put their house up for sale and were fortunate that it sold quickly.

She filed for the divorce and was awarded most of the marital assets. Marlena took most of the furniture when she moved out, as she wanted the children to be surrounded by as many familiar possessions as possible to enhance their sense of security. Since Florida law in 2005, when the divorce was granted and permitted joint custody, this was the agreement, and Marlena was named the primary residential parent with the children with her 55% of the time and with their dad 45% of the time. That meant the children were shuffled back and forth frequently. Leona struggled with her mommy and daddy being separated and having to live in two very different households. He believes Kyle was then too young to recognize all of the changes in his life and just accepted what happened and how it altered his pattern of living. Their differences in child-rearing beliefs became further amplified after the divorce as Marlena sets no limits on them (or on herself). She saw herself as more of a friend than a parent to the children. Gene knew parents needed to model good behavior, set standards, and establish rules and limits and did so when the children were with him. (How confusing this disparity of parental behavior and expectations must have been.) During the time the children were still living with Marlena over half of the time, she would pick Leona up at the aftercare setting intoxicated. One day Leona called him and said, "Mommy's asleep and I can't wake her." (What a nightmare for children to be subjected to.)

Early Postdivorce Period

The divorce "forced" Gene to take a good, deeper, more analytic view of himself, and he embarked on trying to change what he saw as needing change in himself. He rented a furnished apartment near where Marlena was living and tried to be as available as possible to and for the children. He was relieved not to be "walking on eggshells anymore." (This is an expression I frequently hear from clients married to explosive, unstable, and unpredictable partners. They never know what will spark an adult temper tantrum.)

Shortly after the divorce, Marlena's life "spiraled out of control." After her second trip to traffic court for a DUI (driving under the influence), she was thrown out of her rental apartment (Steinglass, Bennett, Wolen, & Reiss, 1987). In late 2005, less than six months after the divorce, she voluntarily brought and surrendered their young children to Gene. Shortly thereafter, she was arrested for possession of crack cocaine and spent a year in prison. By that time she had lost her driver's license. Mr. Goodman had urged her to go into alcohol rehabilitation treatment after the divorce, to no avail, but subsequent to her legal entanglements and arrests, she did.

Finances

Originally Gene was the residential parent 14 out of 30 days, but he still paid full child support – as that was what the judge in the Florida court deemed as fair under the child support guidelines chart. He paid $2,000 a month or $24,000 per year tax-free for four years until he finally was awarded full legal custody of the children, long after she was sent to prison.

Given that the children were now living with him full time and he had total responsibility for them, he filed a motion to reverse the child support order a month after she surrendered the children to him. After that, she only called the children sporadically, whereas he had called them daily whenever they were residing with their mom. Marlena failed to show up at both of the pretrial hearings about a possible change in the child support order and at the full jury trial later scheduled for the same purpose.

The court order for him to pay child support was not rescinded for four years, and then Marlena, who had been released from jail, was ordered to repay the back child support plus 20% that was erroneously paid to her after she surrendered the children (Emery, 1994). It has been and remains very hard to collect from her. During these years, Gene was fully supporting both households, even though the children were never with their mother.

Reactions Pre- and First-Year Postdivorce

Gene felt hurt, rejected, and bewildered by Marlena's roller-coaster actions and her having had one or several affairs. It took him quite a while to realize how disturbed a person she was. He had chalked her behavior up to immaturity and thought with the passage of time she would grow up more, which failed to occur. Also he had glossed over some of the red flags signaling just how sick she was, as he had wanted to save the marriage at any cost.

Since they had not been able to deal with Marlena's serious addiction problems (Orford, 1985) nor their marital conflicts while in counseling during their marriage, Gene decided to try tele-counseling for himself after the divorce. It helped him recognize the severity of Marlena's problems, the huge gulf in their values and life goals, and how much he loved "his two beautiful kids" and wanted to do with and for them. And he has tried to be an exemplary dad since assuming sole residential custody in late 2005.

Initially, after selling their house, Gene lived in a rented furnished apartment in the same development where they had lived as a family. Once the children came to live with him full time, he moved into a larger rental house, again in the same community to maximize the children's sense of continuity and stability. In this house, it feels like he has been able to create a home for the three of them. He likes health and healthy foods and feeds the children wisely and carefully.

Most Disturbing Issues

Gene never told the children their mother had been sent to prison and is not sure to this day if they know where she "disappeared" to. He believes Leona had seen her mother intoxicated often enough and been terribly frightened when she was in the car and her mother was drunk while driving that she felt relieved, safer, and comforted when their mother told them of her own accord that she was taking them to live with their father. But Kyle has never understood where and why his mommy vanished, and he desperately yearned for a mommy. He is good with his school teachers and attempts to get some maternal nurturing from them.

Gene has had to learn how to deal with Marlena's demands, outbursts, and histrionic behavior unemotionally and not overreact or become distraught (American Psychiatric Association [APA], 2004). He now focuses only on issues about the children when he has to deal with her and no longer permits her "manipulations"; however, dealing with the vagaries of the various courts is something he still finds complex, perplexing, and often unfair.

After Marlena had spent approximately a year in prison, she apparently was uncertain where she would go upon her release. Her mother was then living in the southwest, and Marlena hoped her mother would welcome her there. But, apparently after many years of being susceptible to her daughter's fabricated stories, she had finally come to realize what a "liar" she had long been, and she refused to let her come to her home and "mess up" her life again. Instead Marlena moved in with a boyfriend in North Florida for a while, and when that did not work out well, she went to live with her father and stepmother in a northeastern city. She was virtually out of the children's lives for five years. During this time, Mr. Goodman tailored his work schedule around the children's needs, did all of the chauffeuring, helping with homework, preparation of meals, and daily guidance chats children require. (He became the kind of model dad who earns a father of the year award.)

Their daughter, Leona, went to see a psychologist for four visits. She also has gone to Alateen meetings and asked "what is really wrong with mother." Mr. G describes his daughter as bright and an "old soul." She has, fortunately, had some good mothering from some of the "hockey moms" that go to his son's practices, and he has encouraged these relationships. But she exhibits many insecurities and seems to him to be "boy crazy."

In the early months after Marlena's disappearance, Gene reassured Kyle that "your mommy loves you, she just can't be here now." Kyle is now over six years old and wants to know more about how a mommy could suddenly vanish and just as suddenly reappear. For a number of years, he was a strong willed and defiant child and a "real handful" for his dad. But with Gene's consistent presence, guidance, and clear expectations, he has become a funny, cute, and much less defiant child.

Almost a year ago, Marlena moved back close to the area where Gene and the children still live and wanted to resume contact with them. When she was leaving her father's home, he called to warn Gene to be careful, saying, "she's an asshole" and was very critical of his daughter. Gene had never been advised to file for "termination of her parental rights" by any attorney during the years she totally "abandoned" the children and did nothing emotionally or financially to contribute to the children's lives. When he learned of her return, he filed a motion to institute abandonment charges in juvenile court, and this seems to have produced mayhem at *the local court, which was not accustomed to fathers filing to take such an action.* He was advised to withdraw the motion and did. When she returned, she qualified for court-appointed counsel; also an attorney ad litem was appointed to look into the custody arrangement.

Marlena has remarried and is working in a local restaurant. The guardian ad litem recommended they negotiate a reunification plan and what has been worked out temporarily is she is now permitted to see the children weekly for an hour at his home and is paying some minimal child support – well below the amount she was been told to pay by the court. She will not sign any new financial settlement agreement.

Gene is adamant that he does not want Marlena's reentry into the children's lives to be disruptive of the calm, stable environment, and relationships he built with and for the children, to cause chaos in their lives or interfere with the good adjustments they have made.

Most Painful Aspects of Divorce

Walking in on his ex-wife with her lover (Brown, 1991) prior to the divorce was a horrifying experience and a shattering blow to Gene's ego. After the divorce, he briefly experimented with casual sexual encounters and use of street drugs to deaden the pain and compensate for the loss of having his children as part of his daily life. But once Marlena brought and surrendered the children to him, these behaviors stopped, and he modified his work schedule so he could accommodate to their needs. He still struggles with overeating to fill the emptiness of not having a loving partner. He is reluctant to marry again as it is hard for him to trust anyone enough to make such a commitment, and he is concerned about how the children would adapt to a stepmom. (These are among the long-term consequences that color the thoughts of many divorced dads.) He does not want the children to perceive that he is in any way abandoning them in favor of a new partner.

Changes in Personality, Sense of Meaning and Value, and Ideas About Family Subsequent to Divorce

As mentioned earlier, Gene engaged in a good deal of self-examination and entered various kinds of therapy to gain more self-awareness and insight, to make changes he deemed necessary, and to rebuild his shattered self-esteem. He became aware of his own codependency needs and behaviors and how these had kept him hooked on Marlena and unable to see that her actions were so disturbed and unacceptable. When he does go out, he consciously chooses to date women who are "giving" of their time and "compassionate" in their involvement in the community at large with nonprofit organizations. Like many other divorced dads who were deeply "hurt emotionally," he is lonely and would like an enduring love relationship, but too many factors have so far mitigated against his veering in that direction. In addition, he thinks few women want to be wife #2 and that he has not met the "right woman for whom he is the right man." He definitely would not want to "make a second mistake."

Highlights in Relationship to Each Child Post-separation

His children have become "his life's work," and there have been many highlights in their relationship. He has thoroughly enjoyed coaching his son's roller hockey and ice hockey teams. He is often pleased to hear and see his children's good manners and is proud of their many achievements, including that his son repeatedly makes the honor roll in school and his daughter is always designated an honor student. Leona is an "all American cheerleader," and she is in the International Baccalaureate Program at her high school. (He seems to be very successful in fulfilling the goals of his life work.) Among his contributions to his children's lives have been the sense of safety and security he offers, letting them know and feel how much they are wanted, loved, and cherished by him; imparting pro-social and ethical values; encouraging them to be high-achieving students and athletes (within the broad range of their abilities); and introducing lots of fun times into their lives, in and outside of their cozy home. They sing, dance, and play together. Gene has a fine sense of humor and usually maintains an upbeat approach to what he/they do.

Some of the Worst Times, Events, and Memories

Gene became aware that Marlena talked about him with a girlfriend, in front of the children, while the two women sat drinking and smoking. He regrets that the children were subjected to such scenes. He has noted that Marlena still smokes, and this is not permitted when she now visits with the children in his home. He has learned from his daughter that her mom had men coming to the house when they were living with her and that she and Kyle saw men in bed with her. At one point there was a live-in boyfriend and when he left, Kyle announced, "Now I'm the man of the house" (Beavers, 1982). That is quite a role for a four-year-old to assume. Gene was infuriated one day when their very young son wandered out of the house, and Marlena did not even know it. His daughter called Gene when this happened, and he went to help find Kyle. He has done all he possibly can to soften these memories, to offset Marlena's poor and negligent parenting, to be less harsh and nasty, and much more pleasant, predictable, and joyful.

Postdivorce Interactions with Her Family and His

Initially Marlena's mom and stepdad went from being in-laws to feeling like they were "outlaws." They devalued him for wanting full custody after he assumed the responsibility of primary sole and residential parent.

Mr. Goodman's parents were deceased before the divorce and so were not there to also feel the loss or provide him with emotional support or comfort. His brother was and has been understanding. He remarked at the time of the divorce that he "never thought Gene should have married Marlena" – but he was unable to figure out why and so had not said anything.

In the past several years, his contacts with her parents have been limited to several phone calls received from her divorced mom and dad, each unbeknownst to the other, in which they were highly critical of their daughter. They have made few overtures to be in contact with their grandchildren and do not send birthday or holiday cards or presents. Her mom has finally congratulated him on what a great job he is doing with the kids.

Retrospective and Prospective

Gene wholeheartedly believes people should not enter marriages perceiving them to be disposable relationships. He believes happy, long-term relationships need to be founded in and embody genuine friendship, congruent core values, and also be rooted in integrity, honesty, and trust. These characteristics will be essential ingredients in his relationship if and when he chooses to remarry. He also intends to get to know any person he considers selecting very well – before the fact.

He sees Marlena as having a borderline personality disorder with many narcissistic features and a substance abuse disorder. These are diagnoses proffered to him by various professionals who have been involved in treating different family members. He is leery of the recommendations of the guardian ad litem in her plan for reunification of Marlena with the children. In Marlena's recent visits, she again has been trying to be their friend, not their mom, for example, by saying she wants to take them to popular evening entertainment venues – on school nights. This would mean their getting home very late, disrupting the routine they are accustomed to, and putting play above homework. She is unaware apparently of her poor judgment. When he says no, she tells the children their dad is too mean to let them go. She talks to them about matters that fall outside the courts guidelines of permissible topics and tries to set Gene up as "the bad guy." Gene does not understand why the guardian has recommended a reunion plan, based on a short interview with Marlena, filled with her insipid promises, rather than on her 13-year track record as an alcoholic, as a woman who had male sex partners come to the house in the children's presence, and as a negligent and abandoning mother. He hopes the children will see who and what their mother is and stay on the good pathways on which they have embarked for the past five years.

One can only hope the court will exercise wisdom in determining Marlena's permissible involvement in the children's lives and taken into account the well-researched principle that the best predictor of future behavior is past behavior. Perhaps an evaluation by a credible, objective psychiatrist or psychologist should be sought before the reunion plan is finalized so that Marlena's current mental status and personality integration are known factors to the person making recommendations to the court so that they will truly be "in the best interest of the children" (and not contingent primarily on the gender of the parent – when that parent has not shown herself/himself to be "fit").

References

American Psychiatric Association. (2004). *Diagnostic and statistical manual of mental disorders* (4th ed.). Washington, DC: Author.

Beavers, W. R. (1982). Healthy, midrange and severely dysfunctional families. In F. Walsh (Ed.), *Normal family processes* (pp. 45–66). New York: Guilford.

Brown, E. M. (1991). *Patterns of infidelity and their treatment*. New York: Brunner/Mazel.

Emery, R. E. (1994). *Renegotiating Family Relationships: Divorce, Child Custody, and Mediation*. New York: Guilford.

Orford, J. (1985). *Excessive Appetites: A Psychological View of Addictions*. Chichester, England: J. Wiley & Sons.

Rosen, E. J., & Weltman, S. F. (1996). Jewish families: An overview. In M. McGoldrick, J. Giordano, & J. K. Pearce (Eds.), *Ethnicity and family therapy* (2nd ed., pp. 611–630). New York: Guilford.

Solomon, M. (1996). Understanding and treating couples with borderline disorders. In F. W. Kaslow (Ed.), *Handbook of relational diagnosis and dysfunctional family patterns* (pp. 251–269). New York: Wiley.

Steinglass, P., Bennett, L., Wolen, S., & Reiss, D. (1987). *The alcoholic family*. New York: Basic Books.

Chapter 10
Case 9 Dr. Ari Regis: The Relentless Demands and Criticisms Never Cease

Brief Personal History

Born in Athens, Greece, in 1959, Dr. Regis comes from a Greek Orthodox family. Although he has remained affiliated with his religion of origin, he is nonobservant (Tsemberis & Orfanos, 1996). When he was a young teenager, his family decided to send him to a Jesuit high school in the Midwest United States, so he could acquire a fine education and continue to have a strict, excellent, and value-oriented education. After graduating, he chose to remain in the United States and became a citizen. Ari went to college then medical school, and after graduating, he took a residency in oncology. Currently, he runs a medium-sized successful practice, and he is known in his community to be highly ethical and very skilled. In the interview he was composed, articulate, affable, yet emotional about highly charged issues. In appearance and bearing, he is a handsome, well-groomed, personable, and mature adult.

Marriage, Children, and Divorce

When Ari was 26 years of age, he met a cute 19-year-old brunette, Patty. Patty came from a German-Lutheran family that also was not very religiously observant. She was born and bred in the United States. They dated for four years and then got married in 1989, when Dr. R was 30 years old. Their first daughter, Lisa, was born a year later. They waited for five years before having their second daughter, Betsy.

During these years Ari was focused on building his practice, becoming the best dentist he could be, and being involved in professional affairs. He no longer found his young, pretty wife interesting or stimulating – it was as if at the point at which they got married, she stopped growing. They did try marital therapy, but she maintained her usual passive demeanor in sessions and would say little, no matter how the therapist tried to draw her out. There was little contention – just coldness on her part – and he felt less and less affinity toward her. He was terribly sad that the marriage was not viable and dreaded the breakup of the family unit. Until then, he had not seen divorce as an option in his life plan and was dismayed when it came to pass. He was very devoted to his two little girls, then six years and 18 months of age, and dismayed over the prospect of not being part of their daily lives.

From Patty's point of view, Ari did not fulfill what she wanted – which was a more attentive husband and a playmate – much more absorbed in her and her narrow world than in his practice and the wider professional and intellectual world. She too was dissatisfied with their relationship – which she found insufficiently centered on her emotional needs.

Patty filed for divorce (early in 1996) and changed the locks on the house doors, locking him out; a month later she moved out taking their daughters with her. They then put the house up for sale, and she never returned to it again. Ari has always thought she was already involved in an affair before her departure, particularly since she immediately moved in with Mr. X, who is the man she soon married. Two years later she and her second husband had a baby.

The Divorce and Multiple Losses Experienced

Ari went to live with a friend for four months and then quickly decided to rent a condo apartment near the ocean to provide greater pleasure to his daughters when they visited him. But no matter what he did, his eldest daughter, Lisa, blamed him totally for the family's breakup and was often hostile to him, which made their visits tense and put him on the defensive. Her accusations seemed to be parroting comments made to her by an adult as she was too young at ages 6–9 to come up with these charges on her own.

He missed being present for many of the milestone developmental events in Betsy's life. He regretted not having the children easily accessible when his parents and other relatives came to visit from Greece, and his parents rarely saw the children after he and Patty separated (Kaslow, 2007). Nor could he have the joy of easily planning trips abroad with his children to his homeland. He had to arrange time off from his office to coincide with the custody plan and his ex-wife's preferences as to scheduling, and she allegedly did her utmost to place hurdles in his path.

He had always expected to raise his children in an intact family, to have dinner together every night, to help with homework, and to exercise influence over the development of their ideas and values. Not being with the children every night to read to them and help tuck them into bed felt like very painful punishment to him. He considers living together in the family home as symbolic of the stability, security, and continuity each family member needs, and this vanished for all of them when Patty decided to move out. The children now had two new and unfamiliar homes, each minus one biological parent.

The custody agreement called for him to have the children every Tuesday after school for dinner, every Thursday evening for dinner and sleepover, and every other weekend from Saturday morning until Monday morning when he either took them to school or back to their mom's house during vacations and the summer. It fell far short of the time he wanted with his daughters.

Another loss resulted from having to divide the one income (his) to support two households and ultimately two postdivorce families. Now, 15 years later, he is still supporting two families, and the exorbitant cost of living in the expensive area in which both parts of this binuclear family reside remains oppressive.

Finances

Dr. Regis has always been the payer parent. He found the first three years following the divorce extremely tough financially as he had to give Patty $6,000 a month child support and alimony which amounted to $72,000 a year of nontaxable income to her. To do this he worked extra long hours as he had to earn over $100,000 annually just to pay Patty alimony and child support and cover the taxes due on this – for which he remained responsible (as do many dads). This left him little for his own housing, food, clothing, car, personal expenses, and childcare expenditures on the girls when they were with him. In addition to sending Patty child support payments, Ari has routinely covered all of the girls' medical and related expenses, all insurances, and for their vacations, cell phones, and phone bills. (Very little of the literature on divorce elucidates what divorce actually costs the payer dads financially and how hard they work to cover two households with nothing in return from the ex-wife, except often aggravation and alienation of the children's affections.)

In order to have any money for himself, he worked a grueling schedule and only took off when the children were with him. The spousal support ended after three years as Patty had remarried. However, child support has continued at a minimum rate of $3,000 per month for the ensuing years, through to the present as the youngest daughter is still under 18 years of age. There have been several increases in the amount he has had to pay since whenever Patty learned that there were major changes occurring in his life, she returned to court to get a court order for an increase in child support. Some examples of when this occurred are when three and a half years after the divorce, he once again provided his daughters and himself with a lovely, gracious, and stable home environment, leaving his rental condo behind, and when he got remarried – albeit several years after she did and was about to leave on his honeymoon.

When his eldest daughter was working on the details for attending college last year, it was made clear to him that he was expected to defray *all* the costs. Patty's second husband never finished high school, and formal education is something she and her husband claim not to think is important. Therefore, Patty reasons, if it is something Dr. R wants the girls to have, he has to assume total responsibility, and he has. Wisely (as many other divorced dads who support their children do), he let Lisa know when she turned 18 years old that she would have to discuss and work out plans directly with him and that Patty could no longer be the intermediary (negotiator or demander) between them. So far this new arrangement has worked well for

Dr. R and his daughter. She is a good student and appreciative of his investment of time, thought, and money in her college education.

Life Postdivorce and Remarriage

About a year after the divorce, Ari met Nancy, a lovely woman about 16 years his junior. She had never been married and was quite smitten by him. She moved in with him about two years after they began dating; then, it took Ari another four years before he was ready to ask her to marry him, and he thought it was prudent to make a commitment to marriage again and to change the configuration of his postdivorce family that had, for seven years, consisted of him and his daughters only. He also made sure he and Nancy had a bona fide prenuptial agreement (a document that has become increasingly common for those entering second or later marriages and also for many couples entering first marriage. Often one or both is/are more cautious and have become more realistic about the vicissitudes of marriage and want a prenuptial agreement that protects them, their assets, and their children).

Nancy moved into his home, and their marriage, now over an eight years duration (longer than his first to Patty), has experienced some emotional turbulence attributable to the presence, impact, and influence of the prior family on Ari and, therefore, on their life together. (Second and later spouses "know" children will visit and their spouse has a preexisting attachment and loyalty to his children – but how strong it is and what time, behaviors, and costs it entails may not be anticipated sufficiently.)

By the time he remarried, Lisa was 13½ years of age, and Betsy had just turned nine years old. Lisa, who was accustomed to receiving enormous amounts of attention and having their time with dad revolve around them, apparently became disgruntled about having to share the limelight. She particularly disliked (as most children do) whenever Nancy said anything about her mom. As a young teenager, she came to visit her dad "dutifully" on schedule, as she was a "good" child, but she kept herself distant from both of them.

According to Dr. R, Patty has totally blamed him for pursuing the divorce, although she was the one who had decided to move out and had filed for the divorce and moved in immediately with another man, whom she married shortly after the divorce was final. Clearly, Lisa did not have "princess" status at her mom's house and resented losing the sense that she was "dad's best girl" when Nancy moved into the picture, that is, the family, the home, and dad's heart. She also was displeased that her dad was, by her standards, so generous to Nancy. His gifts to Nancy conveyed her importance to him in a very visible fashion.

From Nancy's perspective, he does too much for the girls and is too attached to them, and she feels she is in competition with them for his time, love, and money. Nancy desperately wants to have a child with Ari and create her own family with him, even though he told her *before* they got married that he did not want and would not have any more children. One gathers she has not given up her dream at the same time he is determined to hold to his long-standing decision. [This is not an infrequent problem when a younger woman marries an older man who already has children and does not want more. When he has been honest with her prior to their decision to get married, as was the situation here, the woman engages in self-deception if she believes she can and will cajole him into changing his mind – which is unfair to both and sets them on a possible collision of wills course (Kaslow, 2000). Equally unfair is the man who says he will be willing to have more children, just to persuade her to marry him, when he does not mean this, and then refuses to once they are married. It is crucial that both future partners behave with honesty and integrity about such vital matters and not intend to manipulate, coerce, or deceive their future spouse.] Nonetheless, Nancy feels deprived over not having a child of her own, and this adds to her resentment about the importance of his closeness to his daughters and to his wanting to see friends he had cultivated prior to their marriage or separate from their couple activities and in the professional realm of his life.

When Lisa was 16 years old, Ari, his two daughters, and Nancy all went on a cruise together, and he and Lisa became closer again. She saw him through her own eyes, and this gave her a different and apparently more accurate view of him. He and Lisa are enjoying their newfound understanding and camaraderie. She had been deeply affected by the family breakup and often carried her baby photo album back and forth from mom's house to dad's house. She seemed afraid he would desert her and Betsy when he remarried, which obviously has not been the case. Over time, her fears have dissipated as she has recognized that his loyalty to and love for her and her sister have not diminished.

As Betsy was only 18 months old when her mother decided she wanted to separate and moved out of the family home, taking the two girls with her, she does not recall a time when she did not live part time with each parent in two separate homes. It has always been her lifestyle.

The girls seem to love their mom and not to have resented her moving them away from their dad and their familiar surroundings since their mom had convinced them (brainwashed them into believing) that their dad was solely responsible for the breakup. They never say anything critical or negative about her nor do they convey much information about what goes on in mom's household and life. It does not sound like either of the girls have formed a "heart connection" to Nancy, or she to them, much as Dr. R had hoped this would eventuate over time.

Experience of Divorce

The loss of living with the children on a daily basis was Ari's biggest loss. He realizes he still carries some resentment and much hurt over Patty's rejection of the family unit for selfish reasons and her decision to break up the family and then her continuing to *distort the truth* by telling the children he had wanted the divorce. In his second marriage he expects Nancy to be less dependent and more self-sufficient than Patty was, and he has insisted that she have her own career. She does work, albeit part time, but resents that this is expected of her – especially since he never expected this with Patty. In their community and circle of friends, she believes wives only have to work because their husbands do not earn enough, and she is embarrassed to be working.

Postdivorce Interactions with Ex-Wife/ Her Family/His Family

For a period of four years, she would not allow the girls to have cell phones. When he tried to reach them on the house phone, she did not answer so he was prevented from talking to them or leaving messages, which he found extremely frustrating and aggravating.

Patty will not talk to Ari; instead, she sends him cryptic text messages. These have replaced the phone messages left before she acquired and became adept at using her cell phone for texting. He has grown to actively dislike and disrespect her because of the lack of guidance she has provided to the children, her failure to motivate them to do and be their best, and the false stories she has told them about the breakup. Also he perceives that she is not very emotionally available to their daughters. She sounds much more like a taker than a giver. Dr. R and Patty were not particularly supportive of each other's parenting styles as they have different standards, goals, and values. Ari would have liked to expose Lisa and Betsy to a more intellectual and cultural environment and activities and to a broader, more worldly perspective. Patty's horizons have remained very provincial, and keeping abreast of current events and world affairs is unimportant to her. Ari has introduced them as much as possible to a variety of people, viewpoints, and activities and has used their vacation time with him for traveling. Patty did her utmost to undermine his emphasis on education.

Ari deeply dreaded and resented her periodic petitions to the court to raise the amount of child support she received, especially since she choose not to work, and he never knew when he would receive another court order. He felt like there was *always a shadow hovering nearby*, whenever things were going well in his life. She justified her actions to their daughters by saying "he can pay this and lots more," and he should. Patty always wants her pleasure immediately in the here and now; this contrasts with Ari's philosophy and modus operandi that some money should be saved and allocated for future needs and for emergencies and only some used for immediate gratification. (How confusing the great divergences between them in almost all spheres of life must have been and still are to the girls. When such a schism is perpetuated, as it is between many divorced couples, it falls to the children to try to make sense of their parents' differences and to learn what is expected by mom and at her house and by dad and at his house. The children must do what the adults could not to resolve the disparities or live in a haze of bewilderment.)

Postdivorce Ari's ex-in-law family severed all contact with him. Ari had like Patty's stepdad, and they had had good chats when they were together. But Patty's mom hated him and blamed him for divorcing her daughter, and since she completely dominated her husband, as Patty went on to do with her second spouse, his ex-father-in-law was not permitted to stay in touch with him. Interestingly, his ex-paternal grandmother-in-law told them all to "take a flying leap" and kept in touch with Ari personally and professionally until her death. Ari also remained fond of her. Ari is not a person to be dominated or pushed around; in his personal as in his professional life, he takes a proactive role in shaping the course of events and in making decisions that affect him and his significant others. He and Patty had not been "a good fit" with each other.

For five years after the divorce, Dr. R's parents were still able to make trips to the United States. When they were here, Patty was inflexible about allowing Ari to have the children with him and his parent for any additional time, which caused them all great sadness. He took and still takes the girls on vacation to Greece to visit his family and friends there every other year.

Activities and Life Events He Participated in with Children Postdivorce/His Greatest Contributions to Their Lives

He attended/attends *every* school and extracurricular activity about which he is informed. Since Patty never included him in the birthday parties she made for the girls, he made them separate ones when possible. At Lisa's graduation, Patty and her entourage barely acknowledged him. She and her family took Lisa to lunch; he and Nancy celebrated with Lisa and Betsy at dinner. The children seem to have two parties for everything which keeps the evidence of the dissension in full – and for Ari, painful view. (One wonders, will they need to have two wedding ceremonies, and if so, how sad would that be? Divorce ends a marriage, but not the family connection that continues through the children that lasts "till death does them part.")

He believes he has imparted solid values to them and has been a good role model – exemplifying such behavior as never smoking or using profanity. He also displays high integrity and his expectation that they will embody this. He has given them each a credit card, and they do not overuse these. He has provided consistency of caring and a stable home environment. He has inculcated the importance he places on education and ambition, and both of his daughters have become imbued with these ideals and are focused on their pursuit of learning.

Some of the Worst Times and Memories Evolving from Divorce

Patty had the divorce papers served to him at his office, which was both humiliating in front of his staff and came as a shock, as he had hoped she would not follow through with seeking a divorce. In like fashion, right before he was to leave for his honeymoon with Nancy, seven years later, he was served (again at the office – making his private life all too public) with papers seeking a modification of child support. There were times when Patty did things like taking off for a vacation and leaving the girls, who were still both under 10 years of age, with three different neighbors for a period of four days without asking him if he wanted the option of having them or even letting him know their whereabouts.

Being excluded from their birthday parties, his phone calls not being taken, and not being informed about the children's school events while they were told by their mother that he did not attend because he was "too busy" with other things all added to his discontent and feeling that *they were being brainwashed about and against him* (Clawar & Rivlin, 1991). There was little he could say about any of this without being critical of their mother and challenging the veracity of her statements, which he knew was not in his daughters' best interest. The continuous being pushed into a corner caused him much angst and consternation (Egizli, 2010).

About six months after the divorce, he consulted his physician and a psychologist as he was not feeling up to par nor functioning as well as usual. Both indicated what he had already surmised – he was responding to the external pressures (financial) and emotional turmoil, losses, and disappointments with internal stress-induced reactions. This has resurfaced periodically when Patty has rather hysterically and/or in a self-centered manner instigated various actions to wreak havoc between him and the children and now with Nancy. However, by and large, the solidity of his medical practice, the loyalty and longevity of his staff there and his friends and family network help him to stay emotionally healthy and to maintain an optimistic outlook about his present and future relationship with his daughters, especially as they become older and can figure more out for themselves.

Retrospective and Prospective

Ari still regrets not being able to live out the dream of raising his children in an intact family, having everyone together at dinner almost every night and on holidays, and passing on intergenerational mores and traditions. He handles this as best as he can in his half of the postdivorce/binuclear family (Ahrons, 1983).

Fortunately, recently he has had some rapprochement with Lisa – on the cruise, when taking her to colleges for interviews and helping her move into her dormitory. Nonetheless, sequelae of the divorce persist. For example, even though it was Nancy and not Patty who helped clean up and decorate her dorm room, she thanked her mom. He hopes someday the girls will have the courage to see the reality about the key people in their lives more objectively. (He seems to qualify, as do many of the other divorced dads whose stories are being told here, for the patient, compassionate, father of the year award, even though they have been so very much maligned.) He has and will continue to hang in there "through thick and thin" and enjoy the family he does have as much as he possibly can.

References

Ahrons, C. R. (1983). *The binuclear family: Parenting roles and relationships* (unpublished paper).

Clawar, S. S., & Rivlin, B. V. (1991). *Children held hostage: Dealing with programmed and brain-washed children*. Chicago: American Bar Association Section of Family Law.

Egizli, J. (2010). *The look of love*. Dallas: Brown Books.

Kaslow, F. W. (2000). Prenuptial and postnuptial agreements: Sunny or stormy bellweathers to marriage or remarriage. In F. W. Kaslow (Ed.), *Handbook of couple and family forensics* (pp. 3–22). New York: Wiley.

Kaslow, F. W. (2007). Post divorce relatedness between parents, their divorced sons, and their grandchildren: A pilot study. In C. A. Everett & R. E. Lee (Eds.), *When marriages fail: Systemic family therapy interventions and issues* (pp. 141–156). New York: Haworth Press (now Taylor & Francis).

Tsemberis, S. J., & Orfanos, S. D. (1996). Greek families. In M. McGoldrick, J. Giardano, & J. K. Pearce (Eds.), *Ethnicity and family therapy* (2nd ed., pp. 517–529). New York: Guilford.

Chapter 11
Case 10 Mr. Arturo Miguel: Some Courts Deprive Dads and Their Children of Each Other's Companionship/Love

Personal Background Information

This 59-year-old electrical engineer was born in Havana, Cuba, which is a predominantly Catholic country, and he was raised Catholic. However, his maternal grandmother came from a Sephardic Jewish background, which led him to appreciate different religions early in life. When Arturo was eight years old, he and his parents moved to the United States and settled in the Carolina area. Some of his extended family members have remained in Cuba. He was given no formal religious education nor was Catholicism practiced by church attendance. Education was stressed, and Arturo grew up being proficient in both Spanish and English.

First Marriage, Children, and Divorce

When Arturo was 24 years of age, he married Barbara, a Caucasian Jewish girl who had been born in the United States. The differences in family religious backgrounds did not present a problem. Arturo continued his formal education after they got married and went on to earn a Master of Science in an engineering field. They had two sons together – José, who was seven years old at the time of the divorce, and Jerry, who was a mere three years of age.

Arturo describes himself as having been a "trusting and somewhat naïve" person and states that he still retains these traits but probably to a lesser extent. He was therefore shocked when Barbara literally sprang the news on him that she wanted a separation that would rapidly culminate in a divorce.

This soft-spoken, contemplative gentleman realizes he saw some clues that Barbara might be having an affair. She was often preoccupied and distant – particularly when she returned from a business trip. Nonetheless, she never admitted that she had "fallen in love" with someone she had met while traveling for work and that they had started having an affair prior to the divorce. Arturo was terribly dismayed and shaken when she told

F.W. Kaslow, *Divorced Fathers and Their Families: Legal, Economic, and Emotional Dilemmas*, DOI 10.1007/978-1-4614-5535-6_11,
© Springer Science+Business Media New York 2013

him she wanted to end the marriage (and the existence of the family in the extant form they had created). Arturo has never told their two sons, José and Jerry, about their mother's infidelity and betrayal. He did not think it was "in their best interest" to be told this and doubts that their mother disclosed this fact to their sons as she has sought to cover up her extramarital exploit. Arturo's suspicions were confirmed several times over when mutual friends with whom Barbara worked told him that her colleagues there were appalled as her lover worked at the same firm and they often traveled together. This had made it uncomfortable and difficult for members of the same firm. Also, they were sympathetic with Arturo, whom they regarded as a good husband and father and someone who did not deserve to be cuckolded (author's term) and publicly embarrassed because so many others were aware of the duplicity. The identified man also filed for divorce about the same time that Barbara did and soon he became her next husband.

Arturo wanted joint and equal custody, but in the southeastern state in which they resided, this was not a legal option. According to his report (and that of several of the other dads in this study who lived in the same state at the time of their divorces), the mother automatically was granted sole custody, unless she could be proven "unfit," which was defined by such behaviors as addiction or prostitution. His lawyer advised him that he had no chance of obtaining either sole primary or joint custody, which he found unfair, unjust, and unbearable, and therefore not to even try to petition for it.

This thoughtful, considerate man became distraught when Barbara announced she wanted a divorce and followed through to obtain one. He found separating from her very painful as he still loved her, even though he knew in the core of his being that ultimately he might not be able to recuperate from the pain and hurt (Gold, 1992). But the loss of his boys and being unable to live together with them in one home and household on a daily basis was *devastating*. He had been particularly close to José and had often been able to arrange to spend afternoons after school with him – going exploring, taking walks, and just being together. This close father–son tie was suddenly disrupted, and he had no choice and no say in the decision. He was relegated to being a father on an every other weekend basis only and believes Barbara's decision to divorce accompanied by the court's rubber stamp custody award severely damaged three lives – his two sons' and his (Myers, 1989).

By and large, at the time of the divorce, José was a good-natured, happy-go-lucky, seemingly resilient child who was able to "let things go" and roll with whatever happened. A dyslexic boy, he did not seem to be "troubled" by the schism that had occurred between his parents. Jerry, then three and one-half years old, followed his brother's lead. Barbara decided to send the boys off to boarding school when José was 15 and Jerry was 12 years of age, respectively, and this continued until they finished high school. Although Arturo disagreed with Barbara's choice to send their sons away, his wishes were totally disregarded, and he suffered a second and continuous loss of frequent contact as their being away at school curtailed the possibility of biweekly visitation. Despite his objections to the boys being shipped off from their mother's home to boarding school and his inability to gain custody of them to live with him and attend a local school, he was expected to pay part of the ongoing expensive tuition [the majesty of the court is to serve the cause of justice – but in cases like this, its wisdom and justice are hard to discern (Isaacs, Montalvo, & Abelsohn, 1986)].

When the boys were home and Barbara traveled, she left them with others. On the first occasion after the separation when Barbara was to go away, her sister traveled to their state to care for the boys rather than leave them with Arturo any more time than what was decreed by the custody agreement. Neither Arturo's lawyer (nor anyone else) had advised him to have a clause inserted in the MSA that he was to have first option to have the children with him when she was away – something he would gladly have done, and he was never so much as notified when such a trip was in the offing. (One can only wonder why children are deprived of the opportunity of being with the other parent when the one whose turn it is to have them in residence is unavailable. It would certainly seem to be the advisable option if said parent is willing, competent, non-abusive, and not an addict, all of which applies to Mr. Miguel. What is the motivation, the objective, or the rationale for a nonparent caretaker to be with the children? And how can it really serve the children's best interest? The stark reality of the probable answers is disquieting. It is fervently hoped that laws and judicial decrees will change to redress such deprivation to children and those dads who are dedicated and competent.)

Reactions During Divorce and First-Year Postdivorce

Arturo was quite worried about the impact of the separation and of his moving out of the home on his sons and on their development. He missed them terribly and felt totally empty and bereft. He likens it to going through a long and painful enforced withdrawal from something you cherish. He detested coming home each night, first to a room he took in a friend's apartment as he had no funds available to rent an apartment (see section on "Finances") and later to the empty apartment he rented nearby the family home. He deeply missed any kind of daily contact with "*his kids*." Sadly, at the time he and Barbara separated, she was able to restrict his phone contact with the boys as calls had to go to and through her, and she rarely permitted it. This all occurred during the precomputer and pre-cell phone era.

His hope had been that in renting an apartment that was nearby the former marital home, the boys would be able to walk over to his place and they would see each other more easily and sometimes spontaneously. This plan never materialized; Barbara would not allow it. The rift worsened after the divorce when Arturo confronted her about her betrayal and deception, and she denied it – screaming at him in a horrific temper outburst. After that, the relationship became even more adversarial (Millon, 1996). To this day, she has never acknowledged having become involved in the affair prior to the divorce and sticks to her story that it began afterward. He wonders if he should have colluded with her by not challenging her deception and if this would have made access to his children easier and more frequent. But he recognizes that not to have done so would have severely compromised his integrity in his own eyes.

Although Arturo slowly relinquished his long-held illusion of what his family of creation would be like, particularly living as an emotionally and physically intact unit, he remains bitter and angry about the "injustice of it all." Lo, these many years later, it still feels like the children were *"kidnapped from him"* for no reason. The state law assumed the father was the out of the home working breadwinner parent; the mother was the at-home parenting mom and therefore should not only have sole custody but also have the authority to make all the decisions. The fact that this was not the case in this situation was not considered, and he just had to live with it – as did the kids.

The boys, now 30 and 27 years old, respectively, have never asked him any questions about the divorce, and he has not volunteered any information. He recognizes that Barbara took good care of them when they were at home.

Finances

Before Barbara told him she wanted to separate and that she expected him to move out, she surreptitiously took all of the money they had saved out of their safe deposit box and also withdrew all of the funds from their checking and savings accounts before closing them. All accounts had been set up with either to sign checks, withdraw, or close so it was easy for her to do. Apparently, she had been planning for the divorce for quite a while before she told Arturo, and she had manipulated their finances totally in her favor, leaving nothing in any account for him. Thus, with none of their money available to him, he had no choice but to initially move in with a friend before he could reconnoiter his thoughts and his finances enough to even rent his own apartment.

Arturo was always the payer parent, and Barbara was the recipient, even though she also worked full time. He paid $2,500 per month child support from the time of the divorce until both of the boys reached 18 years of age; there was a slight reduction in amount when José turned 18 years old, 11 years after the divorce. In addition to the child support, he covered all costs of medical, dental, and similar expenses plus half of his son's expenses for boarding school, despite his opposition to their being sent away, and later half of the costs for each of the boys to attend college. Nonetheless, until Jerry turned 18, Barbara continued to return to court to petition for more money. He was relieved when he sent her the last mandated child support check and could then handle financial issues with his sons directly. This arrangement has worked much better for him and for them.

Ways in Which Sons Were Most Problematic

When José decided to enlist in the US armed forces, Arturo did not agree that this was a wise choice. José was in college, and it meant "dropping out" without finishing. Arturo continued to have little influence on his son's thoughts and actions. José went ahead and joined the service and spent 10 years in the military, which included three tours of duty in Iraq and Afghanistan. Since leaving the military, José has been fortunate to find good employment, has gotten married, and has started a family of his own. He is considering returning to college to earn his degree through taking evening classes.

As an adolescent, if his dad set limits with him, Jerry would refuse to visit. As a young adult, he has had difficulty finding his path in life. Despite Jerry's education and many talents, he has had trouble settling on a career.

Arturo continues to regret that he has had so little say about matters of importance in his sons' lives when they were growing up and that he was so unable to exert a positive influence and be a solid role model. This has been his greatest "heartache."

Postdivorce Interactions with Ex-Spouse and Her Family/His Family's Reactions

Barbara kept all contact with Arturo and their sons at an absolute minimum. He was not consulted about their schooling, extracurricular activities, limit setting, and other child-rearing practices, values to be instilled, or anything else. Nonetheless, he does not think she was openly critical of him as she knew that could be damaging to the boys; rather, she chose to ignore his existence to the extent possible (Schwartz & Kaslow, 1997).

He considered his ex-wife's family to be a dysfunctional one; many members of her extended family of origin did not talk to one another. Nonetheless, he is still friendly with her brother; she is not. He did not approve of the way and the reason Barbara exited the marriage.

Arturo's family did not live in the same city as he and Barbara, so there was not much change in any of their relationships. The virtual disappearance of the children from Arturo's life for years was a big loss to his family of origin.

Postdivorce Activities and Life Events He Participated in with Sons, Best/Most Poignant Memories, His Most Important Contributions

Over time, occasionally Mr. M was able to take his sons on vacation and to spend one of their two weeks of Christmas vacation with them. He relished these times and has good memories of their just being together. Though they did the usual father–son things such as going to baseball games and the zoo, the more memorable experiences were often simpler ones. Building forts from sofa cushions, word twists, and silly make-believe games seemed trivial at the time but have created lasting memories. It has been gratifying for Mr. M to see his son José pass these on to the next generation. Unfortunately, he found that it was often impractical for a noncustodial parent to try to provide any "corrective influence" when required as there was no way to follow up or through on what he was trying to implement.

He believes his major contributions were his stability and the consistency of his love and friendship and the boys' knowledge that he was and remains available and "there" for them.

He remembers fondly the times they did visit at his apartment, and they all played together. They got along well, and he is very pleased that they have accepted his second wife, Laurel, and shared in the joys of the pregnancies and births of their two younger half-siblings.

They very much welcome his sons into their family and want this being part of each other's lives to be a reciprocal desire and mutually initiated behavior. His eldest son, José, is now married, and Arturo likes his daughter-in-law and his young grandchild. He is delighted to be a grandfather and sorry that they do not live in the same state.

Changes in Personality, Sense of Meaning, Value and Belonging, and Ideas About Family Occurred During and Subsequent to Divorce

Mr. M states that he remained bitter and angry over the divorce and how he was mistreated for a long time. He became distrustful of women and was not sure he could ever really trust anyone enough to marry again. However, a few years later, when he met Laurel, her personal attributes and, above all, her close connection to José and Jerry made him decide he would marry again but build a different kind of partner relationship and family. Arturo and Laurel have two children together, and he has been extremely involved in raising them. He decided he would really "be there" physically and emotionally for them and glowingly describes their two teenagers as "two great kids." He opted to retire early so he could spend loads of time with them before they grew up and left for college. He and his wife both thoroughly enjoy their son and daughter and his two older sons, and the two younger children are quite bonded to and devoted to each other.

Retrospective and Prospective

For Arturo, the separation Barbara told him she wanted bursts onto their domestic scene like *a train wreck* – unexpected, horrific, and with awful consequences. He adores his sons and regrets having been legally, physically, and emotionally extruded from so much of their lives. He rarely got to share in their everyday school events or sports activities or meet their friends. He detested the years of coming home to an empty apartment and missing his children's presence in his life and his in theirs.

Mr. M has done everything he can to build a loving, interesting, and enduring second marriage with a bright, compassionate woman who has become a successful and well-respected researcher in her professional field. They have been very involved parents with their two children who are currently described as vibrant, talented teen-agers. Arturo retired early to maximize the amount of time he has available for fathering and thoroughly enjoys encouraging and enabling his children and his wife to pursue their interests. Both he and Laurel have done their utmost to make José and his wife and child and Jerry an integral part of their family.

Despite some residual regrets and the scars of his earlier heartache from being pushed into being an estranged father, Arturo seems quite content with the life he has created for himself and with family in the last 20 years and the professional success that made this possible given excessive financial pressures. He is clear that a close-knit family, in which everyone feels free to communicate openly and respect-fully with everyone else and to pursue their own dreams, is a top priority (Kaslow, 1981). He is not only pursuing his dream of being a good husband and father but has taken up an instrument and is writing music and finding both activities satisfying to him and pleasurable for his family.

References

Gold, L. (1992). *Between love and hate: A guide to civilized divorce*. New York: Plenum.

Isaacs, M. B., Montalvo, B., & Abelsohn, D. (1986). *The difficult divorce: Therapy for children and families*. New York: Basic Books.

Kaslow, F. W. (1981). Profile of the healthy family. *Interaction, 4*(1/2), 1–15.

Millon, T. (with Davis, R. D.) (1996). *Disorders of personality: DSM IV and beyond*. Hoboken, NJ: Wiley.

Myers, M. F. (1989). *Men and divorce*. New York: Guilford Press.

Schwartz, L. L., & Kaslow, F. W. (1997). *Painful partings: Divorce and its aftermath*. New York: Wiley.

Chapter 12
Case 11 Mr. Hy Hopes: The Fallout of Crazy in Love

Brief Personal History

This 52-year-old man is nice looking, personable, and articulate. His parents are both Jewish and Caucasian, and the grandparent generation came from Eastern Europe. Religious observances were minimal though the family's Jewish identity was and remains moderately strong. Hy and his brother had a close relationship with one another and with their parents, who for many years worked together as partners in a family business they established in South Florida. A good education, ambition, hard work, ethical behavior, and family closeness and loyalty were the values emphasized by Hy's parents.

Marriage, Child, and Divorce

Hy went off to a good college in the northeast. He earned a bachelor of arts degree and was interested in the world of business. After graduating, he got involved in the financial world for a while and then transitioned into being a management consultant which entailed being "on the road" quite a bit.

After a number of years postcollege during which he remained a bachelor, he met Carolina, a young woman from South America (Garcia-Preto, 1996) who had come to the United States during her mid-20s to get an MBA degree and had decided to stay on after she received it. They met in 1988 when both were 30 years of age and she already had her MBA, which Hy found impressive. She had managed to do her work in English, which was her second language as she was raised and educated in Spanish. Initially, he thought she was independent and self-sufficient.

Carolina came from a "broken home." Her parents were separated for many years but had never divorced. Her mother had had five children in six years. Her dad fathered an additional four more children out of wedlock. Given that the family professed to be staunch Catholics, divorce was not acceptable, but out of wedlock children did not

F.W. Kaslow, *Divorced Fathers and Their Families: Legal, Economic, and Emotional Dilemmas*, DOI 10.1007/978-1-4614-5535-6_12, © Springer Science+Business Media New York 2013

seem to be forbidden! Carolina had never felt financially secure and apparently saw getting a good education in the United States as one step toward becoming economically successful. She wanted to help support her siblings and her mother in the future, a fact which he had not been made aware of until after they were married.

Her background contrasted sharply with Hy's. He came from a home and family that offered both emotional and financial security and stability. He felt a great deal of sympathy for Carolina (and apparently has the good-natured personality characteristic of a person often deemed a rescuer. It may be that her neediness was part of what attracted him at a less than conscious level of awareness).

He fell very much in love with Carolina; in fact, as he describes their long period of going together, it sounds like he was quite captivated by her (Johnson & Murray, 2007). Her Latin background, appearance, and style intrigued him. They socialized mostly with her friends, whom he enjoyed, and she was well accepted by his circle of friends. He saw her as similar to his beloved paternal grandmother, who had a warm, sunny, open disposition. And she seemed to accept him and not to try to change him, which he found refreshing. She always liked to look very attractive and be fashionably attired. She was ambitious and talked about wanting to establish her own business. Carolina was a good listener, easy to get along with, and seemed to fit in with his lifestyle. He was ecstatic when they decided to get married five years after they met.

Once they married, the many assumptions he had made about Carolina turned out not to be grounded in fact. They had not discussed their expectations of each other nor of the marriage. They just took for granted that what they expected and wanted was similar. And there were so many important issues they had never discussed before they had gotten married that surfaced as problems.

One of Carolina's brothers had sought and received political asylum in the United States and came to live with them. Her brother's wife ran off, deserting him, once they were apparently safe in the United States. Carolina was concerned that her brother would be "dragged" back to their native country and felt they had to offer him shelter. Hy went along with this and accepted him fully. He remained with them for 14 months. Next, her sister came and lived with them for about nine months. About three years after her sister moved out, her father came to stay for seven months. Hy had not known he would be running a hotel for her family or that her life plan included being the caregiver daughter and sister. Altogether her relatives lived with them a total of about two-and-half years.

After their marriage was consecrated, he realized that her staunchly religious mother, who still lived in South America, had exerted quite a powerful influence on Carolina's beliefs. In the interview, Hy emphasized that although she was religious, this was not synonymous with moral – for any member of the family.

Their son, Reggie, was born about 10 months after they got married. Carolina insisted that they have him baptized when he was seven or eight years of age, which did not please Hy. Although he had not promised to go along with raising their son in the Catholic faith, she was the more religious partner and was determined to do this. This was just one of the areas they had not discussed prior to getting married, and it has caused him much consternation in terms of both his and Reggie's sense of identity.

Carolina had not become a US citizen prior to their marriage but filed to become one shortly thereafter. She did obtain it and now has dual citizenship, which is allowable by her country of origin and the United States. Hy now wonders if this was perhaps one of the main reasons she wanted to marry him, in addition to hoping to gain access to his family's assumed wealth. She did tell him when they were getting the divorce that she had partly chosen to marry him because "I thought you were from a good family" (i.e., rich?). Looking back he wonders, "Did she ever really love me just because of me or was it more deliberate planning to obtain what I could provide that she coveted?"

Shortly after her brother came to live with them, Carolina went to visit her ill mother in South America. Her mother died the day after Carolina left to return to the United States and Carolina was grief stricken. The doctor there had told her that her mother was out of danger before she left. Hy conjectures that perhaps she never forgave herself for not staying until the end.

About 10 years into the marriage, Hy found an e-mail she left up on the screen on a shared computer. He opened it and found a string of e-mails that had been exchanged with another man with whom he learned she had been involved emotionally and sexually for over a year and a half. He realized she has fallen in love with a married man whom he knew professionally and she had met through Hy's business, when she was doing some sales promotion work for him. He described the man as a "predator" and a "player" and his ex-wife as vulnerable and amenable (Kaslow, 1993). He did not think it was deliberate but rather that despite her being bright enough to get an MBA, he did not see her as "street smart" and thought this was just "carelessness" on her part. Now many years after he discovered her emotional and physical affair with a man who is separated but not divorced from his second wife, he is aware that they remained lovers for a number of years (Lusterman, 1998). Reggie has always been hostile toward him. Recently, he learned Carolina has started dating again.

Her dad tried to talk her out of pursuing a divorce before he died, which was just before she filed papers, but to no avail. By this time, she had drifted from her siblings, who apparently had been embarrassed by her actions. The closeness she had initially purported to want had become less important to her over time.

Hy felt used, cheated, terribly hurt, and disappointed when all of this surfaced. The betrayal seemed even more undeserved given how generous he had been to Carolina and her relatives.

One night after she had initiated the idea of getting a divorce and she indicated she planned to file for one, they were having a verbal spat. He asked her how she thought her boyfriend's wife would react when she found out about the affair and Carolina's identity. She "freaked out" and called the police. Through all of this flare-up, Hy was sitting on the couch with Reggie. When the police arrived and observed what was transpiring, they admonished her not to make false allegations and told her to take a walk and calm down. Hy saw what a "loose cannon" she was.

Carolina would not move out for about four months after she announced she wanted a divorce. It was an extremely tense and conflicted time, and Hy was worried about the impact of the tension and arguing on Reggie. She moved into a rental town house in the same development so that Reggie, by then 10 years of age, could walk back and forth.

Postdivorce

In the divorce settlement, Hy kept the marital home, which he continued to live in for another year after the divorce. Then the house was foreclosed, and he moved into a rental to lower his expenses. Fortunately for him he personally does not need "a lot of things" (material possessions). Instead, the major continuing concern for him is whether he will be able to save enough money to send Reggie to college.

The custody and visitation plan that was involved and approved by the court, after Hy "stood up for what he wanted and thought was best for Reggie," was joint and shared custody – with their son spending alternating weeks with each of them. Carolina had actually petitioned for sole custody and for Hy to have only supervised visitation, but the judge recognized that this was not a wise and fair plan as Hy had come from a much more stable family background, had tried to keep his own family together and to see his son often, and had done nothing to warrant the need for supervised visitation (Kruk, 2012). (By this time they had all relocated from the northeast and were living in North Florida.)

When Reggie was in third grade, Hy saw he was not doing very well in school. He was taken to a well-respected (doctoral level) psychologist for evaluation and the initial diagnosis was ADHD. He was put on medication but that was stopped two years ago at Hy's insistence; he believes his son is quite able to concentrate but is "somewhat lazy." Hy has served as an assistant coach for many of his son's sports activities. During these years, Hy became a fine cook and has enjoyed preparing meals for himself and his son.

Occasionally, Reggie tries to play one parent off against the other and attempts to manipulate his dad with the all too familiar phrase, "Mom lets me," but Hy feels secure and justified in saying "my rules are my rules" and is cognizant of what is normal adolescent rebellious behavior and when his son is pushing the limits. Mostly they have a good father–teenage son relationship. However, he is concerned that Reggie is not a good student and continues to attribute the problem to laziness. Ostensibly, Carolina worries about his being "a bad kid," but Hy does not agree with this despite his concerns about their son's poor grades, his attempts at "back talk," and his occasional lies. Recently, it was agreed Reggie would live with Hy full time until Carolina "gets her life back together" and because Reggie and his mom have problems with each other when they spend time together. Hy and Carolina worked this arrangement out together informally; it has not been legalized.

Relationship with His Family

Hy's family has been his erstwhile support throughout his marriage, divorce, and postdivorce. His mother has been his "cheerleader" and his brother, who still lives up north, has come through with financial support when he has required it.

Carolina had told Hy in front of his parents that she wanted a divorce. They had, at Hy and Carolina's request, financed a wedding reception for them years earlier, and they too felt cheated and taken advantage of (Kaslow, 2007). His dad was disappointed for and with him that the marriage did not work out as he had planned. His mom was furious and wanted him to hire an investigator to learn more about her dalliance. She went so far as to suggest they report her sister and try to have her deported, but Hy did not want to take this kind of action.

Several years ago, Hy's mother decided it was time to retire from her active partnership in the business with her husband. It was agreed that Hy would join his dad on a trial basis, acquire whatever additional training and certifications he needed to be in the business, and actually embark on a different career, and that is where he is now working. His parents remain delighted to have their grandson nearby.

Greatest Losses

Having a close-knit family is something Hy very much valued and tried to create for himself, as his parents had done. *The loss of the dream* of getting married and living happily together *"til death do us part"* was devastating, as has been not having his son live with him full time, until very recently. He was bitter over the betrayal of trust for a long time but has tried to let go of the bitterness and move on (Jacobson, 1983).

Finances

At the time of the divorce, Hy was encumbered with many debts. While they had had two incomes and one home, they were able to manage. When Carolina moved out, each had to struggle. During the beginning stages of the divorce, he suggested refinancing the original marital home, but her attorney advised her against it. By the time a year later when the lawyer told her to go ahead and do the refinancing, it was too late. The house was already in foreclosure. Hy wanted to get rid of all of his debts as quickly as possible, and the costs of keeping the house ran too high.

There has never been any child support exchanged since they both had similar salaries and joint/shared/equal time custody. However, Hy has always covered most of Reggie's expenses. He pays Carolina a nominal $10 per month alimony and is still paying off all debts incurred during the marriage.

Reggie does not need a great deal financially and works to make his own spending money. Hy's parents and brother will "pitch in" when he runs short, knowing how hard both he and his son are working and that they are not extravagant. His son has been the main focus in his life for many years.

Changes in His Personality, Lifestyle, Sense of Belonging, and Ideas About Family

A few years before the divorce, Hy was so distraught about Carolina's behavior, including her rejection of him and her deceitfulness that he went into therapy. The therapist helped him to realize he should concentrate a little more on himself and his needs and encouraged him to acquire some additional relevant professional certifications and also suggested this was a good way for him to keep busy. She also reflected back to him what a fine husband he had been and what a great father he continued to be. In the past two years, he has reverted to his "pre-divorce self," and life has become an adventure once again. He is finally involved in a new relationship with a woman he has fun with and with whom he shares many interests. She has two young teenagers. Because his new girlfriend has gone through an "awful" divorce she does not wish to remarry, so for now at least, they are just enjoying their time together.

Postdivorce Interactions with Ex-Spouse

Hy and Carolina continue to disagree about some of their child-rearing practices and are not fully supportive of each other. Hy is willing to accept the normalcy of some rebellious adolescent behavior from his now 16-year-old son and to clearly set out the limits and adhere to them. He carefully chooses when it is important to battle and when it is not. In a different modus operandi, Carolina is into punishing and gets hysterical when Reggie does not obey her. One time recently she punished her son, and he retaliated by hiding her computer. She called the police, just as she had when Hy aggravated her.

Carolina refrains from maligning Hy too much to Reggie. She learned during the divorce that Hy could use his knowledge of her infidelity as a weapon against her with their son if she criticized or disparaged him (see Chapter 15 on Games Divorcing and Divorced People Play). He is somewhat appalled, although not surprised, that Carolina now has an STD (sexually transmitted disease) which he assumes she contracted from the man who had long been her lover.

Life Events He Has Participated in with His Son and His Most Important Contributions/Poignant Memories

Hy has taken part in every aspect of Reggie's activities that he could – including his bowling matches, soccer and hockey practices, and games. But his most important contribution has been "just being there and available," being firm when needed, having good conversations with his son, and being open and accessible to him.

Hy's most poignant memories of his son when they were all still together were the sadness he felt when he left Reggie and Carolina at the airport on Sunday evenings when he was traveling for business and his sheer joy when he returned and they were there to greet him several days later. When he described this, his fact lit up and his pleasure in the memory was almost palpable. He treasures any and all time he spends with his son and recalls fondly time they spent together with animals. Reggie loves animals and at times asks to stop at pet stores just to see the pets.

Retrospective and Prospective

For Hy, the most painful aspects of the entire divorce experience have been the multiple losses, disappointments, and disillusionment. The shattering of the dream of a long-term happy marriage that both partners would actively participate in to keep vital and satisfying was a tremendous blow to his view of his world and his self-esteem, and the loss of being able to be a full-time live-in dad with his son was very traumatic and depressing. He regrets that they did not discuss their expectations and needs before marrying and that he was so smitten by Carolina and crazy in love with her (which does have an element of both blindness to faults and crazy exaltation of the loved one) that *he did not see her impulsivity, her hysteric responses, her self-centeredness, and her deceitfulness* (Millon, 2011). He remains grateful to his brother and parents for their unflinching loyalty to and support of him, and he is proud of his fathering and the strong relationship he has built with his son.

Hy has resolved his anger and bitterness to the point where he has transformed his thinking and is now able to be in the present and out of the past. He has changed careers and is able to trust enough to be in an ongoing relationship with another woman. He is positive and optimistic about his future and continues to work hard and purposefully to create the life and lifestyle he wants.

References

Garcia-Preto, N. (1996). Latino families: An overview. In M. McGoldrick, J. Giordano, & J. K. Pearce (Eds.), *Ethnicity family therapy* (2nd ed., pp. 141–154). New York: Guilford.

Jacobson, G. F. (1983). *The multiple crises of marital separation and divorce.* New York: Grune & Stratton.

Johnson, W. B., & Murray, K. (2007). *Crazy love.* Atascadero, CA: Impact Publishers.

Kaslow, F. W. (1993). Attractions and affairs: Fabulous and fatal. *Journal of Family Psychotherapy, 4*(4), 1–34.

Kaslow, F. W. (2007). Post divorce relatedness between parents, their divorced sons, and their grandchildren: A pilot study. In C. A. Everett & R. E. Lee (Eds.), *When marriages fail: Systemic family therapy interventions and issues* (pp. 141–156). New York: Haworth Press.

Kruk, E. (2012). Arguments for an equal parental responsibility presumption in contested child custody. *The American Journal of Family Therapy, 40*(1), 33–55.

Lusterman, D. D. (1998). *Infidelity: A survival guide.* Oakland, CA: New Harbinger.

Millon, T. (2011). *Disorders of personality: Introducing a DSM/ICF spectrum from normal to abnormal* (3`th ed.) 242–243. Hoboken, NJ: Wiley.

Chapter 13
Case 12 Dr. Zack Determined: It Is a Strange World After All

Brief Personal History

This interesting, tall, broad, personable 62-year-old man was born in the United States of Scottish, Protestant, Caucasian parents in 1949. He was raised to value close family relationships, a good education, and high integrity. He attended college on the East Coast and then matriculated in a well-respected doctoral program in psychology at a state university. In his middle adult years, he has liked being involved in professional organizations, and he possesses and exercises good technological and managerial capacities.

Marriage, Children, and Divorce

When Zack was 22 years old, he met and married Peggy. Her heritage was Anglo-Saxon and Caucasian, and like Zack, she was raised in the Protestant faith. Although they had attended different Protestant churches, their views on religion were compatible. Zack continued his graduate studies during the early years of their marriage and was proud to be awarded his Ph.D. in 1976.

Peggy had been raised in a much more affluent family and household than Zack had been. Difficulties surfaced between them about money early in the marriage. Peggy wanted more money to spend, and he always felt that no matter what he did and how hard he worked, he simply was not earning enough to suit her. He handled the finances, kept everything tallied on spreadsheets, and tried to explain the income and expense accounting to her, but she had no interest in learning. Her main financial interest was having sufficient funds available to spend for whatever she wanted, whenever she wanted it.

At the beginning of the marriage, she worked in a public government position. Zack commented that he thinks she was a very good worker. Income was combined and shared.

F.W. Kaslow, *Divorced Fathers and Their Families: Legal, Economic, and Emotional Dilemmas*, DOI 10.1007/978-1-4614-5535-6_13,
© Springer Science+Business Media New York 2013

Their first child, a daughter, Sue Ellen, was born in 1976, the same year Zack received his Ph.D. Peggy left her position to become a full-time stay-at-home mom, devoting all her time to the baby, cooking, baking, and sewing. She prided herself on doing everything personally and by hand.

Two years later, a son, Corey, arrived on the scene. Their third child, Lenny, was born three years later, in 1980. Zack loved "having the kids" and thoroughly enjoyed being a father. But by the mid-1980s, when Peggy realized she was pregnant again, she was surprised and more concerned than delighted. They were experiencing some serious marital conflicts, and the pregnancy was unplanned. Zack thinks she was worried that he would be upset because this might mean too many children.

Peggy's mother was a wealthy woman. Her family had owned a profitable manufacturing business. During the time her parents were married, Peggy's father managed the business. He was depicted to me as a scalawag and an alcoholic who fit the stereotype of the heavy-drinking Irishman of the 1950s and 1960s (Windle & Searles, 1990). Her parents fought about finances, and when they got divorced, he was "thrown out of the business." After that, Peggy had "nothing to do with her dad." Later, her mom married again and chose another "no good alcoholic" for her husband. She divorced him several years later. Zack suspects that her second husband sexually abused his wife. In addition, he was told by Peggy that her stepfather physically abused her, which included spanking her, yelling at her, and making sure she was afraid of him. He believes her recounting of these childhood horrors. In protest, Peggy became "very rebellious," and this demeanor was part of what attracted Zack. At the same time that she appeared nontraditional, she was accustomed to and liked having easy access to money. After they were married, her rich mom "lent" them money for a down payment on a home and to buy a car. She was always very generous to and for the children.

When Zack and Peggy both realized their marriage was floundering, they tried a few sessions of marital therapy. The therapist, recognizing the high level of disagreement and tension, suggested they live apart in the same house for a while as a trial separation. Zack moved into bedroom over the garage, but it contained none of the necessities for living except a toilet. He had to go into the house to use a full bathroom, that is, to wash or shower, or to have access to a kitchen. It was terribly uncomfortable, and he could not tolerate these living conditions for more than several months.

At that point, Peggy insisted that he had to move out, even though it was she who wanted the divorce. This meant he had to find and furnish his own living quarters. An example of Peggy's typical behavior, according to Zack, was that shortly after he moved into his own place, she arranged for the children to visit him and each brought him something for his new home. They brought kitchen items like plates, cups, and flatware, as he had taken nothing with him. The children saw this as mom being thoughtful and kind (he thinks that was the intention).

The attorney she retained was not a divorce attorney, rather he was a personal injury lawyer recommended by an acquaintance. Ostensibly, the said attorney had advised her "it would be best if her husband moved out," and she pressured Zack to do so. A mere 10 days after he moved out of his garage apartment, she filed for divorce – charging him with abandoning the home, having physically abused her, and having been "mean to the kids."

Zack believes the attorney encouraged her to lie. The attorney listed the charges enumerated above in a letter he sent to the judge in which he sought temporary and immediate relief for his client. The lawyer also stated Zack had been stealing household items (the ones the children had brought to him) and had purchased a bed so he could have other women "come to visit." He was shocked at the list of falsified charges she had had filed.

At this point, Zack had to hire an attorney to protect and represent him. His lawyer drew up an agreement, which Zack thought was quite equitable, but Peggy refused to sign it. He became aware that her lawyer had told her that unless she did exactly what he advised her to do, that Zack would file for and get custody of the children. Frightened by this warning, she followed his instructions resolutely.

At the same time that all of this was transpiring, Zack's mother lay bedridden. She had had a serious stroke and was not recuperating from it well at all. His father had Alzheimer's disease and was also incapacitated. Zack had been commuting back and forth by plane fairly often for quite a while to visit and help care for his elderly, infirm parents who lived in another state. One day when he was alighting from the plane to begin a planned visit with his parents, he was served divorce papers. Apparently her attorney had told the judge he was only going out of state to avoid being served at his home or office, and this was the only way to corner him. [Shades of the embattled process played out in the classic film, The War of the Roses (1989). It is almost impossible to accuse opposition counsel of fabricating information, so he had no recourse to correct these false statements.]

Weeks later when Mr. D's attorney scheduled an appointment time to take Peggy's deposition, neither she nor her attorney showed up. They learned that her attorney had told her not to go. The interactions became increasingly contentious. Zack learned that Peggy was spending money she inherited from her family to pay her attorney's fees that were running into the tens of thousands. (To him, that seemed an astronomical sum for something that could have been resolved more easily and rapidly in mediation or settlement conferences.) *Zack's attorney was unable to get the other attorney to have his client agree to mediation.* Many motions for many reasons were filed by her attorney. Zack was forced to respond to each new allegation and charge, building up a large attorney's bill. The divorce dragged on and was not finalized until after several years of legal action had transpired. The costs were so astronomical that Zack had to declare bankruptcy.

At the time of the divorce, the children were ages nine, seven, four, and two years. The eldest daughter, Sue Ellen, was quite mature for a nine-year-old and quickly was thrust into the *role* of a parentified child (Simon, Stierlin, & Wynn, 1985) – helping to run the family and take care of the younger children.

Feelings About the Divorce: Pre-, During, and in Early Postdivorce Period

Zack had experienced feelings of attraction to others during his marriage and had engaged in flirtations and brief, furtive sexual encounters. He was drinking "a lot" and his drinking became worse at this juncture; he states he was a highly functional "alcoholic" for 25 years (Bepko & Krestan, 1985). He had a favorite bar, and he frequented it often. Nonetheless, during all of that time, he was committed to his professional work and to being a good father.

About a year after the divorce, Zack's ex-wife, whom he describes as having a "nervous and scattered" personality, evidenced severe anxiety disorder symptoms, spending time in bed, crying frequently, and seeking medical attention. The eldest child, Sue Ellen, took on much of the mothering role. After about a year, Sue Ellen had what was then called a "nervous breakdown" and had to be hospitalized. She remained hospitalized for nearly four months. Zack said that her doctor felt she needed a break from her role at home and some help developing her own personality.

Main Emotions During Divorce and in Early Postdivorce Period

Zack was distraught about what was happening. The separation, legal bickering, and Peggy's drawing the children into the tumult were torturous. It was all so devastating to his disabled mother. Prior to his divorce, when he was in his hometown to visit his parents, he sometimes spent some time with Janie, an empathic childhood friend. He sometimes cried when talking to her and moaned, "I don't want to go home" to the constant abuse from my wife. When he was drowning his sorrows in alcohol, he would tell his troubles to the bartender (Daley & Raskin, 1991). He remembers these as *the most horrible years of his life*! And he believes much of the battling and dissension could have been reduced and handled in a much more civil and rational way – which is what he tried to do. At that time, he did not understand why it was so impossible to deal with Peggy or how to make anything better. He reports having felt completely helpless throughout the ordeal and like he had totally lost control of his own life.

Finances

Zack was designated the payer parent and he paid Peggy child support for 15 years, until the last child finished high school. He took care of the children's health and other insurances and contributed significantly to their college educations. Since Peggy had an inheritance from her family and was independently wealthy, he did not have to pay alimony. Peggy was awarded the marital home which had been purchased partially with a loan from her parents, and she kept possession of a car. He kept his retirement plan.

He continues to help the children, now that they are adults, when they request it, and he thinks it is warranted. Zack always made a reasonably good salary, and during the time that Janie was in his life, she chipped in to help with support for the children, if he ran short. The marital settlement agreement articulated a clearly spelled out custody and visitation plan. Zack was to have the children every Wednesday night, and every other weekend and holidays were to be alternated with each parent. Sadly, too often Peggy would suddenly intercept the schedule by unilaterally changing her plans, thereby disrupting Zack's anticipated visits with his children.

How Long Until Felt Reasonably Settled in a Home and Accepted the Divorce

During the first year of the divorce, Zack rented a house that was large enough that the four children could visit and stay with him comfortably. Three years after the divorce, he bought a home and Janie moved in with him. Occasionally, he and Janie traveled together and took the children along on their trips. He took a sabbatical from the college at which he was teaching and went to France and Italy with her, to spend a semester teaching abroad. Sue Ellen joined them and spent some time studying at the Sorbonne. This was an exciting time for Zack, and he savors fond memories of that sojourn. It also was the refresher he needed to put his thoughts and sense of self back together.

He also had acquired a vacation home in upstate New York. One summer, he took the children there for their vacation with him, and they went white water rafting and had a great time – it was quite a contrast to the kind of activities they were accustomed to in their hometown in the south. He also took them up there in the middle of one cold winter, when he went to visit relatives, and they had a "perfect winter holiday." He did whatever he could to keep in close contact with the children and spend quality time with them.

Children's Relationship with Subsequent Partner

The children always seemed to accept Janie positively. Janie was also divorced and did not wish to remarry.

Children's Reactions to the Divorce: Short and Long Term

The children all became "symptomatic" – exhibiting their distress over the family breakup, dads moving out, the tension between their parents, and then having to live in two households. Fortunately, his eldest daughter has had good psychological treatment in the ensuing years, did well at college and graduate school, and has a professional degree – seeming to identify with and emulate Zack, at least in the professional realm of his life.

When his eldest son, Corey, wanted to move in with him when he was 13 years of age, Peggy refused to allow this to occur. So he moved in with a friend instead. Currently, he remains estranged from his mother. He is now married for the third time, and his father's observation is "he marries women who are very similar to his mom" (which rarely portends well for a marriage when the mother–son relationship has been a fractious one). He is in the medical field in the rehabilitation realm.

The younger two children, Lenny and Tina, moved in with Zack, of their own choice, when he was with Janie. She was extremely "good to both of them." They were both very rebellious teenagers. Lenny's and Tina's behavior got so out of control that they both needed inpatient treatment on several occasions. This was a tumultuous period in all of their lives.

Peggy engaged in "classical borderline behavior" (Zack's words), projecting all of the blame for the children's emotional and social maladjustments onto the kids and/or Zack (Millon & Everly, 1985). Lenny has continued to have a very difficult time as an adult; he is sometimes quite depressed and may bunk in with his father temporarily when the going gets rough. Tina has a tendency to choose to date men who resemble her dad and are alcoholic (also not unusual behavior when a daughter is trying to help another man conquer this kind of battle which she could not help her father handle with the disease of alcoholism).

Most Painful Aspects of Divorce

For Zack, the profound feelings of the helplessness he experienced about the divorce and the children were unfamiliar, depressing, and immobilizing in some ways. It took him several years to re-equilibrate and regain a sense of composure and competence about running his life.

Changes in Lifestyle, Personality, Sense of Meaning and Value, and Ideas About "Family"

After the divorce, Zack faced the truth about his drinking and sought help through Alcoholics Anonymous. There he learned to "Let Go and Let God," to be more accepting of self and others, to relinquish some of his quest for control, and to be "less of a fixer." Over a period of 15 years, he left his administrative position at a university and started his own consulting business, all the while attending AA meetings and working his AA 12-step program. Eventually, he no longer felt desperate and was able to make better choices about his personal and professional life. He finally "felt comfortable in his own skin." He has now been sober for 18 years. Over the years after he became sober, he and Janie drifted apart. She moved away and he began a single life; by then, the children were older and only the youngest was still spending much time with him.

Relationship to Ex-Wife's Family and His Postdivorce

Peggy's parents had long been divorced so Zack had no relationship with her father before he and Peggy separated. Her stepfather was portrayed as abusive and despicable so there had been no relationship with him either. Her mother had been supportive and even fond of Zack. She had indulged her daughter while she was growing up and continued to do so. His mother had died and his father had dementia and was in a nursing facility in New York, so he was unaware of the cataclysmic upheaval in Zack's life. Zack and the children lived in the south and so saw his father infrequently. His siblings were not surprised at the dissolution of this marriage and told him they "never understood what he saw in her." While Zack and Peggy were married, they had chosen to be distant from Zack's family. They liked his later partners much better and became closer to him and them than they had been to him previously.

Subsequent Changes in His Lifestyle

Around 1991, Zack decided it was time for him to really live as he wanted to and felt he had to, and he "came out." By then, he had met Steve and felt much more satisfied in his gay relationship than he had in prior heterosexual ones. When he told Sue Ellen, her response was that she knew he was dating men and was relieved that he was acknowledging it. Janie was confused and saddened by the news. Corey did not want anyone to know and said he would not tell anyone. Lenny, who had had no suspicions about his dad's [sexual] identity, thought this revelation was "cool." Basically, all of his children became supportive and caused him no problems about this. They all had come to accept this by the time they met Steve, who is laid back and fun. Steve had also stopped drinking, and he and Zack have remained sober and together ever since.

Interestingly, stemming from her rebellious days, Peggy had many homosexual friends and was not terribly upset by Zack's revelation. In fact, she then blamed all of their marital problems on this (could she have unconsciously suspected?). Now her stories about the marriage are more a "revisionist history", and she is more cordial to Zack. However, over the years, she has alienated all of the children with her "narcissism and borderline behavior" (Solomon, 1989), and each one found some way to escape her – the two youngest through drug and alcohol use (Windle &

Searles, 1990). (They are apparently the third generation of alcohol abusers in this family.) The children all visit their mother occasionally, but she lives quite a distance away. In her own way, she was a very devoted and doting mom and is proud of their accomplishments.

When Zack and Steve decided to formalize their relationship and have a "commitment ceremony" at a church, his children all volunteered to be involved in planning and attending the celebration. They exchanged vows in an elaborate ceremony that was very affirming of their *marital bond*. The children all visit their father and Steve, and this pair of "grandfathers" are welcome at their homes and are pleased to visit their children and grandchildren.

Retrospective and Prospective

Zack's divorce was tortuous and debilitating. He felt hopeless and helpless as well as rejected. His drinking escalated for a period until he realized it had gotten out of control and he joined AA (Orford, 1985). This helped him put his life back together a little as did his friendship with a loving, solid female friend, Janie. But it took about five years for him to re-equilibrate and feel confident again.

His wife suffered a "nervous breakdown" after the divorce and was hospitalized for about four months. Zack still considers his ex-wife to have "serious personality problems." Each of the children was impacted by their parents' personal difficulties; their conflicted marriage; the wrangling they witnessed during their pre-divorce living in the same house separately period; the shuffling back and forth between mom's house and dad's house – and the difference in emotional climate and expectations in each home – with mom being arbitrary and dad more lenient; dad's two different partners over the next 18 years; and a multitude of other changes (Gold, 1992). Three of the children spent time in residential treatment centers, trying to deal with their individual and family problems as well as the kinds of serious interpersonal confusions and uncertainties that many children of embittered divorces encounter. Through it all, Zack seems to have been able to communicate that he cares very much for and about the children and to have them remain an integral part of each other's lives. He seems as accepting of their vacillations and vicissitudes as he has come to be of his own.

Apparently, Zack and Steve have forged a committed relationship that provides continuity, stability, a sense of integrity, love, and pleasure in living to each of them. Zack is well accepted in his professional community, is seen as a respected leader, and has found healthy outlets for his creative thinking and managerial capabilities. The emotional storms have subsided, sobriety has been maintained, and the future now looks reasonably bright for him, Steve, and at least several of the children.

References

Bepko, C., & Kreston, J. A. (1985). *The responsibility trap*. New York: Free Press.

Daley, D. C., & Reskin, M. S. (1991). *Treating the chemically dependent and their families*. Newbury Park, CA: Sage.

Gold, L. (1992). *Between Love and Hate: A Guide to Civilized Divorce*. New York: Plenum.

Millon, T., & Everly, G. S. (1985). *Personality and its disorders*. Hoboken, NJ: Wiley.

Orford, J. (1985). *Excessive appetites: A psychological view of addictions*. Chichester, England: Wiley.

Simon, F. B., Stierlin, H., & Wynne, L. C. (1985). *The language of family therapy: A systemic vocabulary and sourcebook*. New York: Family Process Press.

Solomon, M. F. (1989). *Narcissism and intimacy*. New York: Norton.

Windle, M., & Searles, J. S. (Eds.). (1990). *Children of alcoholics*. New York: Guilford.

Films

Leeson, M. (Writer), & Devito, D. (Director). (1989). *The War of the Roses* [Motion Picture]. Culver City, CA: Twentieth Century Fox & Gracie Films.

Chapter 14
Case Unlucky 13: My Greatest Loss

Brief Personal History

Dr. Scott Unlucky (SU) was born in Connecticut in 1946. His parents were American, Jewish, and Caucasian. They had a long-term, happy, and solid marriage. The basic value system they inculcated in their children included the importance of having strong family ties, obtaining a good education, and a commitment to dedicated and honest work. He pursued and acquired his Ph.D. in psychology as well as completing a postdoctoral fellowship, both at well-known universities in the northeast United States. He is a board-certified psychologist; one of his specialty areas is family psychology and child therapy.

Dr. Unlucky is a thin, nice-looking man of medium height; he has many diverse interests. He is regarded as a likeable person, as a good conversationalist with a sense of humor, and as a person with a compassionate understanding of others. He has maintained many long-term friendships with male and female friends and colleagues. Some of these friends are childhood buddies.

First Marriage, Children, and the Legal Divorce

Dr. U married when he was 22 years of age in 1968, separated in 1978, and was divorced in 1980. His wife, Sarah, also was Caucasian and Jewish. They were both raised in the same city. According to Dr. U, his wife's family was known to be "obnoxious social climbers." He stated that his major problem in their marriage during the early years was conflict with his in-laws, emanating from their irrationality in competing with his parents and with other families in the community. He also mentioned that his former wife had been previously engaged to a very wealthy man from a prominent local family, until he had broken off with her. After that she agreed to marry a student, him! Dr. U reported that her parents were very disappointed that their daughter did not marry into her prior fiancé's affluent family; they were upset

F.W. Kaslow, *Divorced Fathers and Their Families: Legal, Economic, and Emotional Dilemmas*, DOI 10.1007/978-1-4614-5535-6_14,
© Springer Science+Business Media New York 2013

with Sarah for choosing to marry a graduate student. Sarah was educated as a teacher but admitted that she did not like teaching. She went back to school to study interior design, but she "failed" when she tried to launch her own decorating business.

They had two children together – their son, Bernie, who was seven years old and their daughter, Ilene, who only was three-and-a-half years old when they divorced. After they were born, Sarah had become increasingly discontent and disillusioned with her role as a mother and exhibited symptoms of depression and despondency. She experienced an identity crisis (Erickson, 1968) and *made plans to leave their marriage and their children in order to rediscover herself* in Los Angeles by adopting a different lifestyle. Her parents had taught her to rely upon her beauty and feminine wiles for exploiting men to indulge her in return for her affection and love. She had become the "princess of entitlement" which her husband had failed to recognize due to his youth, his focus upon his studies, and his captivation with her attractiveness. However, before she left for California, she became depressed and confused and subsequently was admitted to a psychiatric hospital for a month by her treating psychologist.

Dr. Unlucky cared for their children during her absence, and the children became very attached to him. The children told their friends and the neighbors that they wanted to be with their father rather than their mother, who was always yelling at them. Dr. U described his wife as attractive, charming, spoiled, self-centered, and completely indulged by her parents. She expected to continue being pampered as she had been as a child.

After her discharge from the hospital, Sarah went to see an attorney who told her to make sure "she kept the kids" which would entitle her to keep the marital house and to receive full financial support. Dr. U stated that Sarah "expected to receive the majority of the marital assets, unrealistic child support and extravagant alimony." Conversely, he was told by his attorney to stay in the house as long as possible so as not to lose daily contact with the children and his position of interest in retaining sole or joint custody. Sarah's mother invited herself to move into the marital residence with them, and their home life became untenable for him and a war zone in front of the children. His wife and mother-in-law were intrusive and showed no respect for his boundaries; they went through Dr. U's clothes and personal possessions while he was at work. To add to this "despicable action" perpetrated against him (which was difficult for him to recount without choking up), *his mother-in-law would hide his work papers, make sure there was no food in the refrigerator when he returned from work, and throw his clothes in a ball on the floor or on the front lawn.*

During their years of marriage, Dr. U had given Sarah money to send to her father because of his financial difficulties and repetitive business failures. This money was used to subsidize his in-laws. Nonetheless, Sarah stole as much money as she could from him, and she would send large sums of funds to her unemployed father.

Dr. U had to move into a separate room in his own house and installed a special lock to keep his mother-in-law and wife from gaining access to his personal belongings and work papers. His mother-in-law was the same person whom he, as a "dutiful son-in-law," had provided financial support for years. Now she was engineering the divorce to "torture and financially exploit him." Her daughter Sarah followed her mother's directives.

The couple tried marital therapy, but Sarah was only willing to attend a few sessions as she was determined to get a divorce to gain her "freedom." Her plan was not to work but to "find herself" while he continued to support her and the children as her attorney and mother had led her to believe he would have to do. In the state in which they resided, there was no statute for "joint custody" awards, and Dr. Unlucky did not want to settle for infrequent contact and loss of parenting involvement. However, once Sarah filed for divorce, he had no choice but to move out of the marital home. *His wife fabricated numerous complaints of domestic violence in her attempt to force him to leave their home.* Several times Dr. Unlucky offered a financial settlement whereby he would pay half of his earnings to his wife and to support their children and proposed each of them would share equally in their time with the children. *Sarah continually refused any settlement offers*; she and her mother reiterated the demand for what he considered an unreasonable percentage of his income, which would have left him with insufficient funds to pay for his basic living expenses.

The only way that he could settle the divorce with no financial disputes and function mentally as a psychologist without the ongoing conflicts, stress, and false allegations was to assume a salaried staff position in a government mental health facility in a nearby state rather than his continuing in a high-level practice and with a university affiliation. He was forced to move in with a friend because his income was insufficient to cover his living expenses. He chose to spend his part of his remaining salary on renting a small one-bedroom apartment in close proximity to the marital residence which was awarded to the wife as part of the property settlement in the MSA. In this way, he had a place to stay during his visitation with his children, initially every weekend and in subsequent years every other weekend. He commuted by car four-and-a-half hours to spend time on the weekends with his children once he had taken a job out of state.

The Early Postdivorce Period

During the first year after Dr. Unlucky moved out of the family home, his son's schoolwork declined; he developed tics and other signs of an anxiety disorder while he defended his mom's "frivolous" complaints and accusations against Dr. U. He was drawn into their battles over finances, visitation schedules, and disputes about education and medical decisions. Sarah withheld all information about the children from their father and removed his name from the children's school records (Isaacs, Montalvo, & Abelsohn, 1986). His son became his mother's spokesperson and called his father denigrating names that were identical to the ones in his mother's vocabulary. He would actually say that his mother and sister had no money for food or activities and that their maternal grandparents had to support them. Dr. U knew that Sarah was receiving his check for child support, but he was unable to convince his son of any contrary explanation to his mother's vicious attacks.

One day when Dr. U went to pick the children up for his Thanksgiving visitation to be shared with *his* parents, his father-in-law appeared at the door of his former marital residence and immediately attacked him with a baseball bat. Sarah's mother had another baseball bat and smashed his car window. The children observed this violent action but blamed their father despite the fact that the incident was provoked by the children's maternal grandparents. Dr. U went immediately to the police station to report the incident and show the police his damaged car. By the time he got there, his wife and her parents had already called the police to charge him with domestic violence and inciting the incident and he was arrested! *It took him hours to be released by the local police until they realized and figured out the obvious, that he only was picking up his children to take them to his parents' home, in accordance with a court order, for their scheduled Thanksgiving visit there.* Other demeaning incidents followed. For example, his former wife reported him to the Department of Children and Families (DCF) on an abuse allegation of striking his son and knocking out his tooth. Dr. U had to obtain his son's dental records to prove his innocence and to show that the dentist had extracted the cracked baby tooth on a specific date *before* the alleged date reported about the incident. The DCF ignored this finding. Later the divorce court ignored the fact that the allegation was a fabrication also. (Note: In family and divorce court, one is often considered guilty as charged and has the burden of proving themselves innocent, which is different from the procedure in criminal court.)

Dr. U was also confronted with the news that his ex-wife had contacted the hospital where he had privileges and reported the already unsubstantiated DCF findings about the charges of abuse against him. The hospital would no longer allow him to see patients in their facility. The medical staff was unwilling to examine the evidence he provided them to show that the allegations were false and the investigation by DCF was one of many unfounded claims.

Over time on the children's scheduled visits with him, they became increasingly hostile, rejecting, and critical of him. They refused to comply with the court-ordered visitation (Quinn, 2008). Eventually both children became severely alienated and refused any kind of telephone contact or visitation with him (Clawar & Rivlin, 1991). It was especially painful for Dr. U to share in his own mother's sadness while she was dying of a terminal illness. She wished to see her grandchildren one more time while she was in the hospital, but it was impossible for him to arrange any way for his children to visit with their paternal grandparents. His parents' real loss of any relationship with their beloved grandchildren tormented him (Kaslow, 2006). Complete contact was terminated with all of the father's friends and family so that the children were totally cut off from their father and his network.

Dr. U described an incident when he went to pick up the children for his customary visit to the new residence of the former wife and her second husband to discover that Sarah had left the house, taking their son with her and the stepfather to attend a church service. His daughter, remaining home, would not speak with him or even fully open the door so that they could have a conversation. She slammed the door on her father and told him she never wished to ever see him again. She said her mother had told her "the truth" about him and she wanted nothing to do with him. His former wife even went so far as to obtain a restraining order against his being in the vicinity to pick up or visit their children. She obtained this order without Dr. U being notified of any court hearing!

Since 1985, he has neither heard from nor seen his children. Gifts and cards were sent to his children but were returned as "undeliverable." He even went as far as to set up a college scholarship fund for underachieving boys, hoping his son might apply and attend one of the recipient colleges so that he would be located in a state away from his "alienating" mother. Unfortunately, he never applied for the special scholarship fund.

Postdivorce Interactions with Ex-Spouse and In-Law Family

During the early postdivorce years, visitation took place, but the transitions and interactions were negative and difficult for the children as well as their father. Sarah was relentless in her attempts to further "exploit" money from Dr. U while she chose to continue being unemployed. He lost any role in shared decision-making, and their mother kept information from him regarding the children and their activities while making unilateral decisions despite the terms of the MSA. Although it appeared as if the father had given up all attempts to try to communicate and maintain a visitation schedule, it was his observation, as a child psychologist, that his children were caught in a web of divided loyalties and devastating conflicts in which they began to show moderate symptoms of depression and anxiety. The only way that he could help his children, following the "Wisdom of Solomon," was to "withdraw from contact with the children so they would no longer be exposed to the battles and caught in the crises in which they were being indoctrinated to express their mother's vehement and toxic emotions against their father." He had hoped that the children would come to realize what their mother was doing, but instead they became programmed and supported the mother's "cult-like actions and fabrications" (Baker, 2007).

His Family's Reactions

Dr. Unlucky's parents and his brothers were relieved when he finally got divorced. They thought he had been treated horribly by his wife and her parents. They were astonished by the unjust rulings of the courts. Their sadness over "the loss of the kids" never went away. Such "deliberate alienation" was hard for them to comprehend and to accept.

Experience of Divorce: Then and Now

Dr. U never felt a sense of loss or regret over his divorce from his former wife. His interest in remaining married was only to keep the family unit intact and to offer his children stability by virtue of his presence. He recognized Sarah's "emotional instability" and worried about the children's well-being under her primary care. He did admit to feelings of devastation over the loss of his close relationship with his children and of the opportunity to help care for and raise them. He talked about his preoccupation with worrying about their safety, health, and development with a mother he viewed as having distinct emotional problems and who had admitted to her dissatisfaction and continual aggravation with the responsibilities of being a mother. In fact, this reminded him of the concept of "parental aggravation" which is defined as "when a parent feels overwhelmed with the needs and requirements of children and has to sacrifice more than they wish to do." (Such a person feels annoyed, aggravated, and/or often angry that they are trapped in the parenting role and must compromise their personal desires and lifestyle.) Her avoidance of direct child care was not Dr. Unlucky's idea of responsible parenting, and he thought it conveyed a message to his children of detachment by their mother. Dr. U posited that when he was a part of the family unit, he had overcompensated for their mother's "inadequacies," but that time had ended when he was totally extruded.

On the day of the interview, he greeted me with the statement: "I only agreed to do this because you are a colleague and friend whom I hold in high esteem, and I think your objective of telling the stories from the divorced dad's point of view is a crucial one for the public." He said that *just knowing we had this appointment and the topic of the research project caused him to have nightmares and experience flashbacks that were terribly upsetting for him.* He stated that "having this interview has brought back awful memories that I have had to repress and brings to the fore the heartache of these years of not seeing or hearing from my children." (These statements epitomize the agony of being a childless father who has children he does not see or know.)

Initially, the children wanted to live with him as they had done when their mother was hospitalized and while she was searching to "find herself" in making plans to become a "California hippie." He recalled a few occasions in which Sarah had reacted to the children with such frustration and aggression that her behavior easily could have been construed as abusive, but he had had insufficient proof to provide to the court for custody litigation.

He still harbors much resentment about the manipulations and exploitation of his ex-mother-in-law who has since passed away. He clearly relived "her engineering of the contentious split" and how his ex-wife followed her commands. He "knows" both women "indoctrinated or brainwashed" the children against him. He also retains much anger toward the judicial system (as do many litigants going through and postdivorce). Like many fathers, he expected the court to mete out justice, and he was disappointed and disgruntled with the way the judges responded to the incontrovertible evidence his lawyer presented. He believes they always rule in favor of the mother and show distinct gender bias. The judge involved issued unfair orders against him. It seemed obvious to him that the judge understood that his wife's complaints were fabricated and had been dismissed as false allegations by the government authorities, but they nonetheless allowed her allegations to prevail as truths. Dr. U, who is a child psychologist, posits he was certainly a "fit father" who loved his children and only wanted to share in raising his children and deserved his right to a joint custodial arrangement. However, the inclination of the court was "pro" motherhood at the exclusion of fatherhood unless the mother did not want the children or she was diagnosed as impaired. Sole custody, at that time, was the over-whelming choice of the courts. He has an indelible memory of the judge saying, "If it exists (what you supposedly did) in her head, and she believes it to be true, then it must be so and I have to rule accordingly." For example, Sarah said she was afraid of Dr. U, but this was without reason and was not supported by any evidence. Nonetheless, the judge issued orders according to what she claimed. Dr. U asserts that she, her mother, and their attorney waged a "well-thought-out campaign" to discredit him, which they never did, but the courts "never recognized her malicious conduct, nor ordered her to cease such destructive actions, nor reprimanded her by imposing sanctions for wasting the court's time and community resources with her false reporting." Although today he regards himself as the birth father, he realizes he is not the children's psychological father as their contact with him was severed by their mother and maternal grandparents' continuous brainwashing tactics (Lowenstein, 2010).

He knows that his children are aware of his address, phone number, and how to contact him, but he recognizes the harsh truth that they have never sought to try. He thinks that if they did so now, it would only be for financial reasons and he has become less amenable to any rapprochement. He still has much stored up rage and bitterness because of his former wife and her mother's "deliberate torture tactics toward him" as evidenced by such actions he described as their leaving a stuffed animal dipped in ketchup on his doorstep with the message that "we soon will have your blood."

The Postdivorce Years

Shortly after the divorce was final, Sarah remarried, which did not surprise Dr. U. He recognized her dependency needs and her wish to be financially secure without having to work. Although Dr. Unlucky never got to know or have any kind of mean-ingful contact with the children's stepfather, he did hear favorable reports that he was a good person and a dedicated stepfather, particularly since he had no children of his own. Many years after the divorce, Dr. U decided to try marriage again and choose a woman who had never been married before and did not have any children. At the time that he remarried, he considered having more children but soon realized that he did not perceive his new wife to be suitable as a potential mother with babies and young children. She had strengths in relating to adolescents, but Dr. U felt that he would have to be the primary caregiver for many years and deal with ongoing conflicts about proper child care with his wife; these concerns precluded his interest in having another family. A few years later, he divorced his second wife because of her "narcissistic sense of entitlement, and lack of empathy" (APA, 2000) – which were much like the qualities he had been so critical of in his former wife.

Dr. Unlucky dated a great deal after his second divorce and seemed to have no difficulty attracting bright, well-educated, interesting women. He would reside with them to become certain about their personality and self-presentations so as not to risk a third marriage and divorce. Currently, he is remarried again to an attractive, intelligent, dynamic woman who has two young adult sons. He respects her as a caring and devoted mother although he thinks she "spoils and indulges her sons." He entered this marriage with a much more realistic and self-protective attitude than he had had before, as he had become less naïve. He remains bitter about the inequities of the justice system and the impact of decisions made by lawyers and judges, his ex-wife, and his ex-in-laws on his life and his sense of well-being, including his ability to trust.

Retrospective

Since his first divorce, Dr. Unlucky has changed positions in the mental health field several times. He has been successful both professionally and financially. His prior obligation of alimony ended when Sarah remarried. He often has cases which involve the interface between law and psychology and finds it particularly meaningful to serve as an expert witness in doing the "right thing for children," according to "their best interests," regardless of which parent or which attorney retains his services. He understands that some parents "lie," that attorneys "represent," and judges "try" to be impartial. Although he knows he cannot control these variables, he states that he can "adhere to his own integrity in doing the right thing (as he perceives it to be) for any of the children involved in the cases in which he is providing psychotherapy to children, divorce counseling or forensic evaluations."

Dr. Unlucky "knows" that his son, his oldest child, with whom he had the closest bond, was "deliberately turned against him" and that his mother and grandmother inveigled him into being their "assistant alienator." (This is a term often used in the growing literature on parental alienation.) He was given the mission of transmitting his feelings of animosity to Dr. U and influencing his younger sister to accept their "propaganda and untruths."

His most poignant and best memory was the occasion, during the time he was still living in the marital home but in a separate room, when his son impulsively said to him: "I want to live with you, Daddy. Mommy makes us say and do nasty things to you which we do not want to say or do." The "we" included his sister. He holds onto this memory, not blaming his children for their change in attitude and affections; instead, he recognizes the forcefulness and dominance of their mother and maternal grandmother in exerting control over their lives. His reality has turned into a prolonged nightmare, totally different from his life dream of "being married forever, till death do us part."

There had been no prior divorces in his family, and the need for his marital separation was traumatic to all members of his family of origin. They supported his divorce and recognized the impossibility of reconciliation with his wife, who was completely controlled and dominated by her "evil" mother (term ascribed to her by his family). To this day, several decades later, he goes on with his life but still suffers the loss of his children while remembering the wonderful experiences and closeness he shared with them during their early years of development. Recounting his story remains emotionally disturbing to him, knowing of the unnecessary loss caused to his children and to him "because of their selfish, insecure mother (APA, 2004) who was blinded by her own mother's anti-social behavior." *He believes the situation is beyond rapprochement* and states he would not be receptive to overtures from the children as he would be suspicious of their motives (how very, very sad for him and his children).

References

American Psychiatric Association. (2004). *Diagnostic and statistical manual of mental disorders* (4th ed.). Washington, DC: Author.

American Psychiatric Association. (2000). *Diagnostic and Statistical Manual of Mental Disorders-IV-TR*. Washington DC: American Psychiatric Association.

Baker, A. L. (2007). *Adult children of parental alienation syndrome: Breaking the ties that bind*. New York: Norton.

Clawar, S. S., & Rivlin, B. V. (1991). *Children held hostage: Dealing with programmed and brainwashed children*. Chicago: American Bar Association Section of Family Law.

Erickson, E. H. (1968). *Identity: Youth and crisis*. New York: Norton.

Isaacs, M. B., Montalvo, B., & Abelsohn, D. (1986). *The difficult divorce: Therapy for children and families*. New York: Basic Books.

Kaslow, F. W. (2006). Familias que han experimentado un divorcio (Families undergoing divorce: A multicultural and international phenomenon). In A. Roizblatt (Ed.), *Terapia Familiar y de Pareja* (pp. 617–639). Santiago: Mediterraneo. In Spanish.

Lowenstein, L. F. (2010). Attachment theory and parental alienation. *Journal of Divorce and Remarriage, 51*(3), 157–168.

Quinn, E. (2008). *Walking on eggshells*. Baltimore: Publish America.

Chapter 15
Case Analysis and Games Divorcing/Divorced People Play

This chapter summarizes the themes that emerged from the data elicited from the 13 dads in their questionnaire responses. It also elucidates the games some divorcing and divorced people play to the detriment of all involved.

Questionnaire Responses

The dads in the study ranged from 20 to 35 years of age at the time of their first marriage. Seven of the 13 men were between 20 and 25 years old, three were between 26 and 29 years old, and the other three were between 30 and 35 years of age. In retrospect, the majority of participants 25 years and under thought they and their ex-wives got married much too young and that they were not aware enough then of what marriage entailed – particularly in the realm of building a *committed, mutually considerate, respectful, and attuned friendship and true partnership*. One or both did not realize it could take years to earn sufficient money to live as well as one or both wanted to and expected they would, and often they assumed that "happily ever after" was to begin right away and happen easily.

Ten of the respondents are Caucasian, one is African American, and two are Latino. Both Latino men were born in Cuba; one spent his early childhood there; the other did not emigrate to the United States until he was 20 years old. Another one of the dads was born in Greece and was brought here to go to high school in his mid-teens and decided to remain. Three of the men have Scotch and Irish ancestry. As to religious background, four of the men came from Protestant backgrounds, two were raised in the Catholic faith, one was brought up in the Greek Orthodox Church, and six were raised by Jewish parents. Despite the fact that the group of respondents is diverse in terms of these and other background variables, the pain, perils, and sequelae of the majority of the divorces (10/13) are remarkably similar across race, religion, ethnicity, cultural, and socioeconomic background.

In terms of educational background, the sample was highly educated, although this was more happenstance than intentional. Six of the men had earned the title

F.W. Kaslow, *Divorced Fathers and Their Families: Legal, Economic, and Emotional Dilemmas*, DOI 10.1007/978-1-4614-5535-6_15,
© Springer Science+Business Media New York 2013

doctor, one an MD physician/internist, who also has a Ph.D.; one a podiatrist; one a dentist; two Ph.D. psychologists; and one an MD psychiatrist. Two more are JD attorneys. Two of the men have degrees in engineering – one has a BS and one an MS. Of the remaining five, one has a BS in Communications and is currently a self-employed salesman, so he can set his own schedule and build it around the children's needs as he is the custodial parent. The other gentleman who has his son with him much of the time (Case 11, Mr. Hy Hopes) also has a BA and is presently working as a financial advisor, so he too has the ability to adjust his schedule to meet his son's needs. The 13th man (Case 2, Mr. Bob Straight) attended technical school for two years and has worked in the area of data processing.

All the dads comprising the sample are currently still working and seem to be from reasonably successful to very successful in their chosen fields. Most not only are earning a living but also are contributing to their professional/business fields and communities. They have come through the bitter storms with their subsequent frequent cloudbursts and rebuilt their shattered lives as best they could – with work as one strong pillar of their recovery, along with the resolute desire to survive and be the best role model they can be to their children – who may now be close to or remote from them. In over half of the cases, the subsequent partner has also contributed to making their life journey a more fulfilling one.

At the time the questionnaire-based interviews were conducted (from February to August 2011), the men ranged in age from *38 years (just one was under 50) to 77 years.* The others clustered between 50 and 69 years. Regardless of age, all shared stories that encapsulated the long-term pain, sense of loss, and bereavement they had experienced and *how difficult it was during their children's growing up years not to be part of their daily lives.* Many emphasized their *continuous sadness* about not being able to have breakfast together each morning, to help with homework, to know their children's friends, to hear the stories of the day at dinner, and to just be together to play games, coach sports, chat, guide, and influence. Only one dad has primary and full custody, so *his* story is different. Most of the others realize, even decades later, that no matter what overtures they have made and/or how much child support, alimony, and other expenses they have covered, there has long been an uneasy gulf between them and their children. It has, for most, seemed irreparable, and the heartache lingers. For this pain, there is no medication. As Sartre said in one of his plays, "If this is Hell, there is *No Exit*" (Sartre, 1946, 1962).

These first marriages, on which this book is predicated, lasted from 6 to 25 years, with four of them having a duration of 6 or 7 years and the other nine were ranging from 12 to 25 years. Most of the men stayed, even when they knew the relationship was faltering and they and their partners had become incompatible, because *they did not want to leave their children.* They had taken their vows of "'til death do us part" seriously and loved being dads. Several left when the affairs their wives were having (seven wives) were so flagrant that they could not be ignored or tolerated, and the wife would not end her dalliance and work to restore love and trust. Two of the men were locked out of their homes and/or found their clothes outside when they returned "home" from work. One was banished to living in the garage, which quickly became unconscionable. In the vast majority of the cases, the women wanted the divorce and informed the husbands "you have to leave." The sense of having been discarded, rejected, and thrown out was pervasive across the sample, and for most of the men, this feeling lingered for years and is periodically reexperienced at children's events, family celebrations, etc., when they are not part of the event planning process, the family inner circle, or the family pictures and, yet, they are expected to pay the majority of the cost of the event. The mom is the pivotal person, and the family rule, spoken or unspoken, written or unwritten, is that both parents cannot be part of the inner circle. The dad's partial banishment continues ad infinitum. And the sense of the unfairness of *his* plight of having been "forced" to leave when *she* wanted the divorce remains baffling and disturbing.

Although a criminal can only be punished for a crime once, divorced dads who have been cast asunder by a certain kind of ex-wife undergo a seemingly perpetual punishment and estrangement. Perhaps that is why some divorced dads ultimately disappear from the scene; it is too discouraging and frustrating to keep trying and feeling rebuffed. Often a return to court offers no relief; a judge may admonish them, as he did in Case 5 – to Dr. Dedicated and his ex-wife – "to act like grownups and follow the MSA." In many cases, there is no oversight to see that orders are followed, and in many times when the moms block visitation, there seems to be no recourse left for the dad short of further litigation.

To build a meaningful life, the man needs to accept the reality that his ex-wife has created and pulled the children into, which is that *he is unwanted, an unnecessary appendage.* Just his support and alimony checks are welcome (though often criticized for being insufficient or stingy), but not the man. What a dreadful situation for the dad and his children. They have become mom's possessions and often been inveigled into being her pawns. Sometimes, as in Cases 6 (Mr. Brogan) and 13 (Dr. Unlucky) and to a lesser extent in Cases 1 (Dr. Blue Eyes), 4 (Mr. Reuben Guy), 5 (Dr. Ron Dedicated), 9 (Dr. Ari Regis), and 10 (Mr. Arturo Miguel), some thought control, brainwashing, and/or parental alienation have been carried out (Bernet, 2010; Clawar & Rivlin, 1991). The techniques used to achieve this resemble those used by some of the pseudo-religious cults (Schwartz & Kaslow, 1982).

Despite their disillusionment and sorrow over the demise of their marriage and families, and often the resolve not to marry again because it is too hard to risk trusting and being betrayed or told they are unwanted again, ultimately 11 of the men have remarried. Most have been married longer the second time around and think their second marriages are based on a more solid and enduring foundation, with shared values, lifestyles, and goals; good, open communication and problem-solving skills; and a more mature "knowing" and "doing" of what it takes to create and sustain a long-term, mutually satisfying, perpetually evolving relationship. Two of the men are on third marriages (Case 10, Dr. Determined, and Case 13, Dr. Unlucky), and my observation is that these are the two whose breakups were most deleterious and degrading. Two of the men who are now in their early 50s have not remarried; they are the two who have their children with them most or all of the time (Case 8, Mr. Goodman and Case 11, Mr. Hy Hopes), and they do not think a "step mother" will be easily accepted nor have they met a woman who they believe is right for them and vice versa. They do not want a second fiasco of a marriage nor another divorce – and being single is tolerable and preferable to that.

Regarding income, all of the men in this sample wanted to continue supporting their children, often beyond what the divorce decree mandated and long after the children had reached the age when support was no longer court ordered. The vast majority covered their children's medical and dental insurances and optometric costs, provided extra allowances, and contributed some or all of the money to cover the cost of college and, in a number of instances, graduate or professional school. Only one father, Dr. Unlucky (Case 13), has had no contact at all from his children in more than 25 years, and his financial responsibility ended when he was no longer under court order to do so in light of the fact that his ex-wife had severed all connections between him and the children years earlier.

Three of the men reported that their present incomes are between $50,000 and $100,000. Two of them have not remarried, because among other factors, they cannot afford to take on more financial commitments – supporting two separate families is demanding enough. The third, Mr. Straight (Case 2), has a wife who earned a doctorate and works full-time and has gradually reached a point of having a good income that has helped them to provide a comfortable lifestyle for themselves, their joint children, plus his sons from his first marriage. Two earn between $101,000 and $150,000, and although they maintain a solid middle-class standard of living, they have not been able to indulge in any extravagances nor live as they would on that level of income were it not for his divorce and the years of supporting, at least partially, two households.

The two men in the $151,000–200,000 bracket are both self-employed and work long hours on schedules over which they exercise control. One has his young children with him full-time and no longer sends alimony to the ex-wife, who was only recently released from prison and is remarried. He lives in an upper-middle-class neighborhood and does his best to provide his children with a lifestyle comparable to that of their peers (Case 8, Mr. Goodman). Dr. Zack Determined, (Case 12) the other man in this financial bracket, has a partner who works also, so they seem to be able to do whatever they please within limits and are comfortable in their lifestyle.

Five of the men reported that their annual income amounts to over $250,000. All live quite well, are remarried, see their children as often as it is feasible, and are generous to them financially – with all of them having taken the children with them on some trips postdivorce and having contributed, often liberally and quite fully, to the costs of their children's postsecondary education, as they would have if they had remained married.

The portraits that appear in the above composite definitely do no resemble those of the deadbeat, physically or sexually abusive, disappearing, or addicted dad that so often make the headlines. Quite the contrary, these appear to have been dedicated, available, devoted dads.

Typology of Divorced Dads

Various authors have tried to classify types of divorced dads. In addition to the four types mentioned above who are so often held out to be the vast majority – that is:

1. The deadbeat dad – He does not send child support or alimony (Boumil & Friedman, 1996).
2. The physically or sexually abusive man – The man who has abused his ex-wife and/or children.
3. The substance abuser (drugs or alcohol) or other kind of addict (gambler, Internet pornography).
4. The disappeared dad – The one who vanished shortly after the divorce and never reappeared (Myers, 1989).

Some researchers/authors have identified other types. In the following, I explicate and add to these designations:

5. *The victimized dad* – He has not gotten an *impartial, objective* legal hearing or marital settlement agreement. His ex-wife and her attorney's criticisms took precedence over his petition, and he lost ready access to his children, got an unfair portion of the asset distributions, etc., and never recuperates emotionally.
6. *The abandoned father* – The children have become estranged from him, sometimes through brainwashing, and refuse to visit him. He feels rejected, deserted, and deprived of being able to have an important part in his children's lives and to live out his own life dream/plan.
7. *The guilty father* – He has been blamed or blames himself for everything that happened or went wrong. He is so worried that the children will not like him or want to visit him that he is overindulgent, pacifies, or placates them and may be afraid to set limits. This phenomenon is exacerbated when the children "give him a hard time" and are unruly and/or the ex-wife tells him the children do not or will not want to visit him unless (a) he takes them wherever they want to go, (b) he gives them (or her) whatever they demand, (c) he lets them stay up later and eat or do whatever they want, (d) he is less strict, (e) etc.
8. *The over-involved dad* – He is so intent on being "a great dad" that he tries to do everything to please his children; makes life in general, including school work and peer relationships, easier for them; places his needs and wants secondary to theirs; and often puts his own personal life "on hold" until they are grown. Often they become spoiled, develop a strong sense of entitlement, and do not appreciate him but rather see him as a "pushover" and take advantage of him or he may try too hard and may be perceived as intrusive.

Games Divorced/Divorcing People Play

Almost five decades ago, Eric Berne wrote a fascinating book "Games People Play" (Berne, 1964). It delineated repetitive patterns observed in relationships that have the predictable outcome of upsetting the partner. The one who initiates the game consciously or intuitively knows that the transaction cycle will lead to a zero sum outcome, that is, no winner, or to a win–lose outcome. These games are not intended to bring about a win–win resolution, quite the contrary. The following uses Berne's game theory, one of his game titles (#1), and then describes different games I often have observed divorcing/divorced couples playing. [Note: Palazzoli, Cirillo, Selvini, and Sorrentino (1989) authored a fascinating volume "Family games: General models of psychotic processes in the family." Their discussion of the moves partners make (like ceasing to use birth control without informing their spouse or pulling a child into a coalition with them against the other parent) is pertinent to and may further illuminate the following exposition of games played in the context of divorce.]:

1. *"Now I've gotcha, you son-of-a-bitch."* This is probably the most frequently played game in divorcing and divorced couples. For instance, in this study, it variously took the form of a wife making such statements as:

   Unless you give me all the money I want (child support, spousal support, extras), you can't see the children.
   Unless you change the dates (for visitation) whenever I want, I will tell the children you are uncooperative, mean, inconsiderate, (or much worse).

   "Sorry, the children are not here now. They went to a friend's, to my parent's, etc., *for the weekend."* (This is not communicated until dad arrives to pick up the children.) At this point, he has no recourse but to leave, unusually feeling frustrated, disappointed, and angry. He has been "had" again. If he decides to go back to court to insist that the visitation/access plan be fulfilled, many of the moms enlist the children on "their side." Returning to court is a costly process, entailing filing a motion, and often leads nowhere.

2. *"You can't make me do it."* Not responding to e-mails, texts, or phone messages conveys, *"I can ignore you, and there is nothing you can do about it!"* It is a shutout maneuver and power play that excludes the father from knowing what is going on in the family. When the children are quite young or they do not have access to the phone or computer, contact with their father is thereby intercepted, is minimized, and can even be kept nonexistent. Ultimately this mother wins, and the father loses this game (or reverse, if dad is the major custodial parent). It becomes a lose–lose game as the children are deprived of their ongoing contact with one parent and either are subtly convinced, brainwashed into thinking (Baker, 2007), or surmise from the lack of overt attention that the non-primary parent does not care about them.

3. *"It's my word against yours!"* In several cases cited, there were seemingly false allegations made by the wife/mother of physical abuse against her and/or the child/children. Although there are myriad cases of substantiated child abuse (physical and sexual) on record against mothers, grandparents, and other relatives, as well as fathers, countless charges are disproven. However, unfortunately, in many divorce cases instead of the usual caveat of American jurisprudence that one is considered "innocent until proven guilty" being the dominant judicial philosophy, often the men accused by their wives of having been abusive during or after their divorces (in this volume – notably Case 6, Mr. Brogan; and Case 13, Dr. Unlucky) were handled as if they were guilty as accused and there has never been a way for them to prove themselves innocent and counter the charges in court or to rectify the damage caused with their children by these accusations. In effect, the person has been slandered. For the children later to come to not believe

the charges would mean their mother, on whom they were so reliant, had lied to them and to the court deliberately, and to think this is untenable for the vast majority of children. Therefore, the father must have been the culprit! What a sad saga, that is, a lose–lose game for dad *and* his children over time.

4. *"Blackmail!" "I can and will have you sent to jail if you don't!"* This threat is often hurled at a dad to force him into doing what his wife, or ex-wife, wants him to, usually pertaining to money. *If* he is late paying child or spousal support, yes, it can be very difficult for the woman and children and understandable that she might feel desperate *if* she has no reserve. But if he is late because he has lost his job due to the recession and a faltering job market, and he is barely managing and he is actively job hunting, such a threat and/or action, if she can manage temporarily, can prove catastrophic. The children may have to face having a father not only who is criticized for being a failure and a deadbeat (Boumil & Friedman, 1996) but also who now has a prisoner identity. Realistically, many MSAs contain escalator clauses that specify that if the man's income goes up, the ex-wife and children are entitled to a percentage of the increase. One can make a case for why this is fully justifiable, at least for the children. But almost invariably there is no downward escalator clause that articulates what is to happen if (1) he loses his job or business; (2) his commissions, bonuses, or other income are cut – as from a severe stock market decline if interest and dividends were part of the original calculations and projections; (3) he has a major stroke, has other serious medical problem, or is injured in an accident and cannot work for a long time (some states have altered their laws regarding this in recent years); (4) and/or he becomes unemployable and unemployed because of the larger economic scene, and the ex-wife is now earning a good living – does she or should she have any responsibility to reciprocate and now pay him (ex) spousal support? For a win–win game, would built-in "turn-about" be the fair-play way? Perhaps divorcing couples and the bevy of professionals who help them could invoke the Wisdom of Solomon on this.

5. *"There is no way I will continue to support you in style."* The reverse game, played by a husband/ex-husband, who has provided all or most of the income and then deliberately decides to take a lesser paying job or to develop some ailment so he cannot work and therefore will be ordered to pay much less child support/alimony, is an equally reprehensible game – sometimes prescribed by attorneys.

6. *"Who do you love the most mommy or daddy?"* This unfair question pulls the children onto the battlefield of divorce and places them in a no-win position.

Clinical Case Illustrations of Game Playing

7. *"Financial Maneuvers" including "Hiding the Money."* Sometimes it is months – even years – before one mentions their intention of seeking a divorce. In the interim, a good deal of preplanning, particularly financial, occurs. To illustrate from my

case files, the "K" files (disguised to protect identity), synopses of two cases, are presented. This also occurred in several of the cases discussed earlier – notably Dr. Ron Dedicated (Case 5), Dr. Ari Regis (Case 9), and Mr. Hy Hopes (Case 11).

Mr. "J" learned his sweet, charming, innocent-looking wife was having an affair. He confronted her and said he still loved her and the children and wanted to work things out. She adamantly denied the infidelity saying, "How could you believe such vicious gossip. People are just jealous of our great life, and you are my one and only." When he had first heard the rumor, he had not wanted to believe it, but when he heard it from a very different source, serious suspicion was aroused. He hired a private detective and, to his dismay, learned that she was having rendezvous at least twice a week. Feeling betrayed, lied to, disillusioned, and angry, he decided to continue in individual therapy after Mrs. J terminated treatment because she thought "our marriage is perfect." (Unbeknownst to me, he then began to map out plans with a divorce attorney he had engaged, who was known to be a "barracuda." He kept his treatment and his legal maneuverings quite separate.) I knew he did not want to act hastily because of his "great love for the children" and not wanting to traumatize them by splitting up the family quickly and leaving them with a mother who could scheme, act covertly, and lie so convincingly. The slowness, which was in the children's best interest, also gave him time to shift some of his monies into offshore accounts and to tie up other funds in his business partnership in such a way as to make them untouchable. He saw this as his only way to strike back for the hurt she had inflicted and the repetitive deception and pretense she had perpetrated. Retaliation was his objective, and he fulfilled it in court, several years later. How different the outcome might have been if she had taken responsibility for her feelings, behaviors, and desire for a divorce or if he had discussed his covert legal machinations with his therapist or had behaved with greater integrity.

Since this type of *financial game playing/preplanning* conceived to outmaneuver the other is not gender specific, one more brief case illustration, from the K files, is proffered with a different twist – same intent. Pretty Mrs. Collette had wanted to enrich her life when the second of her children started kindergarten. She decided it was time to return to a special community college program and finish her training to become an interior decorator/designer. She was talented, was attractive, and had good interpersonal skills. Classes were held during the daytime, so they did not interfere with her wanting to "be with the kids after school and weekends" at that stage of their lives. For the first six months, she was bubbly, enthusiastic, and proud of herself. One day at the end of her therapy session, she abruptly said, "my marriage has hit some troubled waters and I don't know what to do, especially since I met a wonderful guy in the decorating world and he understands me so much better than my husband does."

The following week she opened the session by telling me, "I had to drop out of school; an old back ailment has reoccurred, and I'm in too much pain to sit in classes." As snap decisions were uncharacteristic of Mrs. C, I quickly juggled what I knew about her, I put it together with my knowledge of the matrimonial lawyers in the surrounding counties, and after expressing concern about her pain, I asked,

"Which lawyer did you consult with this week?" Caught off guard by the accuracy of the question, she blurted out his name, and it coincided with my assumption. I knew which lawyers in the area prescribed backaches, which prescribed migraine headaches, etc., for their female clients – all invisible ailments that were hard to disprove – but which provided the reason why the women could not take training to prepare for a career and/or continue working. I asked her what else she was expected to do in this plan devised by the attorney, and she said, "complain a lot, do very little, and wait six months to serve papers." I queried if she wanted to sacrifice her new found sense of achievement, self-respect, and accomplishment and her optimistic view and self-confidence, and the response was, "There is loads of money riding on my being a good actress, and my financial future is at stake." I said, "Please think about your decision and its implications and whether you will respect and like yourself if you collude with the lawyer in this way for the next session, and we can discuss it further then."

The next week, Mrs. C reported that she had spoken to several of her divorced female friends, and they all agreed she should "go for the jugular" and get all the money she could when she could. Her mother was the only one who counseled her against embarking on such a dishonest scheme, and she dismissed her mother as "naïve" and "not on my side." She was adamant about moving ahead and unwilling to explore the emotional implications and consequences of undertaking this deliberate chicanery on her children, who would be living with a mother supposedly in chronic pain that flared into acute episodes for months and who might someday realize she had tricked their dad. But she was fully concordant with the attorney's ideas, thought the plan was brilliant, and was not the least interested in considering issues of integrity. At that point, I told her, "it will be difficult for us to continue with your treatment together as your attorney and I would be guiding you in different directions and adding to your distress. Let's plan to summarize what you have accomplished, look at how you have grown, consider your future goals, and wrap up at your next session." Surprised, Mrs. C gasped, "but this has been so great for me and I am far from finished." Then she took a deep breath and added, "I know you always stress acting in ways that improve one's sense of efficacy and self-worth and you believe that what I am doing ultimately will have self-destructive repercussions. I do get it, Dr. K, but *this is what I want to do*. I do not want to feel poor! But please, can I come back to see you after the divorce is over?"

Sometimes we cannot help clients avert a catastrophe and have to bow out of the picture, as the therapist or coach, as it is *their life and their decision*; they need to make it and live with the consequences, dire as they may be and were in this case. In brief, her husband, a neurosurgeon; his female attorney; and one of his neurologist colleagues were able to figure out what was probably "causing" her chronic back pain, and they decided to use the alleged severity of her condition and her difficulty doing household chores, etc., as the basis for his being awarded "primary residential parent" status. Under Florida law at that time, this meant Collette got very little child support, and instead of the permanent alimony she had anticipated, she was granted five years of rehabilitation alimony, which included funds for medical care for her "back ailment" and to return for training for a future career. Clearly the outcome of this *risky gamble on a financial jackpot game* was unexpected by the initiators – the chicanery backfired and it was a win–lose in the opposite direction.

Unfortunately all members of the family lost a great deal more than they would have if Collette had pursued what I call *"divorce with integrity."* The family's financial coffers were severely depleted with the payment of the enormous legal fees incurred from both "big league" attorneys, and it took over a decade before the animosity between Collette and her husband dissipated. He still does not trust or believe Collette. And as the children have gotten older and have heard gossip in the community (school, church, local clubs, family members) and have witnessed their mother's "miraculous" recovery and high level of physical activity, they have pieced together a rather accurate version of what actually happened. Superficially they handle it by saying, "That's just mommy and what she does. She likes to have fun with us, to look great, and enjoy living." But when it comes to anything important, they turn to dad.

A third case from the K files illuminates another *game* – how a long-term well-thought-out plan devised as a "road to riches" can be played out with skilled gamesmanship by a beautiful, beguiling woman against a surprisingly unsuspecting very rich older man.

8. *The Rich Husband Sweepstakes: A Gambling Game*

Miss Beguiling decides she wants to meet and marry a rich older man who would be thrilled to have her with him on his arm as lovely "eye candy." She may take up modeling, may take up fashion design, or become an esthetician as part of her preparation. She exercises rigorously to keep her body toned and shapely and sports whatever hairdo and color is considered most alluring in the world she wants to inhabit. How to entice and please a man; being provocative, sexy, or shy; and knowing how and when to tease and where to meet the kind of men she is looking for are talents and assets she develops. She learns to play at the best adult playgrounds, to be invited to sail on the right yachts, etc., and soon, she meets and ostensibly falls in love with Mr. Rich. He is so smitten and feels so fortunate to have attracted a young beautiful woman, who incidentally can produce more heirs for *his* family, that he is willing to get married again and to offer her a very generous prenuptial agreement. Adding more children to his "dynasty" is an egosyntonic prospect.

Knowing how much children are worth to him and that he is an honorable man who has treated his ex-wives well, she quickly becomes pregnant. After a few years of living the lifestyle of the rich and famous, meeting all the "right" people, and flattering her husband who is not as physically attractive, vigorous, or sexually appealing as she would like, she feels bored and restless and decides she wants a divorce and to be free to find a younger, more vibrant playmate. Through her network of "girlfriends" who have used similar ploys, she knows which lawyer to hire to get her the "best results." She wants a gladiator attorney, so she will get the apartment they bought in Aspen, on the Riviera, or the house in Cape Cod; lifetime alimony; and liberal child support, a gigantic up-front cash settlement, as well as a huge portion of the assets he has accrued over a lifetime – in addition to what was promised in the prenuptial agreement.

In a conjoint divorce therapy session, when I queried one departing Miss Beguiling as to how much she thought would be enough, as there was an offer of $7,000,000++ up-front, she said, "There can never be enough." This highlights characteristics that are elaborated further in Chapter 18 of *insatiability, self-centeredness, and lack of integrity* that permeate this type of person's way of "being in the world." It also underscores how unerring she is in pursuing a mate who likes to be seen and admired for being generous, for being a gracious caretaker, for being successful, and for being a responsible husband. In a year or two, and often with much accompanying [newspaper] publicity about the sensational divorce, she emerges a very rich divorcée. She has successfully achieved her early "career" plan. Her *gambling game, the rich husband sweepstakes*, has had a huge pay off for her and the child/children financially; it is often unclear if she has enough conscience to be disturbed by her own systematic deceptive game – especially since some of those in her chosen social network admire and applaud what she has so skillfully engineered.

Summary

Members of the postdivorce family remain connected until one of the original partners dies and even long after that. The relatives of the deceased parent, including the grandparents, aunts, uncles, and cousins, may still care very much about the children and want to remain part of their lives. Acting throughout in a respectful, fair, honest, thoughtful manner is urged. Divorce with integrity leads to a much more positive postdivorce prognosis and resolution of issues (Hakvoort, Bos, VanBolen, & Hermanns, 2011; Angarni-Lindberg & Wadsby, 2011). *To play deceitful, manipulative, destructive games is deleterious for all.*

References

Angarne-Lindberg, T., & Wadsby, M. (2011). Sense of coherence in young adults with and without experience of parental divorce in childhood. *Journal of Divorce and Remarriage, 52*(5), 309–320.

Baker, A.L. (2007). *Adult Children of Parental Alienation syndrome: Breaking the Ties That Bind.* New York: Norton.

Berne, E. (1964). *Games people play.* New York: Grove.

Bernet, W. (Ed.). (2010). *Parental alienation, DSM-5 and ICD-11.* Springfield, IL: Charles C. Thomas.

Boumil, M. M., & Friedman, J. (1996). *Deadbeat dads.* Westport, CT: Praeger.

Clawar, S. S., & Rivlin, B. V. (1991). *Children held hostage: Dealing with programmed and brainwashed children.* Chicago: American Bar Association Section of Family Law.

Hakvoort, E. M., Bos, H. M., Van Balen, F., & Hermanns, J. M. (2011). Post divorce relationships in families and children's psychosocial adjustment. *Journal of Divorce & Remarriage, 52*(1–4), 125–146.

Myers, M. F. (1989). *Men and divorce.* New York: Guilford Press.

Palazzoli, M. S., Cirillo, S., Sorrentino, A. M., & Selvine, M. (1989). *Family games: General models of psychotic processes in the family*. New York: W.W.Norton.

Sartre, J. (1946). *No exit*. (J. Huston, Director) Biltmore Theatre, Manhattan, NY.

Sartre, J. (1962). *No exit (French "Huis clos")* New York: Appleton (trans: Hardre, J. & Daniel, G.).

Schwartz, L. L., & Kaslow, F. W. (1982). The cult phenomenon: Historical, sociological and familial factors contributing to their development and appeal. In F. W. Kaslow & M. Sussman (Eds.), *Cults and the family* (pp. 3–30). New York: Haworth (now Taylor & Frances).

Chapter 16
Commentaries on Cases: How Outcomes Might Have Been Different if Other Services or Professionals Had Been Utilized

Part I: Divorce Therapy, Divorce Mediation, and Collaborative Divorce

Florence W. Kaslow, Ph.D., ABPP

Divorce Therapy

Unfortunately, all too often when one or both spouses are discontent to the point of being unhappy frequently and for long periods of time in their marriage, they have difficulty discussing their frustration and disillusionment with one another. They may try to, but each may think the other is nonresponsive, does not really listen to them, or wants to engage in problem solving or glosses over it with "you are going through a midlife crisis" or attributing the problem to difficulties with the children or on the other's work situation. If this continues, one or both may turn outward for understanding and advice – to parents, friends, neighbors, buddies, colleagues, their clergy person – or perhaps their favorite bartender or beautician. Or they may seek (or naively drift into) a new relationship that seems more exciting and ego gratifying and get involved in a clandestine extramarital affair (Pittman, 1989) or seek to escape by using drugs or alcohol.

Sadly, even if one of them has suggested they go for marital therapy, the other may have declined. Sometimes both are adverse to doing so. Ultimately, by the time the relationship has become seriously fractured and the level of conflict – silent or noisy – is very high, they may, as a last resort, go for marital therapy, hopefully to a doctoral-level, experienced person who is imbued with a family systems perspective.

Sometimes in the first therapy session, it becomes obvious that the spouse who is more invested in keeping the marriage together has badgered or intimidated her[1] partner into coming. If the resistant, reluctant-to-be-there person has already moved out, rented a separate place to live, gotten involved in what they consider to be a serious new relationship, or has come to dislike and disrespect her spouse, it will be difficult

---

[1] A single pronoun will be used to simplify sentences, but *it is not meant to be gender specific* throughout section "Divorce Therapy, Divorce Mediation, and Collaborative Divorce" of this chapter.

F.W. Kaslow, *Divorced Fathers and Their Families: Legal, Economic, and Emotional Dilemmas*, DOI 10.1007/978-1-4614-5535-6_16, © Springer Science+Business Media New York 2013

to do marital therapy geared to improving the marriage and healing the breeches of trust, understanding, and desire to be together in a committed, monogamous relationship. The therapist has to sensitively frame the issue in a question form such as "have they come for marital therapy or divorce therapy?" He cannot do both simultaneously nor can he fulfill both requests. He can initially help them sort out the issues and decide whether they both want to first try improving the marriage (Charny, 2006) so that it is satisfying for both or whether one has already decided to leave the marriage and has reached the emotional (and sometimes physical) point of no return.

When "one wants in" and the "other wants out" and refuses to reconsider because they are definite in their choice, the therapists' role may expand to encompass helping the hurt, rejected, disappointed spouse to really hear and accept the finality of the exiting spouse's decision. He can then suggest that he can provide divorce therapy to help them navigate and negotiate the best possible divorce for themselves (Kaslow, 1995).

This may entail setting up an agreed-upon schedule of individual and conjoint sessions, so each can have an opportunity to focus sometimes only on their own needs, wants, and feelings and other times to listen to the other person, who they once loved and said they wanted to spend the rest of their life with. Both can hear from the therapist statements such as "you should try to treat each other as you want to be treated."

The therapist needs to build a strong therapeutic alliance with each separately as well as with them as a couple whose lives together are splitting asunder (Wallerstein & Kelly, 1980). No doubt both will be experiencing the partings as painful (Schwartz & Kaslow, 1997), albeit in different ways. They will each have their shattered dreams, their regrets and recriminations, their hurts and resentments, their desire to blame the other for some of what went wrong, and a certain amount of bewilderment, anger, and worry about the future. They may be irate over any real or imagined betrayal, deceit, financial chicanery, and (hidden) addictions. The rejected party may feel their world is tumbling downhill and falling apart and become seriously depressed, even expressing suicidal ideation. The departing partner may feel self-righteous, entitled, relieved, and also guilty and the recipient of much criticism. He or she frequently may also be deeply concerned about being able to stay emotionally and physically involved in the children's lives – even when the children are already in college or are adults. (If there are no children, the issues may be quite different just as they are likely to be if there has been physical or sexual abuse, and the breakup represents a welcome end to a tortuous relationship.)

Stage 1 – The Emotional Divorce (see Appendix 2 – Model of Stages in the Divorce Process) is a turbulent time, and many decisions need to be made. Some of the most critical and far reaching are as follows:

1. How and what to tell the children?
2. Who is going to move out?
3. What divorce process to engage in: divorce mediation, collaborative divorce, or a litigated divorce?
4. Temporary financial arrangements so both can manage until the permanent distribution of assets' and child and spousal support are agreed upon and each is assured the other will act with integrity and not sequester or squander assets.

The therapist can help support and guide them through the periods of confusion, turbulence, rage, desire for retribution, and revenge until they are able to concentrate on the myriad tasks that need to be accomplished and decisions that need to be made – understanding the external realities and pressures of having to relocate, produce financial statements, notify the children's schools, tell friends and family, and in some way become engaged in a legal or quasi-legal process. And they need to do all of this while experiencing enormous disruption in the children's lives as well as their own. The divorce process has been likened to a roller-coaster ride and to a prolonged nightmare. I often view the parties and their children as pieces on a chessboard, often being moved around by others who become involved in the divorce drama. Such an analogy enables people to better visualize the dizzying dilemmas they face.

A competent, well-trained divorce therapist can offer a calm retreat in which the parties can cry, scream, express joy at breaking free, make contradictory and ambivalent statements, and be whatever they need to be while problem solving, planning how to do what needs to be done, hearing that there is a present and a future as well as a past, and being encouraged to grieve the losses and then move forward to fact the new challenges and opportunities. Some of the sage counsel the therapist can offer in addition to "treat the other person as they want to be treated" should include the following:

1. Do not belittle or denigrate the other parent (or his/her family) to the children. Remember that the child is also their descendant, and if they are portrayed as "rotten, no good, horrible, etc.," then half of the child has a defective core, and this makes it difficult for the child to have a good self-image and a sense of self-confidence. Over time, the child(ren) will gradually come to know the other parent's strengths, weaknesses, and flaws through their own eyes and experiences and will not resent your trying to "poison" their relationship to him or her. They also wonder how, if the person was so terrible, you could have loved, married, and remained with him or her so long.
2. Plan to engage in peaceful co-parenting and make the transitions from mom's house to dad's house as easy as possible.
3. Do not involve the children in any of the continuing battles – these are for the adults to resolve; rather encourage them to love and respect both parents and reassure them you are getting divorced from each other but not from them so that you will each continue to love them and be involved with them in the postdivorce (binuclear) family (Ahrons, 1994).

When the couple decide to move on to stages 2, 3, and 4 – the legal, economic, and child custody aspects of divorce (see Appendix 2) – the knowledgeable, well-trained marital/divorce therapist who knows the resources in his community can explain the options available for the legal divorce to his clients and talk about the benefits and potential pitfalls of each. He can stress *values*, like the best interest of the children (Goldstein, Freud, & Solnit, 1973); the adults postdivorce ability to be at the same place with and for the children with the least amount of animosity and residual rancor; feeling proud of their own behavior and decisions rather than ashamed of how they acted; and help them choose the process of divorce that is most compatible with their core values. It is also valuable if he maintains a list of referral sources who are known to practice with integrity, and who encourage their clients to act fairly and justly, whichever process they select. It is not unusual for only one partner in the couple that is splitting apart to want therapy to help them deal with their dilemmas and feelings of distress or for each to want a therapist's assistance, but with different clinicians. In either event, it is not valid to deny one therapy because the other is not interested or chooses to go elsewhere. The service one is then providing is individual treatment with a major focus on emotional and often practical issues surrounding the divorce. It may be crucial to stress that the client needs also to rely on their support network of colleagues, friends, and family, and if they do not have one, to build or rebuild it. Self-imposed isolation does not help anyone during this trying time. Initially, the therapist may play an ultra-significant role in the bewildered, angry, and/or devastated client's life, and it is important to help him or her connect to significant others in their personal life and that of their children (Kaslow, 2000).

Divorce therapy may continue for several years throughout the formal divorce period until the marital settlement agreement is signed and beyond – if either or both wish to continue or resume treatment postdivorce as they work on re-equilibrating, and rebuilding their lives and doing the best postdivorce co-parenting they can (stage 7 – the psychic divorce – Appendix 2).

Divorce Mediation

The divorce rate in the United States started to escalate in the mid-twentieth century and skyrocketed to the point where well over 50% of all marriages were ending in divorce. Since in the United States one must have a legal document to attest to their marriage being bona fide in the eyes of their state of residence, they must also be legally divorced in accordance with their state's law. In the twentieth century, most divorces were adversarial proceedings, based on an allegation of fault. Frequently, the parties became engaged in very acrimonious, nasty battles (see, e.g., Cases 4, 5, 10, and 13), and often, the schism was never overcome.

In accordance with the American Bar Association's (ABA) Model Code of Professional Responsibility (1981), an attorney was enjoined to represent only his or her client. The welfare and interests of the other partner and the children were not his/her concern since the assumption in law was (is) that these could be properly represented by separate, opposing legal counsel. However, there was no mention of who represented the children in the divorce action. When the case came to court, if the presiding judge determined that the best interests of the children were not receiving sufficient and proper consideration and that he or she needed more information about and insight into the issue of custody needed than could be obtained through standard adversarial channels, then the judge could and might order a custody evaluation and/or appoint a child advocate (see section "The Role of the Child Advocate" of this chapter) or *guardian ad litem*. In the latter instance, there would then be three attorneys involved in the case, each representing a different perspective and "piece" of the family that was being split asunder and restructured. It remained the task of the judge to integrate all of the testimony and to cogitate upon the future welfare of all of the individuals involved as they moved toward becoming a postdivorce, binuclear family, usually still linked economically and through the children for many years into the future.

Given that historically the law governing divorce had cast the judge's role into one of ascertaining which party was "innocent" and which one "guilty," each attorney attempted to show his/her client in the most favorable light – seeking to retain or obtain the maximum financially for the person he/she was representing. At times, the battle became hostile and demeaning, resulting in prolonged bitterness and anguish into which relatives and friends were drawn and children were traumatized by the continuing strife (Kessler & Bostwick, 1977). This was still the prevailing legal context and atmosphere at the time many of the 13 cases discussed earlier in this book were heard in court (Hetherington, Cox & Cox, 1977).

As indicated in Chapter 1, with the advent of divorce mediation, following publications of Coogler's seminal work (1978), and the expanding knowledge base contributed by other pioneers (e.g., Fisher & Ury, 1981; Folberg, 1983; Haynes, 1981; Neville, 1984), couples who wanted to optimize their own choices about the key issues of custody, visitation/access, and distribution of assets and who disliked the idea of litigation finally had an alternative to the adversarial process. Some core principles of mediation, such as empowerment of the parties, consideration of the best interests of *all* family members, full and honest disclosure of assets, cooperative problem solving, and equitable distribution of assets, were and still are congruent with the recognition of the salient principles of attachment theory and family systems dynamics and therapy – alluded to earlier in this volume. The task orientation in mediation of jointly fashioning a mutually acceptable divorce agreement with the least possible distress is also conducive to coping constructively with the manifold problems and tasks which must be handled during the divorce process (Ferstenberg 1992) . Less energy is expended in hostile, aggressive, and vituperative actions. The mediation process contributes to an individual's being able to more rapidly evolve a sounder personality reintegration and lifestyle re-stabilization – that is, reach some closure on and tranquility with the actual divorce. If the couple can cooperatively reach an accord that takes into account the "best interest" of all involved parties, this period can be one during which they learn to express their wants, beliefs, and values and to use their capabilities more fully. As both come to trust their own independent judgments to negotiate assertively, to compromise effectively, and to take charge of redirecting their own lives (Kaslow, 1984b), their sense of autonomy and competency is augmented.

Engagement in the mediation process can help to diminish the feelings of despair, depression, hopelessness, helplessness, self-pity, rage, and/or alienation that often typify the legal, economic, and custody phases of divorce. Innuendos and threats of self-destructive or retaliatory behaviors diminish as the parties are encouraged to decide for themselves how to distribute their assets and what living and financial arrangements to make for their children. Sometimes during the process of mediation, a client's perceptions and behaviors shift from those of feeling like a victim and loser to those of being a creator and winner.

The skills a mediator needs to possess may differ from those many fine mental health practitioners and many talented matrimonial lawyers have. Mediation at its best requires an amalgam of the sensitivity, empathy, and diagnostic and clinical acumen of an excellent therapist; the knowledge of family law, property distribution, insurance, taxes, and court procedures of the attorney; and the bargaining and negotiating skills of the labor arbitrator (Folberg & Taylor, 1984). Consummate competency in such functions as power balancing, conflict management, negotiation, agreement drafting, and interprofessional communication is also vital (Haynes, 1982). Assisting mediation clients in these ways is consonant with a philosophic orientation that values self-determination and self-actualization and considers these to be basic ingredients that enhance recuperation from this often traumatic life event. Conversely, the adversarial process often diminishes the right to self-determination since it functions through having the lawyers do the negotiating and make the trade-offs and the judges ultimately making the final decisions regarding custody, visitation, child and spousal support, and property distribution which shape and profoundly affect the future of the lives of the people involved in the divorcing family.

Similar principles apply to the economic aspects of divorce. Those who are vague about their income and expenses and their assets and liabilities may be shocked when they realize that soon they will have to live on a decreased income and will have to manage their own finances. Procedures such as evaluating financial statements, compiling a list of outstanding debts and all assets, and drawing up budgets, which both partners are required to do, can be an enlightening learning experience. From the successful completion of all of these, each can emerge with an increased sense of self-esteem and competency. To realize one is capable of handling the finances contributes to a sense of independence and autonomy – and decreases one's fear of financial chaos and aloneness. All of the above are key factors in one's ability to progress toward the psychic divorce (see Appendix 2). As the separating parties reach agreement on the equitable distribution of assets, principles of fairness and mutual consideration may become more a part of the interactive repertoire, thus enhancing their self-respect, which has been shattered, and leading toward their being less hostile and more attractive in other interpersonal relationship.

Many consider children the most precious asset in any marriage. Both parents may find the prospect of giving up full-time parenting "untenable" (Erickson & McKnight Erickson, 1988). Most mediators are probably biased in the direction of children having easy access to both parents and both parents staying integrally involved in their children's lives (Kaslow, 1984b). As the mediator explores the wants, rights, and responsibilities of all family members, each adult is encouraged to see and value the other's strengths as a parent and the children's need to remain attached to both without fretting that loving one will be misconstrued as disloyalty to the other. When the children's responses to the divorce, their developmental needs, dreams for the future, and changing perspectives are thoughtfully considered, and any parental selfish wish to hurt the departing spouse by depriving him/her of access is worked through, the agreement written will be able to more substantially be predicated upon attention to the "best interest of everyone." In addition, it will be easier to live with since everyone's needs and emotions will have been taken into account (Kaslow, 1990). When children and their parents remain closely involved with one another in sound co-parental arrangements, the sense of disruption, loss, and abandonment is minimized (Folberg & Taylor, 1984). Grief and mourning reactions, which are common for both children and the noncustodial parent in many post-adversarial divorces, restructuring of the family unit are not as pronounced or long lasting in a mediated settlement. This enhances everyone's potential for emotional health and well-being.

In dealing with custody decisions, it is urged that mediators incorporate both a knowledge of attachment theory (Bowlby, 1988) and a family systems perspective. Often, there is groundwork to be done with the couple to uncover how they have been dealing with the children's perceptions and reactions, to interpret what is happening to them, and to keep them cope with the changing situation and then to reintegrate. The mediator can explain what a profound influence the parents' (and grandparents') behavior will have on the children; that the children need to know that both parents continue to cherish them and will be involved in their lives (Kaslow, 1984b, p. 64) and will not interfere with their loving or being with the other parent. Children's "rights" encompass not having to hear one parent criticize the other and not having to carry reports back and forth from mom's house to dad's house.

Who in the family attends a mediation session should be determined by ascertaining who is and will be making an input into the decisions and who will be greatly affected by the final agreement. Sometimes children should be included, but in most cases, it is urgent that they *not be asked with which parent they prefer to live*. Rather, helping them understand what is happening and the implications and consequences of the divorce may be in order, providing the discussion is consonant with the goal of enabling the parents to arrive at an agreement and the session does not become therapy. It may be advisable to ask youngsters their reasons for preferring to be with each parent (for primary physical residence or sole custodian in non-joint-custody states) and what problems they would anticipate in each household. As parents decide on the actual time-sharing arrangements, queries about after-school chauffeuring, coaching teams, music lessons, doctors' visits, and care during illnesses should be asked to raise the parents' level of consciousness about the demands of single parenthood. A clear and specific parenting/visitation plan should be written and can be attached as an addendum to the memorandum of understanding drawn up jointly by the mediator and the couple (or by a parenting coordinator working in a parallel process with the mediation) and then given to the parties' respective legal counsel for final drafting and filing.

If grandparents are to be involved in the childcare, financial support, or in providing housing, it may be beneficial for them to participate in one or two mediation sessions. They can be instrumental in the implementation of the agreement; if spurned, they can undermine it and serve as a negative influence by inflaming the children's wrath against one parent (as happened in the case of Dr. Unlucky, Case 13).

Each mediator should clarify his/her own pertinent values to the parties indicating a preference for the "best interest of the child." Mediators can indicate they believe parents' attention to their offspring's emotional needs and future well-being are more compelling and far-reaching imperatives than financial concerns. In addition, they can convey that the less argumentative and more cooperative they are as parents, the better the prognosis for the children's emotional well-being. Such a stance is likely to be congruent with the one their therapist is taking (if they are in treatment) and will help minimize the amount of confusion they are experiencing in other domains of their life where conflictual messages abound.

Sometimes participants in mediation will decide that some ceremony is warranted on the day they cosign the agreement as *they* want it to read. Their judicious handling of a very stressful life event has eventuated in a document of which they can be justly proud. Within the ambivalent mixture of emotions, there is a glimmer of relief. Marking this ceremonially expedites their quest to bring finality to a significant chapter in their lives and contributes to their progress toward growth and positive reintegration. It also constitutes a vital successful experience at a juncture when so much else has felt like failure. The completion of mediation may well provide the impetus for entering the postdivorce stage of the process with a more optimistic outlook and a determination to meet the challenges that surely will arise.

Some mediators customarily ask their clients to return at periodic intervals after the legal divorce is concluded. Three-month, six-month, and one-year follow-up sessions can provide clients with a formal opportunity to assess how the agreement is working out and to renegotiate any nonfunctional clauses without having to have motions filed or return to court.

I also suggest that the couple meet with me conjointly again when one or both are about to be remarried and the postdivorce family will again be transformed – necessitating another series of modifications and accommodations in relationships. Sometimes if a particular child's developmental or personality needs are such that a change of primary physical residence might be advisable or if there is a major modification in a parent's circumstances warranting such a shift and the couple are having trouble reaching agreement on their own, a return to mediation might help break through the impasse. New major agreements should be written and appended to the initial legal document and signed by all parties. With these follow-up procedures in place, neither has to dread that whenever a major issue arises a battle will ensue.

Rational continuity and the ability to plan ahead without total guarantees of "forever" are advocated herein. Changes should be anticipated and should not occur in a desperation mode. Rather, the agreement should contain a provision for remediation if and when the occasion arises.

Contraindications

Despite the aforementioned positive aspects of mediation, it is not a panacea, nor is it the marital dissolution process of choice for all. For example, if one party is mentally retarded, brain damaged, and psychotic or has a severe character or personality disorder, that individual's needs may be better served by their hiring a tough attorney to forcefully represent their interests. Or sometimes there is an enormous (seeming?) power gap (Erickson & McKnight Erickson, 1988), and the weaker partner cannot or will not be assertive. If the mediator has to throw too much weight on the side of the weaker party, he/she may lose the neutrality and objectivity so essential to fair mediation. In such instances, recourse to a lawyer may be advisable so that the more forceful, demanding partner cannot take advantage of the more passive, less articulate one. At times, the parties are so embittered that equity is not what they seek. Rather, they may want to fight viciously and prolong the divorce in order to (1) punish their ex-spouse, (2) ventilate and work through the anger, (3) achieve concessions as the price of achieving closure, and (4) stall for time until they are better able to "let go" of the relationship and the vituperativeness and heal psychologically. Litigation, not mediation, can better offer these.

Nonetheless, individuals entering the divorce process can be educated to the fact that when adversarial proceedings are embarked upon, the antagonists are apt to feel "much more helpless and pessimistic than in mediation as the negotiating devolves on the attorneys, with final authority for all decisions resting with the judge. Much anxiety and apprehension colors the ambiguity of the turbulent waiting period until the final decree. A combination of bewilderment, loneliness, anger and grief over all the losses wrought by the breakup of the marriage/family may be further stirred up until a state of desperation prevails" (Kaslow, 1984a). The ordered distribution of valued possessions, accumulated as part of their life together, is often a distressing and disorienting experience. They have forfeited their right to make many of the choices about their own treasures. What a strange phenomenon it is to allow to occur in one's personal life. This is much less likely to eventuate when they have been engaged in client-centered mediation that has been successful (Moore, 1986).

Collaborative Divorce

Collaborative divorce, the newest of the alternative dispute resolution (ADR) strategies, is heralded by Tesler and Thompson (2006), two of the best recognized pioneers of this methodology, as "the revolutionary new way to restructure your family, resolve legal issues, and move on with your life" (cover page of their 2006 book *Collaborative Divorce*). Like the founders of divorce mediation, they describe their approach as a much better way to resolve the complex issues confronted in difficult divorce cases and to avoid the unnecessary collateral damage that is often a by-product of hard-fought litigated divorces.

In brief, this is a process designed to take place totally outside the aegis of the court system. In this paradigmatic shift, the parties help set up a team after gathering information as to who might be available, from a list consisting of various trained, caring specialists. The team includes two attorneys, two coaches, a financial consultant, and a child specialist, when necessary. The objective is for the divorcing couple to work to build a consensus that considers the needs of each person who will be directly impacted by the severing of the marriage. This model, like mediation, seeks to empower the couple to determine the provisos of their divorce agreement and its aftermath.

During the collaborative divorce process, the parties are encouraged to:

- Conserve their expenditure of emotional and financial resources
- Develop long-term feasible financial and parenting plans
- Comprehend and address their children's needs and wants
- Actively design and plan for their postdivorce lives

Tesler and Thomas wisely caution that collaborative divorce is not for everyone; it does entail being willing to talk directly to and negotiate with one's exiting partner at a time when both are likely to be on the emotional roller coaster of divorce (alluded to elsewhere in this book). They posit that the use of impartial coaches who can work with emotionally charged issues in four-way meetings is to help each party address their partner in constructive ways so that the emotional complexities do not cloud their thinking when they meet with the lawyers about the legal issues. They may be the first professional with whom the couple meets. They teach them strategies to reduce conflict and turbulence and be more available to the children – asking questions and providing information on sound parenting, especially given the extra stress.

By way of highlighting one aspect of the collaborative divorce process (Teslor & Thomas, 2006, p. 127), coaches encourage both partners to look at their nonmaterial values and goals so they can author a joint mission statement emphasizing such values as:

- Behaving well
- Ending the divorce amicably
- Maintaining contact with the extended family
- Honoring what was valuable in the years of the marriage (see "The Divorce Ceremony: A Healing Strategy," Appendix 3)
- Allowing an opportunity to forgive each other for the "failure of the marriage"

Much brainstorming of options may occur before resolution of different issues is reached. They often draw up a conflict resolution plan for the immediate present and for the future and sign the agreement knowing they should expect that changes to it may be necessary in the future.

We can definitely speculate that the men and children in half of the cases discussed in this volume would have fared much better if they had undergone either successful divorce mediation – already burgeoning in the early 1980s or collaborative divorce, which started to become available in the late 1990s. We can only wonder why there are still so many high-profile adversarial divorces and people who want their day in court when the sad repercussions reverberate so destructively for so long when more humane, compassionate, and beneficial to all routes to divorce now exist.

References

Ahrons, C. R. (1994). *The good divorce: Keeping your family together when your marriage comes apart.* New York: Harper Collins.

American Bar Association. (1981). *Model code of professional responsibility.* Chicago: National Center for Professional Responsibility.

Bowlby, J. (1988). *A Secure Base: Parent-Child Attachment and Healthy Human Development.* New York: Basic Books.

Charny, I. (2006). Staying together or separating and divorcing; Helping couples process their choices. In C. A. Everett & R. E. Lee (Eds.), *When marriages fail: Systemic family therapy interventions and issues.* New York: Haworth (now Taylor & Francis).

Coogler, O. J. (1978). *Structured mediation in divorce settlement.* Lexington, MA: D.C. Heath.

Erickson, S. K., & McKnight Erickson, M. S. (1988a). *Family mediation casebook: Theory and process.* New York: Brunner Mazel (now Taylor & Francis).

Ferstenberg, R. L. (1992). Mediation vs. litigation in divorce and why a litigator becomes a mediator. *American Journal of Family Therapy, 20*(3), 266–273.

Fisher, R., & Ury, W. (1981). *Getting to yes.* Boston: Houghton-Mifflin.

Folberg, J. (1983). A mediation overview: History and dimensions of practice. *Mediation Quarterly, 1,* 13–14.

Folberg, J., & Taylor, A. (1984a). *Mediation: A comprehensive guild to resolving conflicts without litigation.* San Francisco: Jossey Bass.

Goldstein, J., Freud, A., & Solnit, A. (1973). *Beyond the best interest of the child.* New York: Free Press.

Haynes, J. M. (1981). *Divorce mediation.* New York: Springer.

Haynes, J. M. (1982). A conceptual model of the process of family mediation: Implications for training. *The American Journal of Family Therapy, 10*(4), 5–16.

Hetherington, E. M., Cox, M., & Cox, R. (1977). The aftermath of divorce. In J. H. Stevens Jr. & M. Matthews (Eds.), *Mother-child, father-child relations* (pp. 149–176). Washington, DC: NAEYC.

Kaslow, F. W. (1984a). Divorce: An evolutionary process of change in the family system. *Journal of Divorce, 1*(3), 21–39.

Kaslow, F. W. (1984b). Divorce mediation and its emotional impact on the couple and their children. *American Journal of Family Therapy, 12*(3), 58–66.

Kaslow, F. W. (1990). Divorce therapy and mediation for better custody. *Japanese Journal of Family Psychology, 4,* 19–37 (in English).

Kaslow, F. W. (1995). The dynamics of divorce therapy. In R. H. Mikesell, D. D. Lusterman, & S. H. McDaniel (Eds.), *Integrating family therapy: Handbook of family psychology and systems therapy* (pp. 271–283). Washington, DC: American Psychological Association.

Kaslow, F. W. (2000). Families experiencing divorce. In W. C. Nichols, M. A. Pace-Nichols, D. S. Bevcar, & A. Y. Napier (Eds.), *Handbook of family development and intervention* (pp. 341–368). Hoboken: Wiley.

Kessler, S., & Bostwick, S. (1977). Beyond divorce: Coping skills for children. *Journal of Clinical Child Psychology, 6,* 38–41.

Moore, C. W. (1986). *The mediation process: Practical strategies for resolving conflicts.* San Francisco: Jossey Bass.

Neville, W. G. (1984). Divorce mediation for therapists and their spouses. In F. W. Kaslow (Ed.), *Psychotherapy with psychotherapists* (pp. 103–122). New York: Haworth.

Pittman, F. (1989). *Private lies.* New York: Norton.

Schwartz, L. L., & Kaslow, F. W. (1997). *Painful partings: Divorce and its aftermath.* New York: Wiley.

Tesler, P. H., & Thompson, P. (2006). *Collaborative divorce: The revolutionary new way to restructure your family, resolve legal issues, and move on with your life.* New York: Harper Collins.

Wallerstein, J. S., & Kelly, J. B. (1980). *Surviving the breakup: How children and parents cope with divorce.* New York: Basic Books.

Part II: A Different Lawyer: A Different Result

Sally S. Benson, J.D.

Introduction

(Most of the material contained in this commentary section is predicated on divorce law and its practice in Florida.)

The right lawyer in a divorce case can make the difference between a poor or a great result. Although many of the cases discussed earlier in this book had an unsatisfactory result for the father of the children, probably only some of the outcomes could have been altered by the retaining of a different attorney's services. Certainly, many dissolution cases and their outcomes regarding decision-making, communication, and time-sharing of the children can have a satisfactory result with the use of appropriate counsel. Nonetheless, in my 36 years of practicing law, I have seen many cases where the fathers were shortchanged when it came to their children.

Traditionally, the word "custody" has been utilized primarily as a description of the rights of the mother or occasionally of the father to the children. That word or concept no longer is part of the law in the jurisdiction where I have practiced for three and a half decades. There have been many improvements in the divorce laws of many states, including Florida, in recent years, which had they been in effect years ago, might have altered the outcome in the illustrative cases, even given the same legal counsel.

In the last quarter of a century, there were slow and gradual and, recently, more rapid and definitive changes in the rules governing the traditional laws and the judicial systems regarding the rights of fathers. Some states, like Florida and California, appear to be more progressive than others. As indicated above, in Florida, there is no longer language in the statute referring to "custody"; the arrangement is now one of "time-sharing."[1]

Another change has been the elimination of the presumption rule that if a child is of "tender age" that the mother should have "custody" (Elkin, 1987). That presumption was frequently adhered to in the United States and the United Kingdom throughout much of the twentieth century. It had to be overcome at the level of "preponderance of the evidence" in order to change the presumption. Today, there is no longer such a tender years presumption in many states (Johnson v. Adair, 2004), and a good father who is able to care for a child, who loves the child, and who is involved in the child's life can be awarded "primary time-sharing" or "equal time-sharing" responsibility for a young child, just as the mother can. Nonetheless, in more conservative jurisdictions, the judges may be a bit less flexible in their thinking, and so, even though the law has been changed and places the mother and

---

[1]Florida Statutes §61.13 Title VI, Civil Practice and Procedure, Chapter 61, May 31, 2011. Dissolution of Marriage; Support, Time-Sharing.

father on equal footing, no one ever knows what goes on in the judge's mind. Some still may tend to give, without admitting it on the record, the weight of the evidence to the mother (Pica, 1999). However, as time goes on, this will also tend to change as "more contemporary thinking" judges are appointed and society puts pressure on all of the courts to change. Most laws now exist so as to be fair to both parents, and it appears that it is just a matter of time before appellate case law and judges' rulings "catch up" with the law.

Assessing the Judge and the Client

The focus of this chapter is primarily on the counsel who represent each party. Even an attorney who may do an outstanding job may not be as successful as he/she "should be" because the judge in the case also harbors his/her own beliefs, including thoughts, predispositions, and opinions about the specific attorney and/or the party that the lawyer represents. As a result, decision-making is quite a complex process comprised of many variables, and the attorney representing the divorce client must take into consideration who the judge is, what that judge's reputation is based on both the past experience of that particular attorney when appearing before this particular judge, the judge's reputation in the legal community, and a review of similar cases upon which that judge has ruled in the past. These considerations can provide the attorney with guidance as to where this court might stand in the broad definition of "abuse of discretion" on many issues in the domestic court, especially issues that were previously called "custody and visitation" and now are denoted as "time-sharing" in Florida. It is of utmost importance that the attorney evaluates his/her own reputation with the judge, and if the attorney has had difficulty in obtaining his/her desired results in the past, said attorney needs to perhaps try a different approach in this case. This may entail simply not arguing with the judge, or having case law to present to undergird his or her points on all issues, or being more or less definitive with the judge. The attorney also needs to assess the client – does the client present him/herself well, is he respectful in his demeanor, does he glare at the other side, is he appropriately dressed for court, and does he have an air of aloofness? These factors must be taken into account along with the facts in the case. An attorney who is doing his/her job properly must think about all of this from the outset of the case before going forward. An attorney can give his/her absolute best advice, but if he or she does not have a client who is going to listen and respect the attorney by following it and counsel cannot "control" his/her client, then they will not get the outcome they seek.

I learned many years ago to put a requirement into my *agreement for representation* that the client sign a statement that they *will always be truthful with me*. Even though this does not invariably turn out to be the case, it does seem to put the client on notice that they need to tell the attorney both the "good and the bad." I advise them initially, "if I don't know the '*bad*' and it comes out in court, I will not be able to handle it as well as if you had told me ahead of time and I could perhaps have protected you from ever having that information be divulged, or at least have brought it out before the other side did and used it against you."

The majority of the individual cases discussed herein are not cases which occurred in the last five years. Many of the facts related by the individuals interviewed to the author probably would be different if their cases were brought before a court today. However, it is by using such cases illustratively, where a very capable, qualified father was not granted sufficient access to his children nor they to him or where alienation was perpetrated, and bringing these injustices to light by way of this publication (and others) that professionals can contribute to continuing to bring about the kinds of changes and improvements that we have witnessed in the last few years throughout many, but not all, states.

Relocation Statute

Another area in which there has been improvement is in the Florida's Relocation Statute.[2] In the past years, if a mother who had "custody" of the child(ren) remarried and moved out of the area with her new husband, thereby affecting the father's visitation rights, "that was the way it was going to be." In Florida, there is now a relocation statute that does not permit a parent to move and impact the time-sharing of the other parent without agreement of both parties or the issuance of a court order permitting the move. The statute is very specific as to requiring timely notification, a proposed time-sharing schedule, and then, if no agreement is reached, a legal proceeding must be filed to determine where the children should reside. Many factors have to be considered. Under this statute, there is no presumption that the moving party – usually the mother – should control the child's location. The parent wishing to move has the burden to prove by the preponderance of the evidence that the arrangement to relocate is in the best interest of the child. If that burden of proof is met, then the opposing side has the duty to prove otherwise.[3] The court looks at all factors such as the involvement of both the father and mother in the children's lives; their work schedules; how each parent has dealt with the other and any improper influence exerted by either one as to their relationship with the other parent; the child's preference with consideration of their age and maturity; the reasons for the relocation; whether the relocation is sought in good faith; career opportunities in the current locale and if said person relocates; any history of substance abuse or domestic violence; and whether the relocation will enhance the general quality of life for

---

[2] Florida Statutes §61.13001 Title VI, Civil Practice and Procedure, Chapter 61, June 16, 2009. Dissolution of Marriage; Support, Time-Sharing.

[3] Florida Statutes Title VI, Civil Practice and Procedure, Chapter 61, June 16, 2009. Dissolution of Marriage; Support, Time-Sharing §61.13001 (7).

both the parent and the other person seeking the relocation and the child, not limited to financial and emotional benefits or educational opportunities.[4]

Frequently, the court will say to the parent, often the mother, who wants to relocate, that she cannot take the children, who are to stay in their current community and school. If she decides to stay where she currently resides, the same time-sharing that previously existed will continue. If she chooses to move, then ultimately a new time-sharing schedule will have to be worked out where the children's primary residence will transfer to the father so that they can remain in the same school and have continuity in their daily lives.

Child Support

One of the areas in domestic law in Florida where the "abuse of discretion" standard is not the level of error required for reversal of a decision at the appellate level is calculation of child support. For many years, there has been a specific statute and table with guidelines upon which the amount of child support to be paid by the parent with the greater income to the other parent has been determined.[5] The statute does allow for a 5% leeway in either direction and has other add-ons, if applicable. For example, $1,000.00 monthly base child support calculated on the two parents' net income would permit up to $1,050.00 or as little as $950.00 to be the amount required to be paid. The parties can concur on a bottom-line deviation. There is no ceiling on the amount the parties can agree to on their own. The court currently requires that a Child Support Calculation Sheet be presented in all cases so as to ensure that at least the minimum support is being agreed upon. The statute for determination of child support has been substantially modified wherein it now carefully addresses the number of nights that each parent has with the child when determining the parties' respective child support obligations.[6] The formula no longer simply assumes that one has the majority of the time over the other. There had previously been a modified application of this for a few years in Florida; however, the statute now (2012) is quite specific and has substantially altered the amount of child support that is required to be given from the payer to the recipient parent. One may wonder if the increasing numbers of fathers who ask for 50% of the time-sharing arrangement are motivated in part by this statutory change.

It has been my experience as an attorney that the majority of the fathers quite sincerely want to spend much more time with their children than was granted under prior laws. Because the statutory change is so new, it is difficult to evaluate what effect this will have on some families. There is concern that the lower income earner (frequently

---

[4]Florida Statutes §61.13001(7) (a) through (k) Title VI, Civil Practice and Procedure, Chapter 61, June 16, 2009. Dissolution of Marriage; Support, Time-Sharing.

[5]Florida Statutes §61.30 (6) Title VI, Civil Practice and Procedure, Chapter 61, March 25, 2011. Dissolution of Marriage; Support, Time-Sharing.

[6]Florida Statutes §61.30 (11) (a) Title VI, Civil Practice and Procedure, Chapter 61, March 25, 2011. Dissolution of Marriage; Support, Time-Sharing.

the mother) may fall into hard times economically because she is not receiving as much income in the form of child and spousal support as she would have under the previous statute. Bottom line is that if the children go back and forth and live in both households, *both* parents must maintain living quarters that have sufficient bedrooms and other facilities for the children and provide clothing and other necessities. In effect, these costs do not diminish substantially even though one might no longer be entitled to the level of support that they would have received under the old statute.[7] This must be balanced with the fact that the other parent's expenses for the children's food and clothing have escalated as they spend more time in his or her household and care. Ensuring fairness and justice here may be a difficult balancing act.

Mediation

Compulsory mediation has allowed for a dramatic change in the options available to a father in resolving the time-sharing of the children during the divorce process. Courts have found that the resolution rate through mediation runs about 50%. The courts in most Florida jurisdictions require multiple mediations when a case involves issues that will take more than half a day at trial and if a temporary relief hearing on complex issues is necessary. For instance, the first mediation is required before a temporary relief hearing can be scheduled. This mediation is focused primarily on addressing temporary issues such as what the children's schedule will be, including where they will reside and overnight time-sharing; what support will be paid by either parent on a temporary basis; what marital bills of the family will be paid and by whom; as well as the use of the marital home and other assets while the divorce is pending. The court can order temporary alimony, use of the marital home, the cars, the boat, and whatever other assets exist. The discovery process continues during this temporary period in order to allow counsel to learn what the assets and liabilities are, what the income of each party is, and what is really in the "best interests" of the children regarding a time-sharing schedule. After the discovery process is completed, the parties are able, through mediation and hopefully advice of adept counsel, to agree to the separation and distribution of all of the marital assets and liabilities and the appropriate time-sharing and child support obligations of each. If they are not, then the matter proceeds to trial. The attorneys are involved in all of the mediations as well as in any trial.

Both parent's attorneys must agree on the mediator. A good attorney will assess the important issues of each case and select a mediator who is strong in these areas. Overlaid on this consideration is the attorney who is representing the other side, who at times may have no interest in settling. With all of the creativity and all the reasonable proposals one can make at mediation, if opposition counsel is not interested in reaching a settlement, it probably will not happen as it takes both parties (and their respective attorneys) to agree on the issues at mediation in order to resolve them (Erickson & McKnight Erickson, 1988). As reasonable as one side can be, if

---

[7]Florida Statutes §61.30 Title VI, Civil Practice and Procedure, Chapter 61, March 25, 2011. Dissolution of Marriage; Support, Time-Sharing.

the other side will not compromise, an "impasse" develops and then the matter goes to the judge.

During mediation, the attorney can be most effective and bring all issues to a settlement if he or she is creative, knowledgeable about the law, knows about the judge who is handling the case and what the judge's "normal" rulings are on certain relevant issues, and what each party's needs and desires are. Frequently, a positive result eventuates from focusing on the critical needs (even though they may not be valid) of the other side and structuring a settlement that satisfies those needs but also allows one's own client to get what he or she wants (Folberg & Taylor, 1984). For instance, frequently, the mother has a strong emotional attachment to the marital home. A good lawyer will recognize this and try to structure something favorable to the father that still allows the mother to stay in the house and she sometimes will trade off other assets to keep the house because of her emotional attachment.

Mediation allows parties to personally negotiate their own affairs, whereas a trial does not. The court has its "hands tied" as to what relief can be granted. For instance, in Florida, once a child becomes an adult who is 18 years of age, or 19 if the child is still in high school but will graduate by the time he or she is 19, there is no leeway for the judge to order either parent to pay for higher education of the children. This is a sad predicament for the adolescent, because if the parents are not both reasonable and/or focused on higher education and do not particularly want their children to have what may be best to prepare them to make a decent living, then the child is "left hanging" as soon as he or she gets out of high school. If one parent has the ability to pay and the other does not, the parent with the financial ability will not be required to pay for the child's postsecondary education, and the child will have to decide if he or she wants to take on onerous student loans or go out into the workforce without that education. I find this to be the number one "sad part" of what the judge cannot do versus what the parents could and "should" agree to do. Thus, if the parties have mediated and come to an accord wherein they can agree to both partially contribute toward the higher education of the child or at least to pay for their prepaid college education costs so that at least some of the costs for college will be defrayed at the time the child is ready to enroll in a postsecondary education program, this exceeds more than a judge has the authority to do.

Other issues which the parties can resolve at mediation, but the court cannot do, are the manner in which the assets are divided. The court is more likely to just do a simple division so as not to err in favor of either one of the parties, whereas in a mediated settlement, there is more latitude to divide the assets so that it is done in the best interests of both the mother and father. Thus, annuities, life insurance policies, retirement accounts, or other securities accounts that are more beneficial to one than the other can be divided accordingly and a formula proposed to balance the ledger between the parties (Kaslow, 1984b). A good lawyer can assess the assets and liabilities and look at them from their client's point of view and argue the division of said assets that are in the client's (and children's) best interests.

Another major concern may be credit card liability. There may be some credit cards in the father's name, some in the mother's, and some that are joint accounts. If the credit card debt is to be divided, an effective attorney for the father may want to list the credit card debt in his column, even if it is sometimes disproportionate to do so. Next, the attorney can ask for a disproportionate amount of the assets to offset this. The rationale for this is that if the wife or "soon to be former wife" is responsible for this specific liability, she may be unlikely to make payments on the husband's credit card a priority over defraying her other existing obligations or ones which she will incur in the future. Failure to pay this liability which is in father's name could cause the man to suffer a reduction in credit scores and/or be sued by the credit card company, and he could ultimately have to pay that liability even though it was not his responsibility under the final judgment. Although the ex-husband would then have the right to "go after" his ex-wife for nonpayment, the likelihood of his collecting is slim, and it would cost more in legal fees and emotional strife than it is worth in the majority of cases.

An effective, farsighted lawyer may even negotiate a disproportionate division of the liabilities at times in favor of obtaining a time-sharing arrangement with the children that the father may want. A court would not do this, but it may become something that is important enough to the father that he is willing to "shoulder" these additional liabilities in order to guarantee more time with his children. There are numerous other ways in which mediation can prove to be more beneficial for each party than allowing a judge to make decisions that will chart the future course of the rest of their lives (Emery, 1994).

Although many of the actual cases discussed in Chapters 2, 3, 4, 5, 6, 7, 8, 9, 10, 11, 12, 13, and 14 appear to have been decided when a judge did not listen attentively to the father, it is increasingly common today in Florida to find that if a father wants to spend the time and money to bring to the court's attention, post-dissolution, the improper conduct of the mother in terms of not permitting the time-sharing decreed, the courts are harsh in their reprimands against a noncooperating mother. The real problem here is that it takes an injustice that has been perpetrated against the father and then bringing it before the court; this is expensive and time consuming. Sometimes it is not worth the effort and time it would take away from work for fathers who are very busy trying to make a living to pay their support obligations as well as provide for their own lives financially, that is, support two households. Emotionally it may be something they do not feel they can continue to contend with. Further, it puts the children "in the middle" and may cause them to become unnecessarily alienated from one of the parents (Egizli, 2010).

How an Effective Lawyer Can Help Avoid the Pitfalls

In domestic law cases, many issues regarding dissolution, including those pertaining to the children, are decided at "the discretion of the judge." Thus, unless there is an abuse of discretion by the judge, the appellate court does not have a basis for reversing the decision. "Abuse of discretion" is a broad term, and because of that legal criterion, many cases that might have been reversed with a more limited criterion have not been appealed. Appeals are expensive and time consuming and may keep the parties' lives in limbo for an extended period of time until they are decided. The knowledge that the majority of decisions therefore are not going to be overturned unfortunately serves as a deterrent when someone is deciding if an appeal would be appropriate.

The courts in the past and still on occasion today in some states simply indicate that the time allotted for a father with his children will be "reasonable and liberal." This assumes that the parties are going to be able to work out the time-sharing arrangement; however, if one of the parties, more likely mother, who has the children the majority of the time, decides the father is not going to get his fair amount of time, and if there is no specific schedule for the parenting plan, he is in a difficult position and must document a deliberate and continual denial of his time-sharing and ultimately bring the matter before the court. To establish a deliberate and continual failure to allow time-sharing is not easy. It may mean months of record-keeping of demands, trips to the house to get the children and mother's refusal to let them come with him, before there is sufficient evidence for the father to bring his motion to the court to show that he is being denied his time-sharing. The courts are not likely to punish a mother who on only one or two occasions has denied time-sharing because surely she will present a reason at the hearing, be it a strong or weak reason, and the court will be reluctant to find the mother in contempt.

A good lawyer, in negotiating the time-sharing, will never settle for "liberal and reasonable" without a default time-sharing provision in the written agreement approved by the court which will provide specific times and dates. If the parties cannot agree, this default provision will afford a guarantee as to certain time-sharing for the father. This is a critical issue; its specification can alleviate the necessity of ever involving attorneys and the court again since the father can "fall-back" on this provision. For example, if the Final Judgment of Dissolution provides for liberal time-sharing but the default provision states that if the parties are not able to agree the father will be entitled to time-sharing from Friday until Monday (including the hours for the transitions to occur) and then there is a refusal by mother to allow that, it is a much easier task to obtain a contempt order against the mother for failing to allow the children to visit Friday through Monday than "liberal and reasonable." Where there is a violation of a specific default provision, the courts are much more apt to find the withholding parent in contempt for said violation, especially if it is repetitive.

Some of the cases in this volume involve fathers who had work schedules that were not very consistent. A good lawyer could have negotiated a time-sharing schedule that would have addressed the irregular time schedule of either parent. For instance, if there was substantial business travel involved for either parent and it changed from month to month, the schedule should have a proviso that at the beginning of each month that parent, frequently the father, would outline his travel schedule and provide it to the mother, specifying that he would have the children the days when he was not traveling or specific days of the week when he was in town. This type of scheduling allows both parents, month by month, to know what the time-sharing schedule will be. Further, it enables everyone, including the children, to prepare and plan their calendars and to know where they are going to be on which days. The court is not as likely to grant this type of arrangement by court order so it behooves the father to negotiate this as part of a mediated settlement. (The failure of some judges to spend the time and provide the relief they should may be attributed to the fact that they may never have had children or they are just "fed up" with all of the bickering they have experienced in families, and they therefore do no allocate the time to listen to the evidence and award this type of schedule.) It behooves the parties to try to get this done at mediation. It also depends on the judge's willingness to focus on what the true issues are for the father regarding his time-sharing with the children. Judges are also complex, busy human beings and whether the specific judge will take the time to do a detailed judgment that would address such issues may be a matter of his "mood" on the particular day that the matter comes before him. An attorney is likely to fare much better on behalf of his/her client who carefully prepares an order and parenting plan which outlines specifically what the father wants so it makes the judge's job easier. This is more likely to convince the judge to enter that order since the judge will not have to take the time required out of his or her tremendous workload to put a great deal of detail into the time-sharing portion of the final judgment (see Part IV"Parenting Coordination" in this chapter).

A reasonable divorce attorney representing the other side is not always what one encounters. There are tremendous pressures put on counsel to "win" for the client. The fact that domestic relations matters have so much emotion entailed exacerbates the often fine line clients express between "love" and "hate." Some attorneys can get "caught up" in the "must win" rather than "doing what is right." Only experienced attorneys who are familiar with the rules and procedures of the family court in the jurisdiction where the case will be tried should be retained. These attorneys are the best ones to advise what is fair, what the parameters are, what the law is, what a judge is likely to do, and where the father should ultimately expect to "land" in the case. A sincere father who desires to spend substantial time with his children, who makes the proper request, and who can show by his past actions that he is sincere so that the court believes that his request is not simply a result of a recent epiphany nor a request because of "financial" reasons, like a reduction in support obligations, will more than likely, with a solid attorney who cares about the "rules of play," get a favorable and fair result, from his point of view.

How Could the Results Have Been Different?

We now look at several of the cases presented and consider how good lawyering might have brought about a more just and positive outcome for the father and his children. The right lawyer in a divorce case can make the difference between a fulfilling future family life and a deprived one. Each divorcing dad should select his attorney carefully. The case studies contained herein have illustrated what happens when attorneys do not properly represent their clients.

Although in Case 5 joint custody was awarded to Dr. Ron, his former wife did not follow the order. Even though she went to court twice because she did not comply with the order, she was only admonished. If, in fact, there were serious violations by the former wife, a competent and strong attorney could have convinced the court that more than just admonishment should occur. Frequently, now in Florida, the courts will assess fees as well as award "makeup" time to replace time that has been denied to the other parent. This is used as a frequent sanction against the "wrongdoing" parent. The unfortunate part is it takes a legal proceeding to bring about the relief and redress the grievance.

Mr. Brogan (Case 6) is an illustration of the kind of situation where originally the former wife engages a reasonable attorney and later changes counsel in the middle of the case to a "barracuda." Then the ex-husband feels pushed to retain a similar type of attorney so as to "meet" the aggressiveness of the former wife's attorney. This occurs often; thus, one should not hire the "wrong lawyer" from the outset. It is difficult to change counsel midstream, but sometimes it is warranted if the facts and circumstances change and call for more aggressive representation.

Case 8, Mr. Goodman, is an unfortunate one factually insofar as it took the court system almost four years to put in place an order which he merited years earlier. Frequently, there is little that an attorney can do because the financial restrictions of the court system seem to limit the speed at which the process takes place. Nonetheless, a lawyer who watches date and time limitations and aggressively pursues hearings with the court can speed up receipt of relief somewhat. The extreme amount of time that it took for Mr. G. to get an order for 100% of the time-sharing with the children, even though the former wife went to jail during the interim, was unusual and disheartening. Sometimes this happens, and it has nothing to do with the counsel involved; it is a function of how the judicial system operates (and a serious problem this book hopes to contribute to hastening to help remedy).

Case 9, Dr. Regis, presents a situation where he wanted more time with the children than he was granted and he did not actively pursue his request for more time. Traditionally, this amount of limited time allocation was common, so he had little choice. However, today in many states, if he could show that he was actively involved in the children's lives and desired more time than just Tuesdays and Thursdays and every other weekend, he would obtain it if he had a good deal of interaction and involvement with the children prior to the filing for the divorce. The *prenuptial agreement* that he had drawn up before his second marriage was a good idea, and the possibility of creating such a document is one that lawyers should always raise for discussion with their clients prior to any marriage in the contemporaneous world.

Case 10 would not evolve as it did today if a father would "speak out." Mrs. Arturo Miguel would not be allowed to place the children in boarding school under current law, at least in Florida, without the agreement of the father, or if he disagreed, she would need to obtain a court order. Florida law now requires a parenting plan (McHale & Lindahl, 2011a) and stipulates that the parents must have "shared parental responsibility" and discuss all issues regarding education, religion, and health of the children. If the parties have always had the children in boarding school and agreed upon placing the children in such a school, then the court would say this is reasonable. However, if the children had not been in boarding school while the parents were married, and suddenly at the time of or shortly after the divorce the mother sends the children to boarding school without the father's consent, it would not be the father's financial responsibility to pay for this, nor would the mother have a right to do that if it would deny the father his rights to time-sharing, provided he had co-parented pre-divorce. Without a doubt, the outcome of this case could have been influenced by a good attorney bringing a motion to void the mother's unilateral decision to place the children in boarding school out of the area. The current requirement of a parenting plan and a designation of what address is to be used for the children for school purposes has substantially eliminated the occurrence of this type of situation in Florida.[8]

In Case 12, the former wife used a personal injury attorney who filed many false pleadings and forced the former husband, Dr. Determined, to defend himself against these allegations, which was very costly. This is a reasonable attorney's worst nightmare because it causes said attorney to have to spend substantially more time addressing the false allegations and subpoenaing witnesses, taking depositions, preparing requests for production, hiring investigators, and filing pleadings to prove that these allegations are false. This ultimately costs the father a great deal of money which is money that may not come out of the "marital pot," but simply has to be paid at the father's own expense. By "marital pot," I mean that the court can rule from what source the legal fees are paid – marital money belonging to both parties, one party paying the other's fees or a portion of them, or each paying their own fees. If each pays their own fees, it is out of their own money, post-filing, or out of the money that they would get under equitable distribution rules. It is a different rule of law than the normal division of the marital assets and liabilities in Florida. It is not determined on the basis of who the "wrongdoer" is but on who has "the better ability to pay," which is extremely unfair in many instances, and, as a result, fathers frequently are assigned the greater financial burden. The good lawyer needs to be careful not to get "pulled in" to the "low-life accusations" of a personal injury lawyer, as in this case. The good lawyer must take the "high road" but may very well need to "step it up" a bit because he or she must disprove the allegations. A psychological evaluation of the "soon to be former spouse" may be in order to show that her false allegations have been made primarily to "get at dad" (see section "Family Evaluation in Custody Litigation: Reducing Risks of Devastating Relationships" of this chapter by Dr. Benjamin re family evaluations).

The case of Dr. Unlucky (Case 13) was a situation where a lawyer who was quite aggressive should have been involved insofar as there was allegedly domestic violence perpetrated by the wife as well as by her mother. Specific statutes exist in some states that provide for relief, but it requires the encouragement of a lawyer to the client to pursue that route, and if pertinent facts are alleged, then immediate relief is provided without the necessity of a preliminary hearing. There is then an evidentiary hearing to determine whether or not the allegations are valid and whether an injunction should be

---

[8]Florida Statutes §61.13 Title VI, Civil Practice and Procedure, Chapter 61, May 31, 2011. Dissolution of Marriage; Support, Time-Sharing.

issued. Parental alienation seems to have occurred in this case; that is, the oldest son, Josh, was encouraged to dislike his father by his mother (Clawar & Rivlin, 1991). Her actions were improper, and Dr. Unlucky needed a very strong "litigating type" lawyer who would have brought these injustices to the court showing that Mrs. Unlucky removed the father's name from the school records, did not inform him of the activities of the children, and alienated the children by saying nasty and inappropriate things to them about their dad, which caused them to not want to have contact with him.

The improper allegations of domestic violence by the former wife should have been addressed "head on" since it appears that her personality was strong, aggressive, and unreasonable and her behavior was not easily restrained. Thus, a father in this type of case would require a domestic attorney who was a "frequent courtroom litigator" so as to be able to acquire for Dr. U. what he deserved, as far as time-sharing with the children and a chance to maintain a good relationship with them, and to have the former wife enjoined from acting inappropriately against him directly and/or indirectly.

Sometimes a good attorney can help his or her client realize certain facts about the family dynamics that he or she may not see because he is "too close" to the situation. A competent, savvy, experienced attorney can listen to the facts and analyze them and indicate whether (he/she thinks) the other spouse has been faithful, has a different agenda, etc. This may require the lawyer to immediately recommend the father see a therapist to try to address various issues such as an extramarital affair rather than to have the client "bury" them because they are so painful. Engagement in therapy can be a powerful process to help him gain greater self-awareness, bring some "closure" to painful issues, and enable him to "move on."

References

Clawar, S. S., & Rivlin, B. V. (1991). *Children held hostage: Dealing with programmed and brain-washed children*. Chicago: American Bar Association Section of Family Law.

Egizli, J. (2010). *The look of love*. Dallas: Brown Books Publishing Group.

Elkin, M. (1987). Joint custody: Affirming that parents and families are forever. *Social Work, 32*, 18–24.

Emery, R. E. (1994). *Renegotiating family relationships: Divorce, child custody, and mediation*. New York: Guilford.

Erickson, S. K., & McKnight Erickson, M. S. (1988b). *Family mediation casebook: Theory and process*. New York: Brunner Mazel (now Taylor & Francis).

Folberg, J., & Taylor, A. (1984b). *Mediation: A comprehensive guide to resolving conflicts without litigation*. San Francisco: Jossey Bass.

Johnson v. Adair (District Court of Appeals of Florida, Second District October 29, 2004).

Kaslow, F. W. (1984c). Divorce mediation and its emotional impact on the couple and their children. *American Journal of Family Therapy, 12*(3), 58–66.

McHale, J., & Lindahl, K. (2011a). *Coparenting: A conceptual and clinical examination of family systems*. Washington, DC: American Psychological Association.

Pica, D. A. (1999, January). The tender years doctrine: Is it still the law? *Advocate (Idaho), 38*.

Part III: Family Evaluation in Custody Litigation: Reducing Risks of Devastating Relationships

G. Andrew H. Benjamin, J.D., Ph.D., ABPP

Introduction

The cases described within this book suggest that most of them involved high-conflict tactics that often emerge in the worst of family law litigation. The issues in such cases are not resolved through negotiation or mediation. In the cases described, it appeared that these highly educated litigants were out lawyered so that issues were not resolved in a timely or fair manner. Out lawyering occurs when someone is not represented (the party is a pro se litigant) or the party has selected an ineffective lawyer who fails to respond appropriately to the high-conflict tactics.

An effective method of responding to high-conflict tactics is seeking and obtaining a court-ordered comprehensive evaluation of both parties and their child(ren). If litigants are treated with respect and transparency during such a comprehensive family evaluation, the findings can provide a new foundation for furthering healthier relationships among the parents and the child(ren). The most critical aspects of a standardized evaluation protocol that lead to litigants believing that they have been fairly and thoroughly evaluated are discussed in this chapter.

Divorce for most people involves feelings of failure, anger, betrayal, and loss, especially the loss of earlier hopes for the way the relationship could have been. In addition, the legal process can produce great distress when compared with other types of professional services. The consequences of the emotional and financial stress on family law litigants can be severe (Hetherington, Cox, & Cox, 1985). The worst harm in high-conflict family law cases is that they typically affect the children negatively. A substantial number of children involved in divorce will be placed at significant risk of suffering emotional and behavioral disturbances due to the ongoing exposure to parental conflict. Such conflict can result in a lack of social support, financial insecurity, and disruptive changes in routines, schools, and residences.

Disagreements between parents about child rearing, discipline, parental access, and visitation arrangements may interfere with maintaining positive parent–child attachments. Children may also be subjected to physical or sexual abuse, domestic violence, or the emotional and physical impairment of a parent after a divorce. Longitudinal studies have found that the negative impact of divorce conflict can persist into the adolescent and young adult years for the children (Kelly, 2002; Kelly & Emery, 2003; Lansford, 2009; Long, Slater, Forehand, & Fauber, 1988). The legal, financial, and emotional impact of ongoing conflict between parents increases the risk of trauma to the children, who are frequently drawn into the middle of disputes even when parents have the best of intentions of protecting them. Poor outcomes for the children typically occur when either party is out lawyered. The antipathy of the other party and the engagement of abusive use of conflict tactics will fail to be checked, if one or both parties lack competent legal representation. It then becomes increasingly likely that the negative impact of divorce on the children will worsen.

Parental adjustment problems can lead to such poor outcomes because of grief, impaired conflict resolution skills exacerbated by mental illness or addiction problems, and economic hardship because of financial decline in the residential household of the child (Sbarra & Emery, 2005). Not surprisingly, parents with serious adjustment problems typically employ some of the following behaviors (Benjamin & Gollan, 2003) against the other partner and child:

- Threatens to mistreats or harm my child or me
- Physically or emotionally mistreats or harms my child or me
- Sexually mistreats or harms my child or me
- Tries to control me through finances (e.g., withholding child support)
- Tries to control or scare my child or me through damaging property
- Invades my privacy or monitors my whereabouts
- Threatens or actually physically harm him- or herself in front of my child or me
- Creates or uses conflict in a way that creates distress for my child
- Withholds contact or access to my child
- Refuses to comply with the court order regarding adult or child issues
- Refuses to co-parent with me (e.g., will not talk with me about parenting issues)
- Makes negative comments about me that make my child confused, upset, or sad

Those who litigate divorce are distinguishable from those who divorce more amicably because they are much more likely to engage in such abusive use of *conflict tactics*. Competent lawyering must check these tactics. With competent lawyering, fair settlements rather than extensive litigation will occur.

First Step: Efficacious Lawyering

Judges will not act in ways to support the health of the children unless compelling evidence is provided documenting the psychopathological acts. Simple accusations uncorroborated by any independent evidence from multiple sources will fail to persuade a judge to set aside the arguments of the more efficacious lawyer. In high-conflict family law cases where abusive use of conflict tactics has begun to emerge, the parent must find and hire a first-rate lawyer.

Finding such a lawyer, who can serve also as a counselor at law, is most likely to occur if the concerned party (husband or wife) identifies three possible lawyers from those well respected by their colleagues and the judges within that jurisdiction. They also are more likely to be the presenters of continuing legal education programs, who have kept current with the emerging standards created through common law by judicial activism. For instance, many of the legal factors (used by judges to make findings) about relocation issues ("move away cases") have been developed in this manner. Mistakes in asserting legal rights are less likely to occur.

The party who needs representation should call three possible candidate lawyers. During each of the calls, the party should list the tactics that their spouse has engaged in, how those tactics might affect the health of the children, and ask what the lawyer could do to prevent the other party from continuing to act out. As the party listens to the three lawyers discuss the concerns and the approaches to addressing these, it will become apparent to the party which lawyer would be the best fit. That lawyer is the one to hire. As has been demonstrated in several of the cases discussed, it is worth paying top dollar for the best legal services. Remember the adage: "Penny wise, pound foolish."

A counselor at law will identify the need for services to address the shock of an abrupt ending to the marriage and will make recommendations to help the party move forward in a manner that protects the interests of the party and the children. If the party is planning the ending of the marriage, a good attorney will advise a period of marital psychotherapy with a psychologist to determine whether a breakup can be averted. If an ending must occur, then psychotherapy would continue to prepare both parties for the psychological ending of the relationship. Shocking the other party without any preparation for the termination of the marriage never seems to lead to a good outcome.

Changes in the marital relationship, and conflict between spouses, usually have begun long before initial contact with lawyers. In contacting a lawyer, the party is formally acknowledging that the marriage is close to ending and is requesting practical information and help in deciding how to progress toward formal dissolution. The lawyer's role is often to be a "voice of reason" with respect to both the emotional and legal aspects of the dissolution, helping the client to identify a course of action while reassuring him or her about unrealistic fears and counteracting any punitive urges with objective information. Research strongly suggests that a perceived inequitable process rather than a perceived inequitable outcome most likely contributes to dissatisfaction with the final divorce decree (Sheets & Braver, 1996). Lawyers' best serve the parties by assisting them to experience a fair process as well as achieve an equitable outcome.

Second Step: Comprehensive Family Evaluation

Litigation in custody cases may cost tens of thousands of dollars before the final day of a multiday trial ends, and a judge renders a series of permanent orders. A comprehensive family evaluation, conducted by a competent psychologist, costs a fraction of this expense and, in most cases, will prompt a fair settlement that ends conflict between the parties (Benjamin, Gollan, & Ally, 2007). Compromises based upon an understanding about the concerns of the parties will lead to fairer restructuring of parental rights and responsibilities in relation to the children.

In most family law cases, no lawyer represents the children's interests, yet their best interests are supposed to be served by the divorce process. Often parental values or the way in which parents interpret their children's behavior may differ markedly. Building a thoroughly understood framework about the concerns for the parties through the findings of a comprehensive evaluation is a crucial task to spur divorce negotiations to a closure of the marital relationship.

During a custody action, the initiating spouse has the advantage of having generally anticipated the separation, allowing time to plan and maintain some degree of control in his or her life. The rejected spouse often has had little time to prepare emotionally for the separation, even if the threat of parting has been present. The emotional reactions of both parties are determined by the circumstances of the splitting apart, the meaning the party draws from the culmination of the relationship, and his or her personality characteristics. Generally, the initial reactions of the parties involve surprise, shock, and acute anxiety. A comprehensive evaluation about the concerns of the parties helps to clarify uncertainties about the future. With comprehensive psychological evidence, lawyers will have much greater influence in cautioning their clients against precipitous decisions or unrealistic negotiating positions. Lacking such evidence, each lawyer may misunderstand the toxic interactions of the parties and how those interactions will affect parenting.

Sound psychological evidence permits the lawyers to communicate reasonable expectations and set realistic limits so that dependent or hostile persons do not cause or experience yet additional dramatic losses. Parties experiencing emotional concerns who lack closure are prone to act out in ways not generally characteristic of them, and such behavior can become pervasive if left unchecked (Kelly, 2002). Reaching agreements about how the parties can parent together in high-conflict family law cases becomes quite difficult because of the insidious breakdown in their communication, loss of self-esteem, and loss of respect for each party. As was demonstrated earlier in the case studies, high-conflict cases result in the following types of acting out between the parties:

- A relationship history with multiple reasons for conflict
- Conflict that centers on the alleged lack of parental fitness rather than specific objections about decisions regarding the children's religion, education, health care, or daily activities
- A record of restricted phone or mail contact and access to the children
- A history of involving others in disputes, particularly a partner in a postmarital relationship or an extended family member

Further acting out exacerbates more hostility, blame, and efforts to exert control. Typically, this type of litigant reacts to the legal process with strong feelings of loss, grief, betrayal, anger, jealousy, guilt, failure, and/or abandonment. Reaching agreement may be further complicated by financial concerns and the adversarial nature of the legal process (Halon, 1991). These types of litigants also are most likely to become dissatisfied with their legal representation and are prone to file disciplinary or malpractice complaints. Competent lawyers welcome the rich psychological evidence that is prepared based on a comprehensive family evaluation about the parties so that they can work more effectively as counselors at law.

Increasingly, the legal system has turned to alternative dispute resolution approaches, such as mediation and parenting coordination to settle disputes involving children. These approaches are aimed at relieving the high emotional and financial costs of litigation for families and the burden of increased litigation for the courts. However, parties who are engaged in abusive use of conflict tactics do not mediate well or engage in other forms of therapeutic structuring such as parenting coordination (Brewster, Beck, Anderson, & Benjamin, 2011).

Comprehensive family evaluations can provide findings about the myriad allegations raised by the parties in acrimonious custody litigation. The conclusions are based upon multiple sources of data and often assist in finding resolution through settlement. Research has indicated that such evaluations may serve as a significant "bargaining chip" because the courts are likely to accept an expert's recommendations (Halon, 1991). In addition, an evaluation may function to mitigate risk factors associated with the negative results of ongoing divorce conflict and, if the matter must be resolved before a judge, will provide corroborated findings about rich psychological evidence that will enable the judge to apply "the best interests standard" in a more informed manner.

Components of a Comprehensive Family Evaluation

Many custody evaluations fail to engage methodologically sound practices (Emery, Otto, & O'Donohue, 2005). As a result of procedural errors widespread among custody evaluators, faulty clinical judgments are common because of the following factors (Garb, 1989, 2005): (1) the lack of consistent definitions regarding the characteristics of the subjects under observation, (2) the differing context in which subjects were observed, (3) the differing perspectives of the individual assessors, and (4) inherent errors within the various measurement tools used by evaluators. Clinical judgment is fallible and, by itself, does not suffice to constitute a reliable approach for conducting a comprehensive family evaluation. Further, reliance on protocols for measuring just parental capacity will collude with the adversarial process of the parties. Instead, a comprehensive family evaluation should result in a fair, respectful analysis of each concern raised by both parties.

Key components for reaching accurate results during a comprehensive family evaluation were delineated by careful qualitative research that was designed and implemented while supervising lawyers (guardian ad litem) and psychologists (Benjamin et al., 2007). The evaluation protocol was refined through studies of videotaped interactions with parties and subsequent discussion with evaluation teams, supervising experts, and family court lawyers and judges during more than 900 separate parenting evaluations for court-ordered or self-referred families. Modifications to the protocol occurred whenever interactions of the evaluation process appeared to produce feelings of abandonment or surprise, expressions about the lack of fairness of the evaluation process, or where clinical judgment errors occurred. As a result of the adjustments made during the last 23 years of work, concrete and standardized procedures were developed for producing a comprehensive family evaluation in high-conflict family law cases (Benjamin & Gollan, 2003). The efficacy of those evaluations has been shown by most of the cases settling and no ethics complaints being filed for even one of these cases, a very rare phenomenon.

The results of the research led to the following recommendations for comprehensive family evaluations:

1. Specific referral questions should be clearly established by the lawyers before the evaluation commences in order to minimize the emotional and financial costs associated with mismanaged evaluations. Competent counselors at law should set the stage for fair evaluations to be conducted.

2. Both parties should agree to join in the evaluation by a specific psychologist or the court with jurisdiction over the case should order that both parties participate. Unless one evaluator is able to conduct a broad-based, multiple-measured evaluation of both parties, the biased reporting of just one party may affect the reliability and validity of widely used psychometric tests, interview data, parent/child observational evidence, and collateral evidence (Weissman, 1991). With both parties participating fully during the process, and their fees for the evaluation paid in advance, the evaluator will be more likely to arrive at objective conclusions that are confirmed by multiple measures. The evaluator should be instructed by both lawyers to delineate the specific parental strengths and weaknesses that would affect the best interests of the children based upon the evaluation of all the concerns raised by both parties.

3. The evaluator should limit communication to e-mail or faxed letters for the parties and their attorneys. Except for the structured meetings of the evaluation process, all of the parties and their attorneys must only use written correspondence to communicate with the evaluator. This approach reduces the likelihood of poor communication. Further, written records from these communications rarely cause confusion or a sense of being treated unfairly. It also creates a written record that lends itself to corroborating the findings of the evaluation.

4. Both parties received a standardized agreement and disclosure statement about the evaluation process. Making the evaluation process transparent by describing each step of the process in advance eases the transition of the parties into the process. This step minimizes parties being surprised by any part of the process. The evaluation should not begin until a court order directs both parties into the evaluation process, and the structure of the evaluation has been clarified sufficiently for both attorneys and the parties. Each phase of the evaluation does not end until both parties have engaged in a parallel process so that the data from each phase are assimilated similarly. The greater the evaluator's effort to behave objectively and with fairness, the more likely it is that the results of the evaluation will lead to a settlement rather than to a trial.

5. In advance of the clinical interviews of each party, data are collected about the concerns of the parties, each parent's routine with the children, and demographic and psychosocial history. This generates a standardized collection of data to use to assess the range of allegations from the beginning of the process. These data are reviewed again during the clinical interview of each party for clarity and consistency. By delineating the allegations at the beginning of the evaluation, and by providing repeated opportunities to clarify each allegation, the language of the parties can be used to create an ideographic narrative that represents the characteristics of the parties operationally. Parties are more likely

to feel heard if their voices are quoted accurately. Using a standardized questionnaire to collect these data promotes a comprehensive preview process that identifies details that will prompt additional investigation throughout the remainder of the evaluation process.

6. Structured interviews and standardized psychological testing of the parties should occur so that errors of clinical judgment are less likely to occur (Emery, Otto, & O'Donohue, 2005). Data from the interviews will help to ascertain contributing factors associated with functional aspects of parental capacity and behaviors, the relative stability of both households, and the developmental and attachment needs of each child. The evaluator should be expected to build the evaluation report on the day of the interview so that the narrative details and nuances of the party's behavior can be accurately recorded to further minimize clinical judgment errors. Such errors are more likely to occur with overreliance on memory, confirmatory or hindsight bias, and overreliance on unique data (Garb, 1989, 2005). Subsequently sending each party a copy of their own psychosocial section and allegation section about the other party to make additions provides a further check for accuracy of the interview data. This part of the process increases transparency and models treating the parties fairly. The final report incorporates any additions the parties have made.

7. Observations of parent–child interactions should be conducted in a standardized manner as well as within the clinical office to reduce error variance from viewing the child(ren)/parent interactions in different settings. A structured process that is conducted similarly on two separate occasions permits comparisons of parenting strengths and deficits, attachment and bonding with the child, and parental judgment. After the observation, if the parent being evaluated suggests that the parent–child observation was compromised by any factor, the evaluator clarifies how the observation was compromised and, in light of those facts, conducts a second observation. This serves the interest of fairness.

8. By the end of the parent–child observation phase of the evaluation, hypotheses generated about the data to that point, which would include psychological test results, interview data, and parent–child observation findings should be written up in a discussion section of the report. These preliminary findings about the psychological evidence are organized under the legal factors used by the judges of the jurisdiction to determine the best interest of the children. The discussion section focuses on the consistency of the data across multiple collection points. It notes discrepancies and limitations of the data (e.g., problems with the reliability or validity of the psychometric testing, which is used sparingly and only for hypothesis generation because of the validity and reliability limitations of psychological test data for this population). Allegations that remain uncorroborated by the psychological test results, interview data, or parent–child observation findings are less likely to be substantiated during the initial review of the legal documentation, past professional evaluation or treatment notes, and forthcoming collateral interviews.

9. Writing the preliminary report before reading any of the collateral documentation or talking with collateral reporters lessens the likelihood that evaluator's credibility will be impugned. None of that evidence is reviewed or incorporated into the

report until the evaluator has written the preliminary report. Basing impressions on the direct interactions with the parties and the children powerfully negates any inference that the collateral evidence unduly influenced the evaluator and affected the independence of the evaluation. It also provides an opportunity to anticipate the hypotheses that the collateral evidence may support. When the collateral evidence fails to corroborate the hypotheses, inquiry must occur as to why disparate evidence exists. The report addresses disparate evidence directly. Any discrepancies may be the result of limitations in the manner of collecting the data (e.g., the credibility of the collateral reporter because of his or her limited objectives or experience) or in the interpretation of the data (e.g., evaluator bias).

By the time that collateral documentation is reviewed, the parties have provided declarations or affidavits of firsthand nonprofessional witnesses who witnessed specific instances of poor parenting or harmful adult activity. Each jurisdiction has a declaration or affidavit form that subjects the person to the laws of perjury if facts alleged within the form lack veracity. Such a process helps prevent nonprofessionals from changing the stories as the evaluation process unfolds or the parties from exerting pressure for support. Collateral reporters willing to report their firsthand observations through this process usually provide rich details about the facts that they have observed. Grandparents usually make excellent collaterals. They also are less likely to change their reports about the observations at cross-examination during a trial.

As soon as each collateral interview is completed, the evaluator informs the collateral reporter that, later in the day, a written summary of the interview will be faxed or electronically mailed for review. Such a review deters a party from complaining later that the evaluator misrepresented or failed to insert a detail that allegedly might have affected the outcome of the evaluation. Not only does this approach help to ensure that both parties will believe that they were fairly and thoroughly evaluated, but it also produces a contemporaneous record of collateral reporter's satisfaction with the results of the interview.

10. Each party meets for a closing interview so that the evaluator can delineate each fact that led to the support of a finding about a particular allegation. If a party disagrees with the finding, the evaluator gently challenges any of the inconsistencies or discrepancies that arise during the party's explanations. This type of Socratic questioning is commonly used in empirically supported psychotherapy (e.g., cognitive behavioral treatment), and similar procedures are effective in eliciting information in this therapeutic jurisprudential setting (American Psychological Association [APA], 2006). This step of the evaluation process appears to lessen the anger of the parties and may be integral in a diminishing their desire to litigate. It provides them an in vivo opportunity to challenge the evaluator and the evaluator's findings. After this step, the parties usually believe that they have had a full and fair opportunity to dispute any evidence that emerged from the evaluation process.

Finally, throughout the evaluation and until the completion of the final report, the evaluator remains skeptical about the hypotheses that are generated during the evaluation process. The report includes (1) allegations that lack independent corroborating evidence, (2) hypotheses that have failed to be corroborated by at least two independent measures, and (3) statements made earlier by the parties about who would provide firsthand evidence about contemporaneous evidence concerning an alleged incident that are not substantiated by the declarations from the nonprofessionals, later collateral documentation, or interviews.

Instead of using diagnostic labels, the evaluator delineates adult behaviors or parenting behaviors that might affect current and future parenting competency. Such descriptive examples of behavior help the lawyers understand the complexities of the case. If the data corroborate allegations about impaired parenting skills, the report provides recommendations for protecting a child from harmful parental involvement. Given the findings of the evaluation, the final evaluation report should include recommendations about primary residential placement of the children, access schedule, allocation of the decision-making authority, future dispute resolution process for resolving later disagreements, and psychotherapy or skill building approaches that the parents and children should pursue. High-conflict cases often will require follow-up with therapy for victimization, substance abuse and other addictions, domestic violence, and parenting skills training.

As soon as the final report is completed, the evaluator meets with both lawyers in the case. In the meeting, the methodology of the evaluation is described, all concerns that were evaluated are addressed, and the questions of the lawyers are answered. The final report is given out at that point so that the lawyers can continue the process of arriving at an equitable settlement in light of the findings from the psychological evidence.

Third Step: Alternative Dispute Resolution for Future Concerns

Third, when treatment is needed or communication deficits exist between the parties, a guardian ad litem, case manager, or co-parent psychotherapist (one therapist who specializes in working with high-conflict parties, who will work with each party separately to develop healthier communication skills and remediate parenting deficits) should be designated in the permanent court order to monitor follow-through of orders. The evaluator will have suggested that primary residential placement and access schedules remain contingent on the parties' complying with their treatment recommendations. If either party fails to comply, the guardian ad litem, case manager, or co-parent therapist can report his or her findings as part of the subsequent dispute resolution process. Such an arrangement can further the coordination and participation of both law and mental health professionals in settling future conflicts swiftly.

In postdivorce situations with little conflict and good communication between the former spouses, changes of circumstances that may affect the needs of either parent or any of the children can be accommodated without requiring additional litigation, even if the parents have significant differences of opinion. This requires a sense of trust and an ability to rely on each other. After the divorce, even a contentious divorce, a very gradual transition to a new period of stabilization occurs. It typically takes two to five years beyond the separation for the instability that is caused to the children's lives to settle out and the psychological functioning of the parties to improve significantly (Kaslow, 1991).

New stability, however, can again be threatened by any major change. Typically, stabilization is threatened by remarriage, significant family relocations, new developmental stages in the children (e.g., an adolescent who no longer wants to be bound to a regular visitation schedule), emerging behavioral problems in one or more of the children, a child's refusal to visit the nonresident parent, or major changes in financial circumstances. Poor outcomes are most likely when parties remain emotionally disturbed or hostile toward each other (Brewster et al., 2011).

If conflicts occur, parents should avoid ensnaring the children in the problem and should instead seek impartial assistance through a case manager, co-parent therapist, mediator, or arbitrator to help them resolve the issue. When conflict is high, it is helpful if communication about decision-making is restricted to written documentation (e.g., fax or e-mail). Such a manner of communication dampens conflictual tactics, provides a more leisurely response period that allows for the quieting of impulsive outbursts, and if necessary, provides a written evidentiary record of improper communication. If such communication continues, it may warrant a change to sole decision-making. As has been discussed above, persistent parental conflict is strongly associated with poor child adjustment. Reducing the level of conflict and increasing the quality of parenting are more likely to occur if the embattled parties work with an impartial professional.

If during the evaluation, the professional documents that an unequal bargaining relationship exists between the parties or that one or both parties appear incapable of resolving conflicts in good faith, subsequent conflicts should be resolved by binding arbitration, conducted by a mutually agreed-upon arbitrator. Such an arbitrator should remain available to the parties for at least three years following the settlement agreement or court order. Quick, inexpensive resolution of further disputes will then occur. Binding or mandatory arbitration can result in rapid resolution (less than two weeks) at considerable less cost than returning to court. Many jurisdictions in this nation have enabled arbitration as a dispute resolution process for family law cases. Any impasse, whether it is between the parties or the parties and a mediator, case manager, or co-parent therapist, should be arbitrated. They should agree in advance to use the first available arbitrator among three identified by their lawyers as part of the custody settlement. They should also agree that any arbitration decision shall remain mandatory on the parties. If either party appeals an arbitration decision to the court, the party who files the appeal must pay the retainer fees of the other party. Unless the legal position of the appealing party is significantly improved, the appealing party must pay the entire fees and costs of the action in the court. These agreements deter abusive use of the legal process and will result in a fair, timely resolution about any disagreement.

Conclusion

Divorce is a time of heightened psychological stress and disequilibrium for most couples. It continues to affect many family members long after the legal documents are signed. These divorces require a restructuring of parental rights and responsibilities with respect to the children that can have great impact if not carried out effectively. Based on the research, guidelines have been provided to further the "best interests of the child" and reduce destructive parental conflict through the process of comprehensive family evaluation.

References

American Psychological Association. (2006). Closing interviews in high conflict family law evaluations with G. A. H. Benjamin. American Psychological Association. http://www.apa.org/pubs/videos/4310753.aspx.

Benjamin, G. A. H., & Gollan, J. (2003). *Family evaluation in custody litigation: Reducing risks of ethical and malpractice infractions.* Washington, DC: American Psychological Association Press.

Benjamin, G. A. H., Gollan, J., & Ally, G. A. (2007). Family evaluation in custody litigation: Reducing risks of ethical infractions and malpractice. *Journal of Forensic Psychology Practice, 7*, 101–111.

Brewster, K. O., Beck, C. J. A., Anderson, E. R., & Benjamin, G. A. H. (2011). Evaluating parenting coordination programs: Encouraging results from pilot testing a research methodology. *Journal of Child Custody, 8*(4), 247–267.

Emery, R. E., Otto, R. K., & O'Donohue, W. (2005). Custody disputed. *Scientific American Mind* (October), 65–67.

Garb, H. N. (1989). Clinical judgment, clinical training, and professional experience. *Psychological Bulletin, 105*(3), 387–396.

Garb, H. N. (2005). Clinical judgment and decision making. *Annual Review of Clinical Psychology, 1*(1), 67–89.

Halon, A. (1991). The comprehensive child custody evaluation. *American Journal of Forensic Psychology, 8*(3), 19–46.

Hetherington, M. E., Cox, M., & Cox, R. (1985). Long-term effects of divorce and remarriage on the adjustment of children. *Journal of the American Academy of Child Psychiatry, 24*(5), 518–530.

Kaslow, F. W. (1991). The sociocultural context of divorce. *Contemporary Family Therapy, 13*(6), 583–607.

Kelly, J. B. (2002a). Psychological and legal interventions for parents and children in custody and access disputes: Current research and practice. *Virginia Journal of Social Policy & the Law, 10*, 129–163.

Kelly, J. B., & Emery, R. E. (2003a). Children's adjustment following divorce: Risk and resilience perspectives. *Family Relations, 52*(4), 352–362.

Lansford, J. E. (2009). Parental divorce and children's adjustment. *Perspectives on Psychological Science, 4*(2), 140–152.

Long, N., Slater, E., Forehand, R., & Fauber, R. (1988). Continued high or reduced inter-parental conflict following divorce: Relation to young adolescent adjustment. *Journal of Consulting and Clinical Psychology, 56*(3), 467–469.

Sbarra, D., & Emery, R. (2005). Co-parenting, conflict, non-acceptance, and depression among divorced adults: Results from a 12-year follow-up study of child custody mediation using multiple imputation. *American Journal of Orthopsychiatry, 75*(1), 63–75.

Sheets, V., & Braver, S. (1996). Gender differences in satisfaction with divorce settlements. *Family Relations, 45*, 336–342.

Weissman, H. N. (1991). Child custody evaluations: Fair and unfair practices. *Behavioral Science and the Law, 9*, 469–476.

Part IV: Parenting Coordination

Debra K. Carter, Ph.D.

History and Objectives

Parenting coordination (PC) is a multidisciplinary method of intervention for separated and divorced parents that blends the role of the court with the role of a counselor and a family mediator. It evolved in the early 1990s in the United States as an alternative dispute resolution (ADR) process to protect children from the plight of exposure to harmful parental conflicts and dysfunctional co-parenting arrangements. As the United States embraces ADR opportunities in the family courts, divorcing spouses and the attorneys who represent them have more options available to help them separate, both emotionally and logistically, in a manner that emphasizes the importance of the child's bond with each parent and the significance of developing and maintaining an effective co-parenting relationship.

The impetus for development of parenting coordination may be better understood within the context of cultural and societal norms. Traditionally, fathers were less involved in child rearing, and most of the research with married families focused on the primacy of the mother–child relationship in promoting healthy child development. When families separated, mothers were typically designated as the sole or primary legal custodian of the children. Fathers were often relegated to secondary status and many dropped out of their children's lives entirely (Fabricius & Hall, 2000; Kelly & Emery, 2003; Pruett & Donsky, 2011). The cases in this book provide many examples of such events and the often devastating results for parents, particularly fathers and the children. Fortunately, over the past 20 years, co-parenting as a concept and the father-child relationship have gained increased attention as significant, if not essential, variable in fostering healthy growth and development in children (McHale & Lindahl, 2011b).

In addition to a new focus on co-parenting in the research on divorcing spouses, professionals working within the family law system have long recognized that the adversarial legal system is ill equipped to serve the needs of families or function in the best interests of children. This is particularly true when families are immersed in high-conflict custody disputes, as children and their welfare often lie in the hands of family court judges, attorneys, and custody evaluators who are involved with these families for only a limited period of time (Carter & Harari, 2008; Mitcham-Smith & Henry, 2007).

Similar to other court-mandated parenting initiatives in the United States such as divorce parent education, the aims of parenting coordination are to reduce interparental conflict, improve parenting skills, foster cooperative co-parenting relationships, decrease litigation and court appearances, and indirectly improve the outcomes for and well-being of children of divorced, separated, or never-married parents. It is a process theoretically grounded in family systems theory, developmental psychology, and conflict resolution theory.

Parenting coordination is a multidisciplinary function practiced by psychologists, attorneys, social workers, licensed counselors, and others and requires an integration of professional skills and experience to help families who are caught in conflict to disengage, emotionally and behaviorally, from dysfunctional parenting relationships and to develop child-focused communication and problem-solving techniques. *The well-trained PC serves as a court-ordered, third-party neutral to assist parents who are unwilling or unable to disengage from their conflict-ridden parenting style to learn how to shield their children from the damaging effects of exposure to chronic conflict.* The PC is not an advocate for either parent and should remain neutral and unbiased toward both parents at all times. However, the PC may serve as an advocate for the children when the impact of a parenting plan or a parent's interventions places the children in danger or at risk for harm, either physical or mental.

PC typically begins with a court order or stipulated agreement between the parents or legal guardians that provides the authority for the person serving as a PC to make binding decisions. Courts may appoint, or parents may request and agree to use, a PC at any point during or after dissolution of marriage proceedings or any other civil action involving custody or parenting.

Roles and Functions of the Parenting Coordinator

The primary roles of the PC combine several functions:

- Helping parents resolve disputes about their child or children
- Helping parents comply with the parenting plan established by the court
- Making decisions (i.e., arbitration) if parents cannot settle disputes with the PC's assistance (if specified in the PC agreement or court order)
- Refocusing parents on their child and providing education about their child's developmental and psychological needs
- Communicating with children to understand their views and perspectives
- Helping parents improve the quality of their parenting
- Helping parents develop and maintain an effective co-parenting relationship
- Establishing an infrastructure to provide parents with the support they need to be "good" parents

It is also important to understand the roles that are not appropriate for a PC to assume. *Parenting coordination is not a couple or family therapy intervention for high-conflict parents nor is it a substitute for a custody evaluation* (in some areas known as a social investigation or parenting plan evaluation) *or a psychological assessment. In fact, assuming any "dual role" that includes one of these other functions would be ill-advised and unethical* (APA, 2012).

The Parenting Coordination Process

The PC process is specifically aimed at disarming high-conflict parents locked in battle by helping them develop and implement a *successful dispute resolution framework for co-parenting* their children. This framework includes a comprehensive parenting plan that details time-sharing arrangements and decision-making responsibilities for children. It also includes a system for child-focused communication and problem-solving techniques and enables parents to acquire the skills and tools they need to disengage from a dysfunctional parenting relationship and to develop an effective and sustainable co-parenting partnership. This type of partnership is designed to reduce parental conflict, minimize stress for children, improve the quality of parenting, and encourage parents to *resolve their parenting conflicts without litigation.*

Along the dimensions of conflict and cooperation following divorce, parents generally divide into three types of co-parenting relationships (Kelly, 2006): cooperative (25–30%), parallel (45–50%), or conflictual (≈20%). While a *parallel* co-parenting relationship, which is characterized by emotional disengagement and minimal communication, is less optimal for children than *cooperative* co-parenting, many children do adjust well in these arrangements, particularly when the quality of parenting in each home is nurturing and adequate. However, those parents who have a continuing *conflictual* parenting relationship, with poor communication and little, if any, cooperation (Maccoby & Mnookin, 1992; Hetherington & Kelly, 2002), are the parents who are usually most in need of parenting coordination services (Carter, 2011). This was certainly the case with most of the families highlighted in this book.

The PC must first establish an intervention strategy that prioritizes parents' and children's needs based on principles of protecting children from risk and harm and establishing a safe, structured environment for them. The important factors to consider when assessing the appropriate interventions for divorcing parents (Johnston, 1994) are the extent to which post-separation or postmarital hostility decreases the capacity for co-parental cooperation regarding the needs of the children. Factors associated with high-conflict co-parenting patterns include frequent arguments, sabotage of the other parent's role as a parent, and the absence of frequent attempts to communicate and coordinate with the other parent with respect to the children. This is highlighted in the Blue Eyes, Dedicated, and Guy families where the mothers engaged in a campaign of demeaning the fathers to undermine their parenting role.

In the case of Dr. Blue Eyes, Jamie (his second wife) was clearly placing the children at risk as a result of her untreated addictions. Had a PC been involved, the PC would have insisted that the mother get clean and sober and adhere to her treatment plan in order to have unsupervised access to the children. Depending on the PC's scope of authority as determined by the court, the PC may have been able to refer the mother to treatment without the need to obtain a court order demanding that she do so. The PC could have also recommended a temporary change in the time-sharing arrangement to the court, placing the children with the father until such time as the mother's addictions and inadequate parenting no longer constituted a risk to the children.

Fortunately, with the help of a well-trained and experienced PC, the co-parenting relationship can be modified (Margolin, Gordis, & John, 2001) to help parents move toward a more functional co-parenting partnership (Carter, 2011) as they disengage from a deteriorated marital or partnership relationship. Most high-conflict parents do not know how to make this transition in order to shield their children from exposure to chronic conflict. This was the case with the Regis and Kelly families, and in the Dedicated family, it was the mother's parents who were allowed to expose the children to conflict and denigrate the father. Such a PC intervention involves teaching parents how to redefine their relationship and set different relationship boundaries than they may have had in the past to accomplish this goal.

Separation and divorce bring emotional and behavioral upheaval that can be very distressing, if not damaging, to the children. One of the primary responsibilities of a PC is to monitor the children's adjustment and to ensure the parent–child bond is maintained and reinforced with each parent (Association of Family & Conciliation Courts [AFCC], 2005), *unless* the parent is abusive or placing the children at risk. The lack of involvement of an independent professional with the authority to intervene in parenting arrangements allowed significant amounts of time to pass with no contact between the children and their fathers in the Dedicated and Miguel families.

For example, the Miguel boys were only seven and three years of age at the time of the divorce when the close father/son bond was suddenly and permanently disrupted. Mr. M had little opportunity to have influence over his son's thoughts and actions or to be a positive male role model for them. This loss of a positive parenting figure may not have occurred with a PC involved. The importance of the parent–child relationship for both boys with mom and dad as well as the need for frequent access to each parent would have been emphasized to the parents but also to the court (if necessary) with recommendations for changes in the time-sharing arrangements and a clearly established protocol for effective communication between the parents and for dad with the boys.

A primary intervention in PC is to refer children to a qualified mental health professional who provides regular feedback to the PC about the child's adjustment as well as the quality of the parent–child relationship. This allows the children to have an emotionally safe place to talk about their feelings and to learn how to cope effectively with the traumatic changes in their family and between their parents.

In the Guy family, all four teenagers were exposed to a significant transformation in their mother that allegedly created a "bitter, nasty, and mean person." In addition to the devastation of losing a warm, loving mother figure, their contact with their father was obstructed, and they were left to absorb their mother's "very disturbing and destructive remarks…about their dad." In essence, they were emotionally abandoned by both parents (through no fault of dad's) during an extremely vulnerable developmental phase (adolescence) when so many changes were already occurring in their bodies, their social life, and in the risks to which they were exposed (alcohol, drugs, sexual activity). Had a PC been involved with this family, the PC would have insisted (through court order, if necessary) that these children see a mental health professional. The oldest, at age 19, would not have been subject to the PC's authority (due to being legally considered an adult), but the others would most certainly have benefited from having a safe emotional outlet to process the disruption in their family and to learn how to set appropriate boundaries with their mother and assertively insist on a relationship with their father.

A large body of empirical research highlights the negative impact on children when they are exposed to prolonged hostility and conflict between their parents, including behaviors that put them in the middle of a conflict (Hetherington & Kelly, 2002;

Buchanan, Maccoby, & Dornbusch, 1991). For example, asking the children intrusive questions or having them "spy" on the other parent (Sally Blue Eyes), asking them to carry hostile messages to the other parent, demeaning the other parent in an open and contemptuous manner (Kelly and Dedicated families), or creating a need for the child to hide information from or their feelings about the other parent (Blue Eyes and Guy families) are all ways of putting the child squarely in the middle of the conflict. The PC may need to help such parents identify ways in which they are damaging their child by putting them in the middle as it may not be obvious to the parent who is caught up in their own unresolved feelings of anger, hurt, or betrayal (e.g., Estelle Guy).

The Dedicated family highlights the need for PC prior to the final dissolution of marriage. These children were already at risk of enmeshment with their mother prior to the separation (i.e., mother sleeping with the daughter) and then had two years of virtually no contact with their father during critical development years. Researchers have documented the importance of maintaining the parent–child bond with fathers (Amato & Gilbreth, 1999; Bauserman, 2002; Pryor & Rodgers, 2001) to foster healthy development. When a father is "absent" for an extended period of time (it was not because the father did not want to be present), the bond between the child and father is disrupted. From child development and attachment theory, we know that children do not measure time in terms of clocks and calendars. Depending on the age of the child, two years can feel like an eternity, and the result can be a significant rupture in the relationship that will take a long time to repair, if it can be done at all.

While Dr. D had legal rights to joint and equal custody, the reality was they were not enforced. A PC could have made a significant difference. Not only would the PC have insisted that the children be in therapy but would have also provided education to both parents about the importance of maintaining a healthy parent–child bond with each. If the mother continued to be uncooperative and unresponsive to suggestions that were in the children's best interests, the PC would have been in a position to make recommendations to the court about the harmful effects of this mother's "gate keeping" and the need for a substantial change to allow the father to have access and more control over the children's lives.

Social scientists have found a strong link between parent adjustment and adjustment of children and adolescents (Emery, 1999a, 1999b; Kelly, 2002b; Kelly & Emery, 2003; Pruett, Williams, Insabella, & Little, 2003). Not surprisingly, they have concluded that inadequate and poor parenting abilities have a significant adverse impact on children. Even the most stable and reliable of parents do not function well during and immediately after separation and divorce (Amato, 2000; Emery, 2004; Hetherington, 1999). Maccoby and Martin (1983) found that parents exhibiting more positive mental health tend to have less conflict with their ex-partner. This suggests that interventions designed to assist parents in improving their own mental health may have a direct impact on their ability to establish a more effective co-parenting relationship and, indirectly, produce more positive outcomes for children. For example, if the parent with the most parenting time is depressed or anxious or has a personality disorder or addiction, as was the case with Mrs. Blue Eyes (Case 1) and Mrs. Blue Eyes (Case 2), the children are at much greater risk of developing problems as well. With this family, the PC would have directly intervened in an effort to mitigate the potential damage to the children.

When a parent has an addiction or chronic mental illness, the PC may be involved with a family for many years. Given the severity of Mrs. D's problems, it is likely that the PC would be involved until all of the children reached the age of majority. This serves to ensure that the children's needs are met, they have an opportunity to develop and thrive, and each parent acquires the tools and skills they need to be effective, loving co-parents. Once parents and the family restabilize, the PC may serve more of a "monitoring" function to ensure the stabilization holds and the children are able to reach adulthood with minimal or no damage. Unfortunately, even into adulthood, Dr. D's children are very distant (literally and emotionally) and continue to experience the aftereffects of the loss of a loving, caring father.

Kline and colleagues (1989) found that the actual custody arrangement had little effect on children's adjustment, but *the parents' emotional adjustment to divorce and the post-separation childcare arrangements had significant impact on the children*. In the Guy and Goodman families, mom's poor emotional adjustment had a clear, negative impact on the children. In families where the primary parent becomes anxious or depressed (Peggy Determined and Diane Blue Eyes) or develops serious addiction problems (Jamie Blue Eyes and Zack Determined), the children often develop a high rate of psychological and social problems. Some children also develop physical symptoms (e.g., stomachaches, headaches) and some act out in an aggressive or defiant manner.

The Goodman family illustrates the way in which a PC may be used in post-judgment modification matters. Given Mrs. G's abandonment of the children along with her serious addictions and history of very poor parenting, the father was able to obtain sole legal and physical custody of the children. While this arrangement clearly provided for more stability and consistency in the children's lives, they were nonetheless left "motherless" and experienced all of the attendant losses that accompany abandonment by a primary attachment figure. Mr. G modified his work schedule and behavior to fulfill the role of "primary" parent and clearly exerted efforts to be both a "mom" and a "dad" with good results. However, with the mother's desire to reenter the children's lives after addiction treatment and serving time in prison, the father is understandably frightened about the potential harm her reentry may have on the children emotionally as well as the risk for actual harm due to her continued poor parenting skills. This is where a PC may be most helpful, and it would have been appropriate for the father to ask the court to appoint a PC at the time they appointed a guardian ad litem (GAL) *if* the court in his Florida jurisdiction has this service available.

Often, GALs are not trained in psychology or child development and may only look for evidence of neglect and/or abuse. In addition, GALs are not appointed to "follow" the family once any litigation matters have been resolved, whereas the role of a PC is precisely designed to "follow" the family for many years. At the time when mom wanted to reenter the G children's lives, they were still quite vulnerable (ages nine and six years) and needed the structure and predictability of a stable, loving home environment that had been provided by their father. The PC would have recommended a thorough psychological evaluation of the ex-Mrs. G prior to suggesting any "reunification" plan to ensure that the children's best interests would be protected.

If it were determined that reunification and ongoing contact between ex-Mrs. G and the children were appropriate, the PC would have frequently and consistently monitored the adjustment of the children (usually through regular contact with their therapist, direct monitoring of academic performance through the children's teachers and of records of physical development and any somatic symptoms provided by their pediatrician) to ensure that renewed contact with the mother was not harmful to them. In addition, the PC would have set up a structure to monitor the mother's sobriety and compliance with any treatment regimen as well as insist that the mother attend in-depth parenting classes to improve her parenting skills. This would have provided Mr. G with some assurance that an experienced, third-party expert would be watching out for the children and would immediately intervene should the mother's reentry prove to be harmful or damaging in any way. "Monitoring" by the PC also would have assured the court that any recommendations for changes in time-sharing or decision-making were based solely on the children's best interests and not just reflective of a protective father's fears. With oversight and guidance, ex-Mrs. G may have been able to become a more competent, loving parent which may have mitigated the emotional damage the children had experienced as a result of her earlier abandonment.

In addition to the significant influence that exposure to interparental conflict has on children's adjustment postdivorce, the *quality of parenting* children experience is equally important (Amato & Keith, 1991; Kelly & Emery, 2003). Thus, in addition to monitoring children's adjustment and well-being and each parent's adjustment to the divorce, PCs must also monitor the quality of parenting each provides. Many parents go through an initial traumatic emotional and behavioral upheaval following separation due to the profound and devastating losses they experience. Not only are their dreams and hopes for their family shattered, but parents (historically fathers) experience significant losses in terms of time with their children and the ability to have a meaningful impact on their lives. These circumstances often lead to compromised parenting abilities. For parents with mental or physical problems, the risk of poor parenting is even greater. Therefore, the PC must gather information about each parent's level of functioning as an individual (versus part of a dyad) and assist each parent in getting the appropriate professional help they need (e.g., referral for therapy, substance abuse program, psychiatric evaluation).

For example, in Mrs. Kelly's "roller-coaster" behavior, style and mood swings and her pattern of easily making and then destroying relationships (which led to four different caregivers for Adriana in five years), the potential risk to this child for poor adjustment and emotional damage was high. Mrs. K also used Adriana to meet her own emotional needs and exposed this little girl to episodes of screaming criticism of Mr. K and to threats, which were very frightening to the child. Had a PC been involved, Mrs. K would have been referred immediately for a psychological and psychiatric evaluation and then treatment in an effort to improve her emotional and behavioral stability. If Mrs. K's parenting skills and mental health did not improve, the PC would have recommended limiting the child's exposure to her mother's erratic and abusive behaviors, including a change in time-sharing arrangements in an effort to provide Adriana with a consistent, stable, and loving home environment. This family also illustrates how a very good and involved father can provide a "protective factor" as a critical emotional buffer for a child, even if the "good" parent does not have sole custody (Kelly & Emery, 2003).

The Guy family highlights the importance of establishing a parenting plan with clearly defined time-sharing arrangements, even for adolescents who have constantly changing needs. It is ideal for parents of adolescents to be flexible to allow for developmental and social changes that accompany this phase of life. However, when parents are in conflict, or in this case not communicating at all, it is virtually impossible to have a more flexible parenting plan. Within the structure of a parenting plan or scope of authority as ordered by the court, the PC may make modifications to parenting time schedules that allow for adolescents' evolving needs and desires. With a PC in place to monitor the children's adjustments and needs, he or she can make recommendations (and implement changes in some circumstances) that do not require re-litigating parenting disputes with the attendant emotional and literal costs that accompany "fighting" it out in court.

Mrs. G also displayed several characteristics of mothers who attempt to alienate the children from their father (e.g., refusing to allow access unless her demands were met; "forbidding" the children to discuss anything about her with their father; making disparaging and destructive remarks to the children about their dad, including wishing he were dead). This is where the PC can be of tremendous value. A PC would have either helped the parents craft a time-sharing arrangement and insisted on adherence to it or recommended to the court that a more structured parenting plan was in order. Given the high-conflict nature of the G family, entering into a postdivorce phase with no structure (such as a parenting plan) and no oversight was bound to result in disastrous family circumstances.

Researchers looking at children's outcomes have also emphasized the importance of quality relationships with a larger support network (Bauserman, 2002; Johnston, 1995; Pruett, Ebling, & Insabella, 2004; Pearson & Thoennes, 1990; Smyth, 2009) highlighting the need to maintain extended family and friendship relationships after the separation. Often, grandparents and other extended family members provide a much needed source of affection, stability, and predictability for the children at a time when their parents are struggling to adjust to their postdivorce living and emotional environment. The generational impact of a ruptured parent–child bond as a result of deliberate attempts to alienate the children from their parent (most often fathers) can also be seen in the Dedicated family. Dr. D had grown up in a close-knit family with parents who very much wanted to be a part of their grandchildren's lives and to celebrate their heritage (Jewish) and religious celebrations to reinforce the family unity and sense of history. Unfortunately, the D children did not have the opportunity to experience the joys and benefits that an extended, loving family with a rich cultural heritage can share and transmit. The solidarity across generations (Carter & McHale, 2012) and family unity becomes more challenging with the ever evolving changes in family definition and rising divorce rates. Children thrive when they have the opportunity to grow up in an environment that is loving, consistent, and predictable.

While many states do not recognize grandparents as having legal "rights" to visitation with their grandchildren, the PC would have educated Mrs. D about the damage she was doing to her children by denying them access to their grandparents and her "gatekeeping" behaviors. The PC would have intervened to ensure the father's access to the children and reported violations of the court order (e.g., mother's refusal to honor the time-sharing arrangements) directly to the court. Perhaps with the support and encouragement of the PC, Dr. D may have continued to fight for his rights as a father to parent his children. He did not give up easily (as evidenced by returning to court twice to enforce his joint custody status), but he also did not have the backing of an independent professional with child development expertise who had authority granted by the court to monitor and ensure the children's best interests, as would have been the case had a PC been appointed.

In most of the families described here, the parents would have benefitted from an established communication protocol. Often parents going through separation or divorce are so caught up in hurt, blame, fear, anger, and confusion that their efforts to communicate are ineffective. It is essential that parents, particularly those who are parenting in two separate households, exchange relevant, factual information about the children to aid in their care and to provide consistency and a sense of security. If parents are unable to manage effective communication without outside intervention, then the PC is responsible for establishing a structure for such communication. If necessary, the PC may serve as the conduit of information until such time as the parents are able to manage more consistent and effective communication about the children on their own. *This type of arrangement prohibits all direct communication between the parents (phone, e-mail, text, Facebook, etc.) and requires each parent to follow communication guidelines as established by the PC. These guidelines usually include some "rules" such as no provocative or inflammatory comments, no unsolicited editorial feedback, and no blaming or accusing along with a model of professional, cordial, factual communication.*

Using this structured communication protocol, parents *must send their communications to the PC who*, in turn, *reviews it for adherence to the "rules" before it is forwarded to the other parent.* The same goes for the response from the recipient. PCs may need to help parents disengage from their conflict in this manner for some time until they can learn to follow the rules and guidelines. Once they are able to do so, then the parents may communicate with each other directly but must copy the PC on all communications to ensure they are adhering to the guidelines. The goal is for parents to get to the point where no oversight of their communication is needed. Parents are incentivized to follow the guidelines since they are charged a fee for the PC's time to review, edit, and respond to any inappropriate communications. It is only the violating parent who is charged, so each parent is in control of their own behavior and the fees associated with "breaking the rules."

Summary

Parenting coordination was designed to meet family courts' and parents' needs for consultation and directives from professionals specifically trained to assist with questions regarding parenting plan components and time-sharing arrangements that serve children's interests both during and after divorce. Parenting coordination services should be considered whenever parents have difficulty cooperating and collaborating around the care of their children (Carter, 2011; Kirkland & Sullivan, 2008).

Psychologists' understanding of human interactions and their knowledge of how individuals function within systems allows for interventions not typically afforded by the family court system. Mental health training helps the PC to understand behaviors and reactions of adults and children when the family system is in flux and under stress. Other skills and experience that psychologists contribute to the PC process include understanding the dynamics of divorce, effective parenting, the impact of conflict on child development and adjustment, personality disorders, and ethical behavior. Psychologists also bring their clinical experience in complex case management, establishing appropriate boundaries with clients, and maintaining objectivity in their work to the role of PC. Attorney PCs bring other skills which they should enrich with courses in personality dynamics, child development, and family systems.

Interventions utilized in PC are founded in the social science literature on the adverse impact on children of exposure to parental conflict, adjustment of children and parents after divorce, efficacy of parenting education programs, and mediation (Carter et al., 2012). Proponents of PC programs believe they can mitigate the negative effects of separation and divorce on parent and child well-being; however, given the nascence of the approach, longitudinal research is just at the beginning stages.

PC has now become well established and continues to evolve as a highly regarded, child-focused ADR process in response to a growing demand for services outside the litigation arena that help parents, children, and the court address family needs in a cost-effective and constructive manner. Had PC been available to the families highlighted in this book, many of the ill effects of prolonged parental conflict, poor parenting skills, lack of a structured parenting plans, inadequate time-sharing, and ineffective decision-making arrangements may have been avoided.

References

American Psychological Association. (2012). Guidelines for the practice of parenting coordination. *American Psychologist, 67*(1), 63–71.

Association of Family & Conciliation Courts. (2005). Guidelines for parenting coordination – AFCC task force on parenting coordination. Retrieved from www.afccnet.org.

Amato, P. R. (2000). The consequences of divorce for adults and children. *Journal of Marriage and Family, 62*, 1269–1287.

Amato, P. R. (2003). Reconciling divergent perspectives: Judith Wallerstein, quantitative family research, and children of divorce. *Family Relations, 53*, 332–339.

Amato, P. R., & Gilbreth, J. G. (1999). Nonresidential fathers and children's well-being: A meta-analysis. *Journal of Marriage and the Family, 61*, 557–573.

Amato, P. R. & Keith, B. (1991). Parental divorce and the well-being of children: a meta-analysis, *Journal of Marriage and the Family*, 53(1), 26–46

Bauserman, R. (2002). Child adjustment in joint-custody versus sole-custody arrangements: A meta-analysis review. *Journal of Family Psychology, 16*(1), 91–102.

Buchanan, C. M., Maccoby, E., & Dornbusch, S. M. (1991). Caught between parents; Adolescents' experience in divorced homes. *Child Development, 62*, 1008–1029.

Carter, D. K. (2011). *Parenting coordination: A practical guide for family law professionals.* New York: Springer.

Carter, D. K., & Harari, C. (2008). Addressing myths, misunderstandings, and dilemmas about parenting coordination. *The Commentator*, Vol. XXIII, No. 1, Family Law Section of The Florida Bar.

Carter, D. K., & McHale, J. (2012). Protecting generational solidarities through interventions with divorcing families: Theory, research and practice. *International Society of Family Law.* Lyon, France

Emery, R. E. (1999). Post-divorce family life for children: An overview of research and some implications for policy. In P. Amato & R. Thompson (Eds.), *The post-divorce family* (pp. 3–28). Thousand Oaks, CA: Sage.

Emery, R. E. (2004). *The truth about children and divorce: Dealing with the emotions so you and your child can thrive.* New York: Viking Penguin.

Fabricius, W., & Hall, J. (2000). Young adults' perspectives on divorce: Living arrangements. *Family Court Review, 38*(4), 446–461.

Hetherington, E. M. (1999). *Coping with divorce, single parenting, and remarriage.* Mahwah, NJ: Lawrence Erlbaum.

Hetherington, E. M., & Kelly, J. (2002). *For better or for worse: Divorce reconsidered.* New York: W. W. Norton.

Johnston, J. R. (1994). The future of children. *Children and Divorce, 4*(1) Spring, 165–182.

Johnston, J. R. (1995). Research update: Children's adjustment in sole custody compared to joint custody families and principles for custody decision making. *Family and Conciliation Courts Review, 33*, 415–425.

Kelly, J. (2002). Psychological and legal interventions for parents and children in custody and access disputes: Current research and practice. *Virginia Journal of Social Policy and Law, 10*(1), 129–163.

Kelly, J. B. (2006). Children's living arrangements following separation and divorce: Insights from empirical and clinical research. *Family Process, 46*(1), 35–52.

Kelly, J. B., & Emery, R. E. (2003). Children's adjustment following divorce: Risk and resilience perspectives. *Family Relation, 52*(4), 352–362.

Kirkland, K., & Sullivan, M. (2008). Parenting coordination (PC) practice: A survey of experienced professionals. *Family Court Review, 46*, 622–636.

Kline, M., Tschann, J. M., Johnston, J. R., Wallerstein, J. R., & Wallerstein, J. (1989). Children's adjustment in joint and sole physical custody families. *Developmental Psychology, 23*, 430–438.

Maccoby, E., & Mnookin, H. (1992). *Dividing the child: Social and legal dilemmas of custody.* Cambridge, MA: Harvard University Press.

Margolin, G., Gordis, E. B., & John, R. S. (2001). Coparenting: A link between marital conflict and parenting in two-parent families. *Journal of Family Psychology, 15*(1), 3–21.

McHale, J., & Lindahl, K. (2011b). *Coparenting: A conceptual and clinical examination of family systems.* Washington, DC: American Psychological Association.

Mitcham-Smith, M., & Henry, W. J. (2007). High-conflict divorce solutions: Parenting coordination as in innovative co-parenting intervention. *The Family Journal: Counseling and Therapy for Couples and Families, 15*(4), 368–372.

Pearson, J., & Thoennes, N. (1990). Custody after divorce: Demographic and attitudinal patterns. *American Journal of Orthopsychiatry, 60*, 233–249.

Pruett, M. K., Williams, T. Y., Insabella, G., & Little, T. D. (2003). Family and legal indicators of child adjustment to divorce among families with young children. *Journal of Family Psychology, 17*(2), 169–180.

Pruett, M. K., & Donsky, T. (2011). Co-parenting outside the lines: When divorce changes who's an insider. In J. P. McHale & K. M. Lindahl (Eds.), *Co-parenting: A conceptual and clinical examination of family systems.* Washington, DC: American Psychological Association.

Pruett, M. K., Ebling, R., & Insabella, G. (2004). Parenting plans and visitation: Critical aspects of parenting plans for young children interjecting data into the debate about overnights. *Family Court Review, 42*, 39–59.

Pryor, J., & Rodgers, B. (2001). *Children in changing families: Life after parental separation.* Oxford: Blackwell.

Smyth, B. (2009). A five year retrospective of post-separation shared care research in Australia. *Journal of Family Studies, 15*, 36–59.

Part V: The Role of the Child Advocate

Lita Linzer Schwartz, Ph.D., ABPP

When parents decide to divorce, each of them has an attorney who is primarily concerned with his or her respective best interests in dissolving the marriage. However, in the event that the parents cannot come to a custody agreement, who is looking out for the children's respective best interests?

There are varying roles related to the children. Hopefully, the judge who is hearing the divorce suit will appoint someone to protect the children's rights and "to voice their interests and concerns at formal hearings" (Engel & Gould, 1992, p. 112). This is generally an attorney, appointed as a *guardian ad litem*. This individual will be asked to evaluate the child's abilities and needs and report these to the court, along with recommendations for custody, visitation, and any therapeutic needs. It is also a responsibility of the *guardian ad litem* to "Protect the children's financial interests with regard to support, visitation, health, education, and future needs" (Engel & Gould, p. 113). (A *guardian ad litem* may also be appointed for one or both of the parents if he or she is seen as inadequate to care for him- or herself.) Fees for the *guardian ad litem* are generally paid by one or both parents, depending on their ability to pay (presumably determined by the court).

In Florida's Twelfth Judicial Circuit, there is also a volunteer *guardian ad litem* program, where the volunteer *guardian* is responsible for advocating for the best interests of children, interviewing the parents and all others involved in a child's life, and making recommendations to the court (Guardian ad litem [GAL], n.d.). In Seattle, a Court Appointed Special Advocates program (CASA) was begun in 1977 which also uses volunteers as officers of the court to serve as advocates for children (Johnson & O'Sullivan, 2002). As of 2002, there were more than 900 such programs throughout the country with close to 50,000 volunteers, many of whom were pediatric nurses.

The Pennsylvania Bar Institute (PBI) introduced a training seminar program for child advocates in 1997 and has run such programs ever since (PBI, 1997). In another related area, the Bar Institute published a manual for attorneys representing children that include material related to the custody of children in domestic relations as well as other cases (PBI, 2006).

The child custody evaluator, preferably a child psychologist (APA, 2010), must be able to communicate effectively with children at their age level. "The purpose of the evaluation is to assist in determining the psychological best interests of the child" (APA, p. 864). As the second guideline to evaluation states, the "child's welfare is paramount" (APA, p. 864). The evaluator does not want to press the child into expressing a preference for one parent or the other, but rather would ask questions to gather factual information about which parent takes the child to school or the playground or sports activities, which one helps with homework, which one takes the child to the doctor or the dentist, and what activities and interests the child shares with each parent. The evaluator might also ask what problems the child anticipates if and when he/she lives with the mother or with the father. The evaluator may transmit the child's responses to the person who will be the child's advocate, or may end up serving as the advocate as well.

It should be noted that children are often witnesses to parental verbal aggression, physical or sexual abuse, and domestic violence, all of which occur in a number of the cases discussed below. Sometimes they may be direct or indirect victims of such negative behaviors. Whether they are witnesses to violence and/or abuse, or the direct victims of it, the effects on the children can be severe and may be long lasting (Teicher, Samson, Polcari, & McGreenery, 2006).

Consideration must also be given to the child's relationships with both maternal and paternal grandparents. In optimal situations, neither parent has attacked the other parent's relatives to the child. Indeed, truly concerned and wise parents may attempt to maintain at least a cordial relationship with their former in-laws for the benefit of the child. Again, this was not true in some of the cases included here (particularly Case 5, Mr. Reuben Guy; Case 6, Mr. Bill Brogan; Case 13, Dr. Unlucky).

Where one (or both) of the parents has had an extramarital affair during the marriage and prior to the divorce, and the child becomes aware of it, what is the effect on the child's opinion of and relations with the adulterous parent? With the other parent? Clearly, the reactions will vary with the age of the child, with what the non-adulterous parent has told the child, and even with what the adulterer may have told the child. If one or both parents remarry subsequent to the divorce, where does the child fit in the new family? If the stepparent has children, how does this child relate to him or her? Hopefully, the child is given permission to form an attachment to the new stepparent and is not convinced that bonding with that person will be a betrayal of them.

Yet another problem arises if primary custody is awarded to each parent for a year or two at a time. If they live in fairly close proximity to each other, the child may be able to continue in his/her school, maintaining the same friends, remaining engaged in the same activities without a problem. However, if the parents live at a distance from each other, whether the next town or across the country, these factors in the child's life will probably become negative rather than positive. Not only will the child's education be affected because each school has a different emphasis, thus placing the child at an academic disadvantage, but the friends who are familiar and would normally be supportive are not there. A helpful book for both parents is Marc Ackerman's "Does Wednesday mean Mom's house or Dad's?" (1997). One suggestion included in this book is for the parents to try to put themselves in their children's shoes in an effort to understand what the children's feelings are as the parents argue, threaten, cajole, and separate. It is urgent to keep in mind that children are people, not property, as was pointed out in an article about relocation by Rotman, Tompkins, Schwartz, and Samuels (2000). The child advocate's role is to emphasize developing a sensible and workable living arrangement that is best for the child or children (Schwartz, 1987).

Obviously, complications arise when there is more than one child in the same family. How old are the children? What is the nature of the sibling relationships? If one is essentially an infant or toddler, and the other siblings are all school age, does one of the older children take a special interest in helping to care for the youngest?

Should the siblings be separated in the primary custody arrangements? After all, the mother (if not alcoholic or otherwise a potentially "bad" mother) is usually given primary custody of a very young child, although that may not be the case with the older children. In general, the siblings should not be separated as they can and often do provide a mutual support system.

Some or all of these factors have to be considered in examining the cases presented in this book.

A Child Advocate in Action

It is appalling that in none of the cases discussed in Chapters 2, 3, 4, 5, 6, 7, 8, 9, 10, 11, 12, 13, and 14 did the children have an independent child advocate or a *guardian ad litem*. Each parent had an advocate (aka attorney) who argued for him or her, and the courts appear to have had their own predisposition in favor of primary or sole custody for the mother with financial support by the father, whether or not the mother was employed. This may vary to some degree from state to state. Thus, it is difficult to know how much a child advocate could have done. No one was available to help the children avoid their mothers' lies, to help them deal with the adultery of one or both parents, or to try to maintain positive relations with grandparents and other family members. Too often, as well, there was no effort to promote positive sibling relationships.

Let us consider the persona and role of the child's advocate for a moment. The advocate would most likely be appointed by the court, report to the court, and be paid by the court. Unless a volunteer, the advocate would presumably be paid his or her regular hourly fee, unless a flat fee is negotiated beforehand or has been established for this service within a specific jurisdiction. The American Academy of Forensic Psychologists recommended, in 2003, that one:

> Get a court order that specifically names you as the court-appointed evaluator. This is essential to gaining judicial immunity for your work. The order should at a minimum require cooperation of the parties with requests for records and other collateral data, should spell out who will pay you and when and (if possible), should designate the questions the court wants addressed. You may need to consult with counsel and/or the court to identify these questions. If the questions are impossible to resolve, negotiate them or reject the case.

In Case 1, for example, Dr. Blue Eyes was denied access to his children by their mothers, despite his efforts to be a good father. It is difficult to be a good father when one is denied visits for a variety of reasons concocted by the mothers. He was not able to develop a father–daughter relationship because of this, and it was not until his son reached age 18 that they developed a good relationship. A child advocate would have tried to rectify this situation many years earlier.

Divorced after 20 years of marriage, Reuben, now age 77 (Case 4), is a devoted and supportive father and grandfather. Ex-wife Estelle has "forbidden" the children to discuss anything about her with their father. He had tried to get her to go for marital therapy with him, but she refused, threw him out of their house, and has not spoken to him for more than 35 years. It is rather late now for a child advocate to speak to the grown children, but years ago an advocate might have spoken to them about the hostility prevalent in some divorces and tried to neutral- ize the effects.

In Case 5, a child advocate could have worked with the children to help them understand why divorces occur and what they entail. An advocate might also have been able to restore the father's parents' contacts with their grandchildren. Whether the child advocate could have influenced the court with respect to the mother's seizure of all assets and her eviction of her husband is a good question. Might the child advocate have obtained evidence of the mother's theft (if this was in the advo- cate's purview)? Might the child advocate have had the joint custody ruling enforced sooner?

Married at age 22, BB (Case 6) remained married for 26 years, although his love for his wife had begun to fade. The family went for a six-month cruise, but in living together in a confined space, the negative aspects of the marriage were exacerbated, and he then filed for divorce. His wife not only threw out all his belongings but also told the children lies about him and denigrated him. Whether a child advocate could have reduced some of the resulting turmoil and animosity is unknown. He attempted, after marrying a psychotherapist, to become reconciled with his children by sending them a "letter of reconciliation" in which he tried to undo some of the damage, but to what degree it was effective is also unknown.

Terry's wife not only did not like being a mother (Case 7), but she also was not a faithful wife. Given joint and equal custody, *her* response was to leave their daugh- ter with a nanny. She changed nannies often, which was not in the child's best inter- ests. A child advocate is needed here primarily to provide support, in addition to the father's, for the girl, and to serve as an independent "ear" to listen (and then respond) to the girl's questions, doubts, and needs for reassurance.

In Case 8, the mother obviously could not provide good parenting or be a good model for the children to emulate. Although dad eventually won legal custody, the children were still moving from one home to the other, and not having a very good experience while at their mother's home. The child advocate could work with and for the children to rectify this arrangement in court and in their lives. Perhaps she might have sought a ruling that the children have limited, and supervised, visits with the mother.

It is difficult to say how much a child advocate might have done in Case 9 other than explain some facets of divorce and remarriage situations, and reassure the chil- dren of their dad's love, even if he has remarried. His second wife, Nancy, could use some counseling, too, about handling her situation with more equanimity as she surely knew of the girls' existence before marrying Ari, and of his devotion to them.

As in so many locations where maternal custody is favored, despite her weak- nesses, the children in Case 10 were wrongfully deprived of contact with their father. A child advocate, fully informed about both parents' behaviors, might have been able to prevent or undo some of the damage caused by the mother and could have reassured the children that their father loved them and wanted to be with them (despite the mother's lies). As it was, he apparently was able to communicate his affection and, as a result, has gone on to have good relations with his sons, their spouses, and their children.

Reggie, in Case 11, might have profited from a child advocate's intervention – fewer problems with his mother (was religion a factor in this case?), and possibly earlier attention to assess and reduce his learning problems. As in some of the other cases included here, having a father who was frequently absent due to his business travel obligations contributed to Reggie's problems. When Hy changed jobs (which several of the other dads also did), he was better able to be available and to demonstrate his affection for Reggie.

A child advocate might have helped daughter Sue Ellen in Case 12, in a number of ways: to care for her younger siblings, persuaded Peggy to assume more of her maternal responsibilities and also not to disrupt Dr. Zack's visiting schedule. Whether the child advocate could have helped the younger children to deal with their mother's weaknesses is debatable, but he or she could have tried. It is interesting that the children had no problem with Dr. Zack revealing that he was gay, and no problem accepting his partner.

In the case of Dr. Scott Unlucky (Case 13), he was unlucky, indeed. As in some of the other cases, he had to deal with his wife's lies to their children and her mother's extreme hostility. How much a child advocate could have helped the children is a matter of conjecture, although a child advocate might have been able to communicate their father's love, even though, given who was raising them, they might not have believed the advocate. The advocate might also have been able raise questions, in court, about his wife's allegations. The whole negative picture here has meant that Dr. Unlucky has had no contact with his children for more than 25 years. At this point in time, it is doubtful that a child advocate could undo any of the damage. As a therapist himself, he recognizes that he is attempting to deal with a very sad, and very difficult, situation.

In summary, it can be seen that a child advocate appointed early in the marital dissolution process could have helped many of the children in these families that were splitting asunder to deal more effectively with the trauma being generated. However, this is unlikely to have occurred early enough in most of the cases, as the parents typically were telling lies, having affairs, preventing positive father–child visits, and generating other problems with each other for some time (months, years) before one or the other sought a divorce and thus the needs of the children for an advocate might have come to the attention of a judge. The children would not have known to seek an advocate themselves because they probably would not have been aware of the existence of such a person, and if they were would have been unlikely to want to reveal family dysfunction. And the grandparents might have been equally reluctant to do so for fear that they would lose connections with their grandchildren.

The challenge is to be able to utilize the services of well-trained advocates early in the divorce process to help minimize the damage to everyone, smooth the transitions, and lead to a more positive aftermath for all.

References

Ackerman, M. J. (1997). *Does Wednesday mean mom's house or dad's?* New York: Wiley.
American Psychological Association. (2010, December). Guidelines for child custody evaluations in family law proceedings. *American Psychologist, 65*(9), 863–867.
Engel, M. L., & Gould, D. D. (1992). *The divorce decisions workbook: A planning and action guide*. New York: McGraw-Hill.
Guardian ad Litem Program (n.d.). Florida: Twelfth Judicial Circuit.
Johnson, M. O., & Sullivan, A. L. (2002). The advocate: Children and the courts: Advocacy roles for pediatric nurses. *Journal for Specialists in Pediatric Nursing, 7*(4), 171–174.
Pennsylvania Bar Institute. (1997). *The child advocate's training seminar*. Mechanicsburg, PA: Pennsylvania Bar Institute.
Pennsylvania Bar Institute. (2006). *How to handle a child abuse case: A manual for attorneys representing children*. Mechanicsburg, PA: Pennsylvania Bar Institute.
Rotman, A. D., Tompkins, R., Schwartz, L. L., & Samuels, M. D. (2000). Reconciling parents' and children's interests in relocation: In whose best interest? *Family and Conciliation Courts, Review, 38*, 341–367.
Schwartz, L. L. (1987). Enabling children of divorce to win. *Family and Conciliation Courts Review, 32*, 72–83.
Teicher, M. H., Samson, J. A., Polcari, A., & McGreenery, C. E. (2006). Sticks, stones, and hurtful words: Relative effects of various forms of childhood maltreatment. *American Journal of Psychiatry, 163*, 993–1000.

Chapter 17
Why Can Some Individuals Share Their Children, While Others Cannot, or Will Not? Is Personality a Major Key?

Personality Patterns

Neither the large body of psychological nor legal publications about divorce have paid a great deal of attention to the personality patterns of the parties involved in separation and divorce. The emphasis is most often on the legal issues to be decided, the essential actions that need to be taken by each of the parties involved (see Appendix 2 – Model of Stages in the Divorce Process), and what each party wants regarding distribution of assets and child custody arrangements. Much less attention has been paid to the personalities, character, or behavior of the partners during their marriage as well as pre-, during, and postdivorce. When the personality variables are not considered, one's understanding of the process is often shallow, circumscribed, stereotyped, and fallacious. This applies to the understanding of those drawn into the divorce process itself – that is, the entire bevy of professionals involved including but not limited to the lawyers, judges, child custody evaluators, guardian ad litem, mediators, therapists, advocates, parenting coordinators and collaborative divorce specialists, as well as extended family members and friends.

Portrait of Many of the Women

The men in the study who were not psychologists, psychiatrists, or other kinds of physicians who had difficult divorces all described their ex-wives in remarkably similar ways. They said the women could be very "*charming*," and they often considered them quite delightfully so at the beginning of the relationship. Over time, the charm seemed to be superficial and shallow, to be a quality that could be "turned on" when the woman wanted to entice her husband or someone else into doing her bidding. The charm was not part of her essence, and she could and would quickly flip from being charming and beguiling to being nasty and hostile when she did not get her way. Most of these women were perceived as self-centered and selfish.

F.W. Kaslow, *Divorced Fathers and Their Families: Legal, Economic, and Emotional Dilemmas*, DOI 10.1007/978-1-4614-5535-6_17,
© Springer Science+Business Media New York 2013

Several conveyed that joy for their former partner was making someone else suffer and that she was quite proficient at keeping them "off balance."

Another adjective frequently used to depict the ex-wives was *manipulative*. She would go beyond attempts at reasonableness and persuasion to get her point across and get her way by *plotting, deceiving,* and *misrepresenting* the facts and outright *lying,* exploding in outbursts of rage, or "pushing all the buttons" she knew would upset her husband. Each of the men found it was hard to live with someone like this since if one does not think in nefarious ways, they are ill prepared to anticipate what someone who does will scheme to do next. They are frequently surprised and unnerved by what they hear, see, or find out. And these particular adult women's volatile temper outbursts frightened their children and left them feeling helpless and unable to cope with their mother's sudden and capricious displays.

They perceived their wives as *sulky, disgruntled, angry,* and *combative* – *complaining* that the *husband* was too busy working and *did not pay enough attention to them*. Although all of the wives wanted the husbands to be excellent financial providers, they were not willing to have the husband invest the enormous amount of time and energy necessary in the early and middle years of marriage to build and sustain a lucrative client-, patient-, or customer-centered career/profession/business. They wanted the husband more available to meet their needs and be a frequent playmate. This left him caught in a classic double bind – whichever choice he made was unsatisfactory to her (Watzlawick, 1963). There was little desire on the part of most of their wives to build their own careers, engage in meaningful philanthropic or vocational activities, etc. *He* was to imbue her life with meaning and value and provide for all of her financial needs or wants.

The women, separately and as an aggregate, allegedly engaged in *turning people against one another* – the children against their father, their husband against his or her parents, or both – perhaps only to reverse this later, and, subsequently, friends against her ex-spouse with statements like "if you are really *my* friend, you won't stay friends with him. That would be disloyal to me." This is a technique known as *splitting,* and many of the ex-wives of the respondents in this study, as well as Mrs. Collette, the woman described in one of the cases from the K files, were masters of this technique. This is a ploy frequently engaged in by individuals diagnosed with a borderline personality disorder and goes along with many of the behavioral traits described above (American Psychiatric Association [APA], 2000).

All of the men alluded to the fact that when anything went wrong in their marriage or family, they were to *blame*. There rarely was a rational discussion of what went awry. He was blamed both for what he did not do that she wanted and what he did do that she thought was wrong. Somehow, it always turned out to be *his fault* (Lachkar, 1992). Nothing he did pleased her for long, and it was *never enough*. Her needs, often seemed *insatiable,* and her ability to engage in *projecting* the blame and *not taking responsibility* for her part in shaping their everyday lives were overwhelming. Projecting of blame and chronic insatiability or emptiness also typify individuals with certain personality disorders, particularly those who are borderline and/or narcissistic (Kernberg, 1975; Linehan 1993); Solomon, 1996) or histrionic (Nichols, 1996).

Some of the wives became *angry, enraged,* or *irate* when they did not get their way, and *life with them was frequently chaotic.* These husbands described being around them as feeling like *"I'm always walking on eggs"* lest "I do or say the wrong thing" (Mason & Kreger, 2010; Quinn, 2008). Others had to contend with dramatic *outbursts of tears,* instead of with *screaming.* Many had been particularly appalled when their children were subjected to such *displays* and so had done their best to avert such scenes by "giving in" and not attempting to engage in joint problem solving. But brushing important matters off and capitulating over and over out of fear of an outburst had cost them dearly in terms of clarity of thought, self-respect, and self-esteem. They also came to abhor modeling for their children that avoidance or giving in to their mom was the best way to manage her emotional liability and get along with her. These descriptions are congruent with those often given for individuals with histrionic personality disorders (Millon & Grossman, 2007) who often exhibit poor impulse control.

Seven of the 13 wives of the men interviewed were (known to have been) involved in extramarital affairs, as was Mrs. Collette in the case from the K files (Brown, 1991; Glass & Wright, 1996). Along with *outright lying,* there were other evidences of lack of candor, integrity, and trustworthiness in their behavior (as there was in the K file case of the man who sequestered funds offshore before filing for divorce – see Chapter 15). Clearly there are various kinds of infidelities perpetrated by "disturbed" and "disturbing" spouses.

Thus, what emerged were a *cluster of common personality factors and behavioral traits,* albeit described differently in lay terms by the non-psychologist/psychiatrist/physician respondents and in diagnostic terminology by those trained in the behavioral and mental health sciences. As indicated above, the women as described by their former husbands *seem* to fall in the category of people who exhibit personality disorders – mostly of the borderline spectra (APA 2004) – which Millon (2011) now subsumes under unstable styles because they frequently are "emotionally dysfunctional and maladaptively ambivalent". "Borderlines" seem "unable to take a consistent, neutral, or balanced position" between polar opposites such as dejection and euphoria (Millon, p. 890). In addition, they were able to create a distorted sense of normalcy until the man came to accept that life on a roller coaster was what was normal. Some of the wives were described in ways that place them more in the narcissistic, histrionic, dependent, or antisocial categories. Most apparently lacked concern for and empathy with how others were impacted by their moods, statements, and actions.

Reciprocal Portrait of the Kinds of Men Who Were Attracted to Many of Them

One might ponder what originally attracted many of these men to these specific wives. Given the holistic, integrative family systems approach that undergirds this book, it is vital to try to extrapolate this. Many of the women were portrayed as charming and attractive, fun loving, popular, and good company. This combination of factors made them appealing and desirable, and the men considered themselves lucky to have attracted such a person. *Some of the men did not look much deeper.* They wanted a personable, charming, and likeable partner who was a good "playmate" and appeared to be understanding and supportive. Prior to marriage, the couples often did not discuss issues revolving around finances; whether the wife wanted to work and, if so, for how long; or their thoughts and feelings about motherhood and parenthood. Both just assumed their views and goals were similar and they would work out problems as they arose. Almost all of the men mentioned having come from families of origin in which they were taught strong family values, to be devoted and loyal to their parents and later to their spouses, and to be hardworking and good providers, as well as caretakers. They were naïve, optimistic, and "fell very much in love."

As is (almost) always the case, one's choice of partner is multi-determined, and some of the predisposing variables are unconscious when one "falls in love." Most of the ex-husbands interviewed thought their beloved was "the love of my life" – they considered themselves to be in a passionate, enduring love story that would last "'til death do us part." The choice of a partner is not a mistake at the time it is made – based on a heart and soul connection and physical attraction. But over time as each one realizes the actual partner is not the idealized partner they had believed him or her to be, the disillusionment and disgruntlement set in, and the dreams of happily ever after crumble. This is the scenario that got played out in the majority of the cases contained in this volume. (This is part of stage I – the emotional divorce – see Appendix 1 on the Stages of Divorce.)

In *Crazy Love*, Johnson and Murray (2007) discuss how to understand "weird" partners and why some people are attracted to someone with a personality disorder (also see Nichols, 1996; Solomon, 1996). Among other variables included is the potential partner's appearance or behavior which is so beguiling (as stated earlier) that it overshadows numerous danger signs, such as the person's intensity, risk-taking behavior, and/or "smooth talk" which was compellingly attractive, and that they *may have had some qualities the potential partner recognized he or she lacked* (pp. 17–18). All of these factors played a part in some of the 13 cases. These authors provide memorable and picturesque terms applicable to the kind of personality disorders we found most often in the 13 case interviews and the cases drawn from the K files.

The Stormy Partner – The Borderline Personality
The Theatrical Partner – The Histrionic Personality
The Self-absorbed Partner – The Narcissistic Personality
The Sticky Partner – The Dependent Personality
The Rigid Partner – The Obsessive–Compulsive Personality
Hopefully, these phrases further illuminate this discussion. (p. viii)

Several of the husbands emphasized how indulged and spoiled their ex-wives had been by their parents and that they expected to continue to be so by their husbands – who had thought she would outgrow this sense of entitlement. This type of individual wants immediate gratification and does not want to wait to acquire possessions or delay expensive vacations. The men recognized too late how unrealistic their assumption was. They felt underappreciated for who they were and what they gave and did. Many of these young, naïve, straightforward, and trusting men were very much in love, happy with their choice, and eager to be married. They did not have much of an inkling of the turbulence that lay ahead nor, in several of the cases, particularly Case 11, Mr. Hy Hopes, and Case 13, Dr. Unlucky, of the over-involved role their in-laws would play in their marriages.

Reflections and Summation

Whether the portraits of the ex-partners were painted in technical terminology by the medical and psychological professionals in the study or by those not immersed in the world of personality diagnosis who used everyday language, the profiles were remarkably similar. They also are congruent to the personality images that emerged in the K file cases. Perhaps these data may be one of the most important contributions this book makes in (1) generating future research on the topic of how and which personality factors and couple combinations may be precipitants of divorce; (2) guiding people not to choose a life partner characterized by these types of personality constellations because "what you see and pick is what you get" and to realize love alone is not enough to bring about deep, lasting commitment and personality change that is difficult to achieve without excellent therapy geared to bringing this about with the clients' consent and cooperation (Johnson & Greenman, 2006; Linehan, 1992; Millon & Grossman, 2007; Millon, 2011); and (3) professionals, including lawyers, judges, therapists, mediators, and child custody evaluators involved in working with clients/patients who exhibit moderate to severe personality disorders (this should be evaluated and diagnosed by someone well trained in testing and personality assessment), so they will be cognizant of the client's penchant for deception and manipulation in order that they are not "taken in" or "bamboozled" or do not believe a craftily constructed story, and do not fall into the trap of making less than the most optimal recommendations and decisions that will effect and affect everyone in the family system for many years to come.

It appears then that the personalities that are manifested in one's thought patterns and behaviors *are* key factors in the actions and transactions that occur prior to and during the divorce process and long into the aftermath of divorce sequelae. The more severe the personality disorder (Linehan, 1992), rooted partially in an insecure attachment style *that evolved in early childhood* (Bowlby, 1988), the more contentious the divorce is apt to be. Sharing children amiably, encouraging them to love and respect the other parent, and making the transitions from mom's house to dad's house easy and pleasant are rarely the goals of such unhappy, distressed, and dysfunctional individuals. An individual with a borderline and/or narcissistic, histrionic, or antisocial personality disorder is more likely to select the most garrulous, contentious, least settlement-oriented attorney he or she can find and to eschew the value of a less adversarial, more jointly acceptable solution-focused process like divorce mediation or collaborative divorce (Nurse & Thompson, 2009). If they do select one of the latter, it is likely to be extremely difficult for all parties involved in the process, and they may ultimately sabotage it, no matter how skillful the professionals are.

Clearly then, *personality is a key factor*. If one partner is determined to play an "I win/you lose game" and the children are considered part of the bounty to be won, then that party will not be willing to share the children peacefully and equitably (Pruett & Barker, 2009). "The best interest of the children" is just a slogan to be bantered around, and much in the custody, judicial, and legal system of divorce needs a major overhaul to really fulfill this promise and minimize the myriad hypocrisies that currently characterize aspects of the process.

Fortunately, in couples where neither wife nor husband has a moderate to severe personality disorder (see, e.g., Case 3, Dr. Perez) and they are considerate of one another, they usually can and do share the children equitably and rationally and can eventually have a relationship between themselves characterized by some equanimity, trust, and mutual consideration. And some couples can and do arrive at this kind of peaceful plateau by using some of the healing strategies discussed in Chapter 18. Such an arrangement minimizes the harmful impact of divorce on children and leaves them freer of fears and worries about what will happen when their parents are, or should be, at the same place and event at the same time or of having to listen to complaints and/or criticisms of one parent by the other. The children can look forward to their own graduations, weddings, birth of children, and other family events, sad as well as happy, without fearing that if they invite both their mom and dad and their parents' respective new partners – if they have them – the occasion will be uncomfortable or fraught with stress. Instead of marginalizing some members (Hawthorne & Lennings, 2008), the postdivorce family can at times be inclusive and expansive.

References

American Psychiatric Association. (2000). *Diagnostic and statistical manual of mental disorders IV-TR*. Washington, DC: Author.

American Psychiatric Association. (2004). *Diagnostic and statistical manual of mental disorders* (4th ed.). Washington, DC: Author.

Bowlby, J. (1988). *A secure base: parent-child attachment and healthy human development*. New York: Basic Books.

Brown, E. M. (1991). *Patterns of infidelity and their treatment*. New York: Brunner/Mazel.

Glass, S., & Wright, T. (1996). Reconstructing marriages after the trauma of infidelity. In W. Halford & H. Markman (Eds.), *Clinical handbook of marriage and couples interventions* (pp. 471–507). Hoboken: Wiley.

Hawthorne, B., & Lennings, C. J. (2008). The marginalization of nonresident fathers. *Journal of Divorce and Remarriage, 49*(3/4), 191–209.

Johnson, S. M., & Greenman, P. S. (2006). The path to a secure bond: Emotionally focused couple therapy. *Journal of Clinical Psychology: In Session, 62*(5), 599–610.

Johnson, W. B., & Murray, K. (2007). *Crazy love*. Atascadero, CA: Impact Publishers.

Kernberg, O. (1975). *Borderline conditions and pathological narcissism*. New York: Jason Aronson.

Lachkar, J. (1992). *The narcissistic/borderline couple*. New York: Brunner/Mazel.

Linehan, M. M. (1992). Behavior therapy, dialectics, and the treatments of borderline personality disorder. In D. Silver & M. Rosenbluth (Eds.), *Handbook of borderline disorders* (pp. 415–434). Madison, CT: International Universities Press.

Linehan, M. M. (1993). *Cognitive-behavioral treatment of borderline personality disorders*. New York: Guilford Press.

Mason, P. T., & Kreger, R. (2010). *Stop walking on eggshells: Taking your life back when someone you care about has a borderline personality disorder* (2nd ed.). Oakland: New Harbinger Publications.

Millon, T. (2011). *Disorders of personality: Introducing a DSM/ICD spectrum from normal to abnormal* (3rd ed.). Hoboken, NJ: Wiley.

Millon, T., & Grossman, S. (2007). *Moderating severe personality disorders*. Hoboken, NJ: Wiley.

Nichols, W. (1996). Persons with antisocial and histrionic personality disorders in relationships. In F. W. Kaslow (Ed.), *Handbook of relational diagnosis and dysfunctional family patterns* (pp. 287–299). Hoboken: Wiley.

Nurse, A. R., & Thompson, P. (2009). Collaborative divorce: A family centered process. In J. H. Bray & M. Stanton (Eds.), *The Wiley-Blackwell handbook of family psychology* (pp. 475–486). NY: Wiley.

Pruett, M. K., & Barker, R. (2009). Children of divorce: New trends and ongoing dilemmas. In J. H. Bray & M. Stanton (Eds.), *The Wiley-Blackwell handbook of family psychology* (pp. 463–474). NY: Wiley.

Quinn, E. (2008). *Walking on eggshells*. Baltimore: Publish America.

Solomon, M. (1996). Understanding and treating couples with borderline disorders. In F. W. Kaslow (Ed.), *Handbook of relational diagnosis and dysfunctional family patterns* (pp. 251–269). New York: Wiley.

Watzlawick, P. (1963). A review of the double bind theory. *Family Process, 2*, 132–153.

Chapter 18
Harken All Professionals Involved in the Tragedy of Divorce! The Urgency of Humanizing the Legal, Judicial, and Psychological Aspects of Divorce

First, to the professionals of all disciplines and theoretical persuasions, *DO NOT BE TAKEN IN BY THE GAMES*. As Chapter 15 reveals, many of those who are divorcing and divorced are masterful in the art of deception and do so very cunningly. Although all of the cases used here (except the one about a male counterpart from the K files) depict women who are skilled manipulators, many men are also well schooled in and use the arts of chicanery and connivery. Professionals need to recognize what their clients are doing and not collude with them *if* they truly are interested in seeking justice and seeing that *the best interests of the children are met*.

Second, to obtain an accurate, objective psychological profile of all individuals in the divorcing family, the best method is to have a standardized, validated battery of psychological tests administered and scored by an *impartial, well-trained, doctoral-level psychologist who is not already involved in the case in any capacity*. Psychological tests are the X-rays of the personality, intelligence, and cognitive processes, just as CAT scans are the X-rays of the body. They reveal what is really there inside the mind and heart when properly interpreted! This produces much more reliable data than anyone's clinical impressions can yield – no matter how astute the clinician. Such evaluations should be conducted on the parents as well as the children in high-conflict cases. This type of family evaluation is described in Chapter 16 by Benjamin.

Third, it is important to bear in mind that divorce is radical heart surgery of the family and is very painful, and the scars take a long time to heal.

Aggregate advice to the various groups:

1. *Divorce therapists*
2. *Divorce mediators*

Although these were listed separately, most of the men pooled their answers for these two groups. They cautioned these professionals to tell their clients:

- Divorce is in itself a family tragedy. Focus on all members of family, not just the couple, including the extended family, and the likely impact of divorce on all. See if the couple is first willing to try to resolve differences and save the marriage, as divorce is so devastating, painful, and irreversible.

F.W. Kaslow, *Divorced Fathers and Their Families: Legal, Economic, and Emotional Dilemmas*, DOI 10.1007/978-1-4614-5535-6_18,
© Springer Science+Business Media New York 2013

- Do not be judgmental, and do not take sides, especially not prematurely.
- Listen carefully and fully before drawing any conclusions.
- If either partner wants reconciliation, see if that is possible before jumping on the divorce bandwagon of the other partner.
- Have a good grasp of the (Axis II) Personality Disorders (American Psychiatric Association [APA], 2000) and how they might affect the marital relationship, one's spouse, the divorce, and the children in any specific case. (This is explicated in Chapter 15.)
- Do not hold stereotypical views of men/women and fathers/mothers. See the people involved in each case as individuals, and evaluate them as to their child-rearing abilities, practices, and attitudes; their interests; and their relationships with their children.
- Remember both parents need to have big roles in their children's lives. Do not assist in pushing either one out of the picture.
- "Do not take someone's kids away from them." It just is not right! And it will cause serious negative repercussions.
- Many dads care as much about their children as the moms do. Many give much more than they are required to postdivorce, and "we" have been unfairly labeled as a group of "deadbeat dads." The vast majority of us "take our role and duty as dads seriously and love our kids immensely."
- A father's relationship with his children, including his daughters, can be as strong, significant, and essential as mom's, even though it may be very different.
- Avoid engaging in brainwashing or any form of parental alienation (Egizli, 2010). It is detrimental to everyone's emotional health and well-being and places children squarely in the middle of a loyalty battle, an untenable position (Byrne, 1989). Turning a child against a parent also turns a child against him or herself and contributes to more negative emotional and behavioral outcomes in these children across their life span (see, e.g., Chapter 13).
- If a parent is planning to "come out of the closet" as lesbian, gay, bisexual, or transgender (LGBT) at the same time they are getting the divorce, this may make it ultra-difficult for their spouse – who feels utterly deceived, betrayed, and foolish (yes, often they do not know or guess) – and for the children, who now have not just one, but two major life transitions to contend with and adjust to in their own family. Some discussion of timing for this revelation and consideration of the needs of "the others" may be called for. This might be particularly important in religiously fundamentalist and politically conservative communities as well as elsewhere where there is not a sizeable LGBT population.
- Do not be biased toward the woman and do not collude with her against her husband.
- Dads are people, too, with feelings and needs that should be respected and considered in deliberations. (Most) fathers are concerned about every aspect of their children and their lives and want the child to know this.
- Be impartial. Just because the mother is very possessive and overly protective about "my children," do not be fooled into thinking the father does not care and they are not "his children," too.

- Try to help partners resolve differences without resorting to aggressive, destructive, adversarial procedures. Let them know that on the battlefield of divorce, too often the children are used as the weapons. Simultaneously they are also the unwitting victims of the "shots" fired by the parents.
- Do not try to get a settlement agreement or cut a deal too quickly. Listen more so you can help tailor an agreement for "this family."

Tell parents to:

- Only tell the children what they must know to understand what is happening. Too much detail will overwhelm them.
- Not expect children to take care of them. Allow them *"to be kids."* "You are the parents."
- Give children permission to enjoy both mom's house *and* dad's house.
- Help them learn how to handle the different sets of rules and expectations at each house.
- Do all they can to make the transitioning back and forth from mom's house to dad's house pleasant and easy.
- Do not involve the children in the sessions, unless they are 16 years of age or older.

3. *Child Custody Evaluators*

- Go into the evaluation process without "preconceived" notions.
- Interview and assess both parents in the same way.
- Stress that the divorcing partners should be honest with the evaluator.
- Probe deeply into what you are being told. Do not be easily "duped" by mother's pathology and miss seeing if she is emotionally abusing children and/or parentifying one of them (also remember you have a duty to report to Child Protective Services if there is an allegation of abuse on the part of either parent).
- The evaluator must fully evaluate each parent in person, (see Chapter 16 – section on "Family Evaluation in Custody Litigation" by Benjamin) and not turn in a report on either adult based on what the other parent says or what the children convey – as they may have been coached. If you think these remarks are pertinent, they should be included in a separate section of the report, duly marked "husband or wife's comments, children's comments, etc.," and not be incorporated as data objectively derived from psychological tests, or from clinical in-office and in-home interviews conducted separately with each parent and with the child (or children).
- Listen carefully during the evaluation to each party involved.
- Testing, scoring, interviewing, and report writing should rigorously follow nationally accepted guidelines for child custody evaluations promulgated, field tested, and periodically revised by the American Psychological Association (APA, 2010) and/or the Association of Family and Conciliation Courts
- Identify any personality disorders in the parents, and note these and the potential implications of same as they apply in this case in the report.

- Be less maternal centric. Get to know each parent.
- "Fathers suffer broken dreams and broken hearts." Do not add to their heartbreak.
- Do not assume the woman is always the better provider of emotional care or more fit to be the main custodial parent.
- Take a long-term, systemic, life-cycle perspective that encompasses flexibility as children's and parents' developmental needs and abilities change over time when making your recommendations.
- Determine if parenting plan should include any recommendations about continuing contact with grandparents and other extended family members (Kaslow, 2007).
- Recommend a treatment plan for either or both parents and/or children, as you deem advisable in recommendation section of report.
- In making recommendations, be decisive and back them up with well-substantiated facts.
- Think outside the box, and do not feel obligated to use the standard agreement. Recommendations should be tailored to the specific family.

4. *Ex-wives*

- Live by the Golden Rule in the affirmative (do unto others as you would have them do unto you) and in the negative (do not unto others as you would not have them do unto you).
- Take a good, hard look at your part in the failure of the marriage; accept responsibility for your behavior and for perhaps not meeting his needs!
- Leave anger behind. Trust him to "do the right thing." You chose to marry him – he must have many good qualities. Do not deprive the children of knowing him.
- Fathers (both parents) are very important to their/your kids. You cannot cut them out of the children's lives or minimize their influence without causing the children (and the man) irreparable harm (Kaslow, 2000).
- *Child support is supposed to be used for the children.* (Not for the wife's needs – especially items like plastic surgery, cosmetic dental procedures, personal travel).
- No one enters marriage expecting it will fail. In marriage and afterward, do not expect to always get your way. "Your ex-spouse is not your enemy and should not be treated as if he is."
- Treat your ex like a friend. You will probably have to see him at children's events long into the future. Not to be pleasant, or at least civil, causes the children and everyone else discomfort and stress.
- Keep in mind what kind of parent *you* need to be, and trust him to do the same without trying to exercise control.
- Remember the child is and should be *part of two postdivorce families* (Wallerstein & Blakeslee, 1989).
- Do not undermine children's respect for dad and for his authority.
- Avoid locking horns with ex-spouse and being adversarial.

- Remember that marriage is a *sacred covenant*. It is a betrayal to spillover and malign your partner (or ex) to your friends *(both male and female)* and relatives about the intimate details (your version) of your marriage. Choose a therapist or a special trustworthy confidante to talk to, but not loads of people.
- *There is no free lunch.* No one is entitled to receive love, attention, money, and support and give little to nothing in return.
- Engaging in parental alienation is a destructive activity with many long-term negative sequelae (Vassiliou, 1998).
- Pots, pans, furniture, and pictures can be replaced. Angry scenes between parents, presence of police, and other horrific events when things are being moved out are traumatic for children and the departing partner and are difficult to erase.
- Be positive about going on with *your* life. Seize the challenges and opportunities.

5. *Children of Divorce*

    (a) From a professional:
    - Both parents love you very much, and they will do all they can to make everything okay. Do not despair.
    - Always remember the divorce was not your fault. You did not cause it. You are blameless.
    - Know your parents as you experience them – not as others tell you about them.
    - Think about whether your parent did what he or she believed was best for you (most of the time) rather than for himself or herself.
    - Reflect on whether one parent acts in ways that were intended to be mean and hurtful to the other, to interfere or not support your seeing the other.
    - Listen to your inner voice whenever possible. Try to find your truth. Speak up to both parents about your needs and ask for changes when you want them. Verbalize your feelings, both positive and negative, to your parents. Avoid being rude.
    - Disagreements and fighting are your parent's problem. Stay out of it. These are for them to resolve. Ask your parents not to put each other down. Tell them it is upsetting to you and does not make them appear considerate and kind, nor does it set a good example.
    - Honor and respect both parents. They gave you the gift of life and have invested a great deal of time and love in raising you.
    - Try not to be pulled into taking sides or choosing a favorite parent. Chances are you have only heard carefully selected parts of the story, and being told too much by either parent is crossing a boundary between parent and child.
    - Because your parents could not get along, it does not mean your father, who was the one told to move out (if he was), does not love you or wanted to be separated from you.

- Best parenting is knowing and being cared for by both parents on an ongoing basis.
- Divorce makes some children stronger. It forces them to learn how to cope with tragedies that happen and to learn young that life is not always smooth sailing. But some children fall apart. You have some part in the choice of how you handle it.

(b) From the parents to their children:

- Keep reassuring them "*I will never abandon you* – I will always be your dad (mom) and love you, and I/we will figure out how to resolve the problems."
- "We are so sorry we did not give you a better family life." "I will never stop loving you." "Try hard not to make the same mistakes."
- Parents make mistakes too, and I am so sorry for mine. I never intended to hurt you or make your life more difficult by getting divorced.

6. *Matrimonial Lawyers*

- "Do no harm." You can represent your client well without seeking to destroy the other party emotionally and financially.
- Do not manufacture additional problems. The parties have enough to contend with.
- Justice and integrity should be compatible for you and your client. Chicanery and half-truths are unjust.
- If your client is the rejected, hurt, or overwhelmed one, encourage him/her not to "give up" but to remain involved as children need to know both parents love them and care about them by seeing their continued engagement in their lives.
- Money is not the paramount or only issue. Civility and mutual respect in the postdivorce family are more important for your client's well-being than money is in the long run.
- Stop being the "worst of the worst" human beings and so "self-serving." Be less concerned about how much money you can make, and "consider what is best for the kids. That would be serving the cause of justice."
- Do not think you have to make every case into a major battle – fair settlements are better than destructive wars.
- Place your focus truly on the best interest of the child (or children); they are your unseen clients. Do not set them up to be *pawns* on the chessboard of divorce.
- "Don't make matters worse, or heat up the battle, by stirring up extra animosity" or instigating more issues to fight about. Indulge in less rhetoric and nastiness.
- Remain neutral and do not pass judgment. Remember, children's interests should be the focus of decisions, and that children need both parents.
- Do not use the woes of troubled people as an excuse to "keep ratcheting up bills" and dragging the case out needlessly. *Fulfill your commitment to pursue justice.* Stop battling to make more money out of each case while destroying lives.
- You can represent your client well without colluding with her to "grab all the man's resources."

- Do not advise the wife to issue a restraining order or call the police for the times he comes to get his belongings. Tell her to have a friend or two there so it can be peaceful and not upsetting.
- Write the MSA so that it finalizes the distribution of marital assets and so that no future renegotiation is permissible.
- Put an end to the possibility of returns to court to keep financial battles going, so each can get on with their own personal lives separately.
- How can you fight for a client you know who is mean, selfish, unfair, and vindictive? How can you live with yourself and sleep at night?
- Fathers should not have to give up everything – children, home, and assets – and then keep on giving and giving for years to the ex-wife. It is completely unfair and inhuman. Most men do not deserve such punitive treatment.
- If clients are abusing or otherwise harming their children, this is the province of a criminal attorney, and charges should be pressed. You should not collude to cover up these facts and subject the child to further harm, hiding behind attorney–client privilege. An endangered child should not be further endangered, and you have a "duty to protect" the child and to report to the designated authority.
- *Summation*
- Overall there was much bitterness and animosity expressed against many of the matrimonial attorneys encountered – primarily those utilized by their ex-wives. Yet, many of the men were also critical of harsh, duplicitous ideas recommended by their own lawyers. This is captured vividly in a quote from one of the respondents: "I would like to drown many of them. They are despicable." The men believe that lawyers should be more concerned about the emotional well-being of the family members during and postdivorce than about inciting greater antagonism between the splitting spouses, dragging the case out by filing multiple motions and counter motions, and needless other stalling techniques, making the process unnecessarily costly and charging outrageous fees for their services. The repetition, which appears in the various tidbits of advice, is to emphasize the depth of the wrath and desire for change in lawyer orientation.

7. *Family Court Judges*

- Insist on your court using excellent custody evaluators and/or guardian ad litem. Read their reports and recommendations thoroughly. Consider these in relation to what the lawyers, mediators, or others involved present, other information you have, and what you hear and observe *before* arriving at your decision.
- Remember the MSA is a "blueprint" for the rest of the lives of the members of this family. *What happens to them is now determined by you – a very weighty task.*
- Permit, even encourage, individually tailored custody/access/visitation plans for different children in same family, when necessary. For instance, a nursing infant may need much more time in mom's house and to have dad visit there. A physically or emotionally challenged child may not be able to go back and forth as often as his/her healthier siblings, and/or one parent may be much more skilled in caring for this child. There may be

compelling reasons why one child should be with the same gender or opposite gender parent. One plan does not fit all.

- Allow flexibility from the standard visitation plan, so each parent can continue to share activities with the child that they have in the past – that is, soccer, ballet, football, music lessons, and sports they coach. The plan should be modifiable easily when the child's activity time schedule is altered without parental battling.
- There are two sides to every story. Look at both sides, and see the whole picture.
- Listen to the male side more, and do not be swayed by a woman's tears or overly sad (often embroidered) story. Avoid the female bias that is so prevalent. Remember the judge's order exercises control over much of the rest of the persons' lives.
- Kids need to know their dads and to be with them. If not, they feel rejected, neglected, and abandoned.
- Permanent alimony is a permanent financial prison sentence for the payer and a free ticket to easy street to the recipient.
- Fathers have hearts and dreams too. Do not punish them unfairly by severely limiting their contact/access to the children. Consider their needs and wishes too.
- "Be ultra-fair. Remember everyone is nervous. Encourage all to be respectful of one another."
- Instruct parents to be as cooperative as possible. Make sure clients understand they are to *abide by* the agreement.
- Make sure there have been thorough and reliable psychological evaluations of *each* parent, when they are needed.
- The laws are based on too many generalities and platitudes. Individualize the cases and study the personalities of the partners.
- Understand the partners you are dealing with before making your decisions; they have permanent consequences for all involved.
- Be aware of your own self-righteousness and hypocrisy.
- If you or someone close to you is/was divorced, do not project your knowledge of and feelings about that divorce onto the couples whose future lives you shape in your courtroom. You are endowed with the sacred trust of judicial authority and must be objective and wise.
- Impose sanctions on clients who make false allegations.
- Make provisions for schedules to be reviewed by parents if need be with a mediator or therapist, as children's school and activity schedules change each year and as parents' work and other schedules are modified *without need for return to court*.
- "Parenting classes are a joke. They are too superficial and not useful." "All you have to do is sit there, and many don't even listen."

The American Bar Association (2008), Section of Family Law, has posted on its website (www.abanet.org/family) civility standards for family lawyers to be followed in their dealings with clients, opposing counsel and the court. They emphasize that *civility is an important obligation of the lawyer*. If lawyers and judges were to adhere to these civility standards promulgated by their own profession, they actually also would be following many of the "tips" so sagaciously recommended by the dads in this survey, plus those of this book's main author. These standards are totally concordant with the thesis and objectives of this book and its recommendations. We earnestly press the bar to enforce them. In the reality of everyday life with clients in therapy, mediation, etc., and with divorcing colleagues and friends and interactions with some matrimonial lawyers, we see and hear many violations of these civility standards.

Kruk has recently proffered *16 arguments in support of an equal parental responsibility (EPR) presumption* in contested child custody cases (Kruk, 2012) and provided empirically supported research data to undergird the validity of adopting this presumption as a viable alternative to sole custody. Increasingly others have also made a compelling case for EPR (Fabricius & Luecken, 2007; Firestone & Weinstein, 2004; Kelly, 2007; Millar, 2009), but as yet it does not appear that any jurisdiction has fully implemented the EPR presumption. Kruk hypothesizes (p. 48) that among the barriers to the passages of EPR, legislation and child custody law reform are the threat posed to some lawyers and judges of the curtailment of their power in the domain of child custody. Another barrier is the concept of "parental deficit" held by many divorce practitioners drawn from the several fields of practice, who believe one or both parents are deficient in parenting skills. Below some of Kruk's arguments are enumerated in paraphrased and combined form. These reemphasize and summarize some of the points that have been made earlier in this book.
Equal Parenting

- Preserves children's relationships with both parents.
- Maintains parents' relationships with their children.
- Decreases parental conflict and prevents family violence allegations, which, if made, should be investigated and, if need be, prosecuted in criminal court.
- Considers both children's and each parent's preferences and ideas (unscripted) about their needs and best interests.
- Reflects actual parent/child caregiving arrangements prior to divorce – there it was always co-parenting. It enhances the quality of relationships – neither parent is overwhelmed by sole parenting responsibility.
- Minimizes parental focus on "mathematizing time" and reduces additional litigation.
- Fosters incentive for parental negotiation, mediation, and developing parenting plans.
- Provides clear, consistent guidelines for judicial decision-making and facilitates enforcement of parenting orders.
- Diminishes risks and incidences of parental alienation (Clawar & Rivlin, 1991).

- Addresses social justice mandates pertaining to protection of children's rights as well as those regarding parental authority, responsibilities, equality, rights, and autonomy.

ON THE BASIS OF ALL OF OUR COMBINED CLINICAL EXPERIENCE, PLUS KNOWLEDGE GLEANED FROM OUR OWN RESEARCH AND STUDY OF THE LITERATURE WE TOO POSIT THAT EQUAL PARENTAL RESPONSIBILITY SHOULD BE THE USUAL PREFERENCE UNLESS THERE ARE CLEAR INDICATORS THAT ONE PARENT IS UNFIT, UNAVAILABLE, OR UNWILLING TO ASSUME THIS MAJOR AND CONTINUING RESPONSIBILITY.

Additional Comments

- Courts and legislatures should continue to rethink the entire divorce process and make it less adversarial, less cumbersome, and more humane, people centered, and open to being tailored to each divorcing family.
- Laws should be changed to really expedite serving the best interest of children, and often this will mean being less mother centric.
- Neither party should permit "failure" of marriage to undercut their self-esteem.
- Marriage should be viewed and lived as a *sacred covenant*. Marriage vows should be taken seriously and not be violated or quickly terminated.
- Adults make a long-term commitment, when they choose to have children, and should fulfill it. With this commitment, the children's needs "should" supersede the parents, at least until they are adults.
- Much of our society condones and accepts divorce and has made getting one too easy. It "should" become more difficult, less sanctioned, and less acceptable [unless there has been a physical, sexual, or emotional betrayal that cannot be rectified and forgiven or perpetration of egregious behaviors (like abuse) that go untreated and are repetitive].
- Permanent degradation and suffering are too high a price to pay after a spouse's rejection and nasty divorce.
- Sometimes the damage is irreparable between the husband and wife, and forgiveness is not possible. It is important, however, that each party comes to accept responsibility for their part in the demise of the marriage and stop projecting the blame.
- Children who have been abused by a father or mother need to be protected from that person. *If* the offending parent has been in treatment and the (*credible*) treating therapist writes a letter indicating he or she believes that child can be safely left with that parent, supervised visitation and ultimately unsupervised visitation may be resumed when reasonable certainly as to the child's safety is established. The child should be told to report any further difficulty to a guardian ad litem or another person designated by the court. Some people can and do go into recovery programs and/or treatment and change their attitudes and behaviors.

- A formerly abused child may later reconcile with that parent, posttreatment or rehabilitation, *and* after a sincere apology and efforts at healing the breach and extending forgiveness are made. *But* children who have been purposely poisoned emotionally and alienated against a targeted parent (in the cases presented here – fathers) rarely reconcile – unless and until the mother dies, or something momentous happens and they are shocked to learn the truth about having been brainwashed (Baker, 2007; Ben-Ami, 2011), or they decide on their own to turn to their father for financial help and reach out to him to seek a rapprochement, and he comes through, being the kind of father he always would have been if obstacles had not been erected.
- One respondent reported:

Going through the interview was gut-wrenching. It dredged up horribly painful memories I have tried to bury and caused me many sleepless nights wondering what happened to the son and daughter, whom I loved so much, who were torn from me 30 years ago. I agreed to participate because the fathers' side of story desperately needs to be told and I respect your ability to do it objectively, but for me it was very disruptive and disheartening to participate. The pain lingers for decades and can easily be ignited. No matter how much I have tried to let it go, it lurks in my memory and is just below the surface.

Recommendations for Less Adversarial Divorces and to Improve Postdivorce Healing and Well-Being

1. Couples should use a psychologist or other mental health *mediator* to facilitate reaching an agreement that the couple feel they authored and own, whenever possible. These professionals have a better understanding of the entire family system, the personalities of the people involved, and the emotional impact of what transpires than do most adversarial lawyers who favor litigation.

2. As in client-centered divorce mediation, collaborative divorce (Nurse & Thompson, 2009) is a cooperative process that encourages consideration of the needs and wishes of all family members. It is less combative and destructive than litigation. The parties often emerge satisfied with the MSA; they played a major role in crafting and are proud of their own ethical behavior. They have a smoother time sharing the children postdivorce, and relating to one another entails much less anger and desire for retribution.

3. Parents, siblings, and friends of divorcing parties can be most helpful by being accepting and noncritical and just "being there" – available if the person wants to talk, cry on someone's shoulder, complain, go out and have fun, or sit in silence. The divorce process is like a roller coaster, with rapid ups and downs that do not stabilize and come to a halt for several years, on the average. Criticism, negative comments, and unsolicited advice are rarely helpful or welcome. But these significant others should be there to offer optimistic thoughts and encouragement about the person's future without negating their need for a period of grief and mourning, sorrow, unhappiness, and bewilderment.

4. Family therapy postdivorce, with a knowledgeable and skilled family psychologist, family psychiatrist, or family therapist, can be valuable in fostering understanding of the new configurations and nuances of the two postdivorce families in which the children now live and may prove very beneficial. Sometimes different subsystems or pairings in the family, rather than everyone together, should be seen, such as all the children (the child subsystem), minus the parents. And when new stepparents are introduced, parents may need to be encouraged and assisted to give the children permission to accept and like the new stepparent without fear that their biological parent will feel jealous or deserted.

5. Do not be harsh on yourself. Initially accept and do what is most pressing that needs to be done each day. Later, consider your own reasons for the choice of that particular partner and why it did not work for you as well as pondering your role in the demise of the marriage. *Forgive yourself* and do no repeat any behaviors you regret. Choose someone quite different in the future – and for all the right reasons for you.

6. *Consider whether forgiveness between you and your ex-spouse might be possible*, and if so, seek ways to bring this about (Bonach, 2007; Hill, 2010). If it is feasible, it will reduce the anger and desire for recrimination (Jones, 2007) if you have that and facilitate your own *healing* (Ransley & Spy, 2004) and completion of State 7 in the Stages of Divorce – the Psychic Divorce (Appendix 2). It can also facilitate co-parenting postdivorce. However, sometimes forgiveness of the other is not possible, because the deception, betrayal, and hurt are too deep, and distancing emotionally so one is no longer vulnerable to the ex-spouse's machinations is a safer, healthier route to pursue.

7. Consider mindfulness meditation and whether it may enable you to focus more on the present and not keep going back to ruminate over the past. You cannot change the past but can change how you deal with it *now,* and this can help you in "letting go."

Postscript

It has become abundantly clear that a marriage in which there are children may be terminated, but the couple remain bound to one another across time and space as some form of co-parenting continues in their postdivorce family, "'til death do them part." In a reasonably civil and equitable divorce, where the best interest of the children was and genuinely remains the major concern, the healing and re-equilibration process for each adult, if they are reasonably healthy emotionally, takes two to five years to be accomplished – that is, both parties have journeyed into their new, separate lives and are finding them meaningful and gratifying. They share the children easily and can be together when necessary, without discomfort and animosity. Changes in schedules are handled as a routine matter without having to turn to attorneys or go back to court, and children have been encouraged to love, value, and respect both parents and their respective families. The children have access to, know, and are free to love both sets of grandparents. One or both parents may have remarried or decided to stay single because that suits them better for now. They are living in the present and are at least cautiously optimistic about the future. They are not stuck in ruminating about the past or seeking revenge. Perhaps their healing has been assisted and encouraged in therapy, as was true in a number of the cases presented earlier, and this helped the men gain needed insight and rebuild their shattered self-confidence and self-esteem.

A quote from a note I received some years ago from a former male client postdivorce illuminates this point more cogently than additional description can:

> Thanks for helping me believe in myself again! You have had a tremendous influence on my life. I know that I will face many challenges and disappointments in the future, but I know that I am equipped to handle them. In one session a long time ago (with [C] present) you observed, 'you are a very spirited guy – that optimism just keeps bubbling out.' I did not see that in myself. Noticing that characteristic, believing it, and developing it has changed my life. Thank you.

Some divorced individuals also feel the need for a modicum of affirmation of what was worthwhile in the marriage – to help them balance and let go of the deep hurt, grief, and sense of loss. After years of being told about this by male and female patients alike and finding that many people who were married in church or synagogue also want their divorce to be recognized and honored in their church or synagogue, I researched what was transpiring and found that only Orthodox Judaism has long had a formal ceremony of divorce. Of course, religions that do not accept divorce will not have such a ritual, and even those which tacitly accept it have done little to formalize one and offer it. Thus, I created a quasi-spiritual-therapeutic ceremony to fill the gap which I have utilized with patient/client families in my office since 1980 and have demonstrated at workshops on divorce around the world after finding it very effective. Other therapists have adapted it for use in their own practices, and some churches have made progress in incorporating divorce ceremonies as one of the kind of services they can offer. Basically it is a ceremony that reaches beyond the residual anger to affording the ex-partners the opportunity to express appreciation to their former spouse for what was good in the marriage, and especially for having had the children, and gives the children a chance to tell their parents what they need and want from them now (See Appendix 3 and do feel free to use it). It also provides them with the knowledge and/or reassurance that they were conceived or adopted because their parents were very much in love and wanted to have a child/children together. For the preponderance of children involved in such a ceremony, this has a resounding impact and stirs deep emotions of joy – to an inner refrain "I was wanted and treasured." Such a ceremony fosters forgiveness and healing for those who seek it, but is definitely not for everyone.

As has been indicated throughout this volume, in situations where there is or has been deceit; duplicity, deliberate chicanery, and lying; purposeful brainwashing and/or alienation of the children; horrific manipulation to achieve an unfair financial settlement and leave the husband in dire financial straits out of meanness, a desire to punish and/or destroy him; legal battles that erupt into all-out war, etc., it sometimes is hard to impossible to forgive the former partner. There may be a realization that the person continues to have an eruptive borderline personality disorder, or just be selfish and mean, and cannot be trusted. It seems worth reiterating that to forgive is then to set oneself up for future hurts and disappointments. In such cases it is best to limit contact to the minimum necessary, keep it focused on issues about the children, control one's emotional reactivity, and be dispassionate in one's interactions. As much as possible, one should go his or her separate way, extricate from the "clutches" of the former spouse, and maintain as much distance as feasible.

As we encounter older adolescent, young adult, and middle-age adult children of divorce and find they want to ascertain a clearer picture of their biological (or adoptive) and emotional heritage, we can help them re-sort the pieces of the jigsaw puzzle of their lives. We can guide them to reconnect with their parents differently – turning inward to search their own experiences and longings, so as to find *their own truth*, and outward – to ask their parents, grandparents, and other relatives their own questions about the fractured marriage, the severed relationships, and their childhood perceptions. In that way they can reformulate their life story or narrative more accurately and, when desired, make a bigger place in their lives and hearts for those divorced dads, like many who told their stories in the pages of this book, who felt discarded, disregarded, or unappreciated. It is often crucial to rebuild and cross these bridges for the dads and also for their children – so both can go on to trust enough to allow themselves to love and be loved by one another and ultimately to make a solid commitment to a partner of their own if that is what they choose to do and so that each can develop a *sense of coherence* (Antonovsky, 1987) in their search for meaning and self-actualization (Maslow, 1968) in their own lives.

Hopefully, in the next period of the history of divorce decision-making and into the future, as more jurisdictions move to a presumption of equal parental rights and responsibilities as the preferred option and alimony tailored to the specific situation, many of the horrific, costly, painful battles like those enumerated herein will be relics of an era no longer operative in the present.

References

American Bar Association Section on Family Law. (2008). *Civility standards.* Retrieved from www.abanet.org/family.

American Psychiatric Association. (2000). *Diagnostic and statistical manual of mental disorders-IV-TR.* Washington, DC: Author.

American Psychological Association. (2010). Guidelines for child custody evaluations in family law proceedings. *American Psychologist, 65*(9), 863–867.

Antonovsky, A. (1987). *Unraveling the mystery of health: How people manager stress and stay alive.* San Francisco: Jossey Boss.

Baker, A. L. (2007). *Adult Children of Parental Alienation Syndrome: Breaking the Ties That Bind.* New York: Norton.

Baker, A. L., & Ben-Ami, N. (2011). To turn a child against a parent is to turn a child against himself: The direct and indirect effect of exposure to parental alienation strategies on self-esteem and well being. *Journal of Divorce and Remarriage, 52*(5), 472–489.

Bonach, K. (2007). Forgiveness intervention model: Application to co-parenting post-divorce. *Journal of Divorce and Remarriage, 48*(1–2), 105–123.

Byrne, K. (1989). Brainwashing in custody cases: The parent alienation syndrome. *Australian Family Lawyer, 4*(3), 1–7.

Clawar, S. S., & Rivlin, B. V. (1991). *Children held hostage: Dealing with programmed and brainwashed children.* Chicago: American Bar Association Section of Family Law.

Egizli, J. (2010). *The look of love.* Dallas: Brown Books.

Fabricius, W. V., & Luecken, L. J. (2007). Post divorce living arrangements, parent conflict, and long term physical health correlates for children of divorce. *Journal of Family Psychology, 21*(2), 195–205.

Firestone, G., & Weinstein, J. (2004). In the best interests of children: A proposal to transform the adversarial system. *Family Court Review, 42*(2), 203–215.

Hill, E. W. (2010). Discovering forgiveness through empathy: Implications for couple and family therapy. *Journal of Family Therapy, 32*(2), 169–185.

Kaslow, F. W. (2000). Families experiencing divorce. In W. C. Nichols, M. A. Pace-Nichols, D. S. Bevcar, & A. Y. Napier (Eds.), *Handbook of family development and intervention* (pp. 341–368). Hoboken: Wiley.

Kaslow, F. W. (2007). Post divorce relatedness between parents: Their divorced sons, and their grandchildren: A pilot study. In C. A. Everett & R. E. Lee (Eds.), *When marriages fail: Systemic family therapy interventions and issues* (pp. 141–156). New York: Haworth Press.

Kelly, J. B. (2007). Children's living arrangements following separation and divorce: Insights from empirical and clinical research. *Family Process, 46*(1), 35–52.

Kruk, E. (2012). Arguments for an equal parental responsibility presumption in contested child custody. *American Journal of Family Therapy, 40*(1), 33–55.

Maslow, A. H. (1968). *Toward a psychology of being.* New York: Van Nostrand Reinhold.

Millar, P. (2009). *The best interests of children: An evidence-based approach.* Toronto, ON: University of Toronto Press.

Nurse, A. R., & Thompson, P. (2009). Collaborative divorce: A family centered process. In J. H. Bray & M. Stanton (Eds.), *The Wiley-Blackwell handbook of family psychology* (pp. 475–486). NY: Wiley.

Ransley, C., & Spy, T. (2004). *Forgiveness and the healing process: A central healing concern.* New York: Routledge.

Vassiliou, D. (1998). *Parental alienation syndrome: The lost parent's perspective.* Master thesis, McGill University, Department of Educational Psychology, Montreal, QE.

Wallerstein, J., & Blakeslee, S. (1989). *Second chances: Men, women and children a decade after divorce.* New York: Ticknor & Fields.

Appendix 1

Questionnaire Divorced Dads

Note: All responses are confidential. The material in this chapter about *your* story will be carefully camouflaged, so your real identity will be protected. Any person who is a participant in helping to tell the story of divorced dads' emotional experience will be offered the opportunity to read and comment on a draft of this chapter about his aspect of his life's ongoing narrative before the final draft is readied for submission to a publisher. All respondents will receive a complimentary copy of this book.

Some items on the questionnaire like highest level of education attained will also be used for summary and interpretive statements in the opening and closing chapters so that in addition to individual stories, a composite picture will be presented along with the tips recounted in the individual narratives on how to improve difficult relationships and reinstate disrupted ones.

F.W. Kaslow, *Divorced Fathers and Their Families: Legal, Economic, and Emotional Dilemmas,* DOI 10.1007/978-1-4614-5535-6,
© Springer Science+Business Media New York 2013

1. CONTACT INFORMATION				
Name:			D.O.B.	
Preferred address:				
City:		State:		Zip:
Phone contact:				
Work:		Home:		Mobile:
E-mail address:				

2. PERSONAL DATA				
Highest educational degree: (Check the one that applies)	High School	College	Graduate	Professional school
Your religion:	Your cultural or ethnic background:	Your ex-wife's religion:	Your ex-wife's cultural or ethnic background:	

3. YOUR MARRIAGE AND DIVORCE SAGA

A: Your age at time of your first marriage?_____ Date married_____ Date divorced_____ Date married_____ Date divorced_____ Current Age:	E: Who initiated idea of divorce? Why?	
B: How long married?		
C: Age at time of separation?	F: Who filed?	
D: Age at time of divorce?	G: Who moved out of marital home?	
Did either partner have an affair prior to the separation?	Yes:	No:
If yes, which one?	Husband:	Wife:
Was other partner aware of the affair?	Yes:	No:

If so, briefly describe the reaction of the partner:

Were the children aware of this extra marital activity?

If you have remarried, briefly describe relationship of your children to your subsequent wife (wives) and any part the mother of your children played in the nature of the relationship, as you perceive it.

Describe how you felt emotionally about the divorce. Was there anything you would have like to have done at the following time intervals?

A) Pre-divorce – when you realized divorce was going to happen?

B) During divorce and first year after post divorce

C) What were your main emotions and thoughts re the divorce and children after the first year post divorce? Where did you live? How long did it take for you to feel reasonably settled in a "home" again?

4. CHILDREN			
How many children did you have together?			
Their ages at time of divorce?	1)	2)	3)	4)

Where there any stepchildren?	Whose children? Gender?	Husband	Wife
Ages at the time of new marriage?	1)	2)	3)	4)

When you made a custody and visitation plan, were you satisfied with the arrangement? If not, what would you have preferred?

Legal provisions as to time at each home	Mother	Father

How did children react to divorce?

To one parent moving out?

To living at two homes?

To being part of two families post divorce?

5. FINANCIAL ARRANGEMENTS	
Child support arrangement:	
Payer: Amount (if willing to state) Other expenses covered Any escalator clause?	Recipient:

Current income range:

Less than $100,000

$101,000 – $150,000

$151,000 – $200,000

$201,000 – $250,000

More than $251,000

How many years did you pay child support?

How many years did you pay alimony/spousal support?

Are you still paying either or both of these?

For how much longer?

How have you been able to manage financially?

What other financial responsibilities do you carry for the children?

In what areas or ways (were) (are) the children most problematic?

6. YOUR EXPERIENCE OF THE DIVORCE

What were the most painful aspects of the divorce for you?

What, if any, changes in your personality, lifestyle, sense of meaning and value, sense of belonging, and ideas of "family" occurred?

What have been some of the highlights in your relationship with each child post separation?

Have you remarried? Yes: No: If yes, how many years post legal divorce?
If no, why not?

7. POSTDIVORCE INTERACTIONS WITH EX-SPOUSE & HER FAMILY

When you have had concerns about your children and/or your relationship with them, have you been able to discuss this with your ex-wife and if so, has she been helpful, hostile or indifferent? How would you describe her reactions, if these descriptions do not apply?

Were you and your ex-wife supportive of each other regarding (a) child rearing?	Yes	No
(b) limit setting?	Yes	No
(c) school?	Yes	No
(d) sports?	Yes	No
(e) other activities?	Yes	No
Comments:		

Please recount three incidents or experiences that typify or exemplify how the children's mother contributed to making your relationship with your children difficult – such as – undermining your authority, criticizing your behavior, indicating if children loved you they were betraying her, making negative remarks about you, intercepting your attempts at communications. If she did not do these things, please say so.

If your relationship with your in-law family changed after the divorce, what were your 3 major responses to and feelings about the changes? Did they talk about you to your children, and if so, were comments supportive, neutral, critical, or derogatory? Were you included in family functions they have had postdivorce?

What were the reactions of your parents and siblings to the divorce? Was there a change in their relationship to your children, and if so, in what way?

What were some of the activities and life events you participated in with your child(ren) post separation?

Did you experience any illnesses that you think were generated by the stress and turmoil of the divorce?

What do you believe have been some of your most important contributions to your child's life?

What made you feel stymied thwarted, left out, and unable to be as much part of your child's life as you wanted to be?

Did you see any differences based on the children's gender in terms of their mother's comments about you specifically, men generally, or her attempts to bind their loyalty to her first and foremost?

What have been some of the worst times, events, and memories for you?

What are three of your best or most poignant memories?

How did what evolved differ from your dreams of and plans about being a dad?

8. CONTRIBUTING TO MAKING IT BEETTER FOR DADS AND THEIR KIDS

If you could address the following in a group, what you want to tell them; that is what facts would you want to make them more aware of from the father's point of view:

1) Divorce therapists

2) Divorce mediators

3) Child custody evaluators

4) Matrimonial lawyers

5) Family court judges

6) Ex-wives

7) Children of divorce ·

Please add any additional information or thoughts you would like to share

Thank you for participating.

Appendix 2

F.W. Kaslow, *Divorced Fathers and Their Families: Legal, Economic,*
and Emotional Dilemmas, DOI 10.1007/978-1-4614-5535-6,
© Springer Science+Business Media New York 2013

Model of Stages in the Divorce Process
Florence W. Kaslow, Ph.D., ABPP

Divorce process	Stage	Phase feelings	Behaviors and tasks	Therapeutic interventions	Mediation, litigation, or collaborative divorce
I. Pre-divorce	1. Emotional divorce	A. Disillusionment	Avoiding the issue	Marital therapy (one couple)	
A time of deliberation and despair		Dissatisfaction Alienation Anxiety Disbelief	Sulking and/or crying Confronting partner Quarreling	Couples group therapy Individual therapy	
		B. Denial	Withdrawing (physically and emotionally)	Marital therapy (one couple)	Contemplation of mediated, collaborative, or litigated divorce
		Despair			Deciding which is best option
		Dread Anguish	Pretending all is fine Attempting to win back affection	Divorce therapy Couples group therapy	
		Ambivalence	Asking friends, family, clergy for advice		
		Shock Emptiness Anger Chaos Inadequacy Low self-esteem Loss Depression Detachment Grief Confusion	Changing of residence for one or both		

Stage		Emotions	Behaviors	Therapy	Tasks
2. Legal divorce	C.	Self-pity	Bargaining	Family therapy	Ascertain parties' understanding of three alternative legal processes
		Helplessness	Screaming	Individual adult therapy	Set the stage for mediation-oriented session
		Desire to retaliate	Threatening Attempting suicide Consulting an attorney or mediator	Child therapy	Define the rules of mediation or collaborative divorce
II. During divorce – a time of legal involvement 3. Economic/financial divorce	D.	Confusion	Separating physically	Children of divorce group therapy	Identify the issues, and separate therapeutic issues from mediation issues
		Fury Sadness Loneliness Relief Vindictiveness	Filing for legal divorce Considering financial settlement: distribution of assets, child, and spousal support	Child therapy Adult therapy Sibling system therapy	Focus on parental strengths, children's needs, and formulation of best possible co-parenting and residential arrangement
4. Co-parental divorce Issues of custody, access, residence, contact/visitation, time-sharing (of the children)	E.	Concern for children	Grieving and mourning	Same as above plus family therapy	Negotiate and process the issues and choices
		Ambivalence Numbness	Telling relatives and friends Reentering work world (unemployed woman)	Collaborate with parenting coordinator, family evaluator, child advocate	Reach agreement
		Uncertainty	Feeling empowered to make choices		Analyze and formalize agreement
		Fears of losses over end of intact family	Relocation of one or both households		Take to attorneys to finalize and file
		Rage	Arranging childcare		

(continued)

Divorce process	Stage	Phase feelings	Behaviors and tasks	Therapeutic interventions	Mediation, litigation, or collaborative divorce
	5. Spiritual/ religious divorce	F. Self-doubt Desire for church approval Fear of God's displeasure or wrath	Gaining church acceptance Having a religious divorce ceremony Making peace with one's spiritual self	Adult therapy Pastoral counseling Children Child play therapy Child group therapy Sibling system therapy	
III. During and early postdivorce	6. Social, community, extended family issues	G. Indecisiveness Optimism Resignation Excitement Curiosity Regret Sadness Uncertainty Loneliness	Finalizing divorce Reworking relationship to in-law family Interpreting changes to extended family Reaching out to new friends Undertaking new activities Stabilizing new lifestyle and daily routine for children Exploring new interests and possibly taking new job	Adult and adolescent individual therapy Children Child play therapy Child group therapy Sibling system therapy Singles adult group therapy	Give children over 16 years of age and perhaps 14, if mature, a copy of the MSA. It is a clarifying road map for their future and one of which parents should be proud

IV. Postdivorce A time of exploration and reequilibration	7. Psychic divorce	H. Acceptance Self-confidence Energy Self-worth Wholeness Exhilaration Independence Autonomy	Resynthesizing identity Completing psychic divorce Seeking new love object and making a commitment to some permanency Becoming comfortable with new lifestyle and friends Helping children accept finality of parents' divorce and importance of their continuing relationship with both parents	Parent–child therapy Family therapy Group therapy Children's activity group therapy Individual therapy when alienation and rejection have occurred Divorce ceremony for total family	Return to mediation when changed circumstances require a renegotiation of the agreement

Sources:

Kaslow, F. W. (1984). Divorce: An evolutionary process of change in the family system. *Journal of Divorce, 7* (3), 21–39
Kaslow, F. W. (1988). The psychological dimension of divorce mediation. In J. Folberg & A. Milne (Eds). *Divorce Mediation: Theory and Practice.* New York: Guilford

For earlier versions see Kaslow 1984a, 1988, 1995, 1997 (in Schwartz and Kaslow). Table periodically revised and expanded
Note: This is a revised and expanded version, small part originally excerpted from Bohannan (1973). The processes of mediation and collaborative divorce were not included in the initial dialectic model (Kaslow, 1984). These have been added to illustrate the interface between the emotional process of divorce and the legal processes. Collaborative divorce, family evaluation, and child advocacy incorporated in 2012

Appendix 3

The Divorce Ceremony: A Healing Strategy

Florence W. Kaslow, Ph.D., ABPP

Introduction and Background

This intervention deals with sadness, loss, healing, renewal, and resiliency. It contains a beacon of optimism in that ultimately this different kind of parting permits "letting go," sometimes generating empathy and/or forgiveness and the freeing up of bound energy to begin a new phase of one's individual and family life cycle. (Kaslow, 2010). This intervention as I have created and modified it over time has its rationale in several highly regarded theoretical schools upon which well-accepted treatment methods are predicated.

In the United States and in many other countries around the world, a majority of people have both civil *and* religious marriage ceremonies. Couples either chose and/or are required to be married in a church, synagogue, or mosque before the eyes of God (and their relatives and friends). For many, the religious service supersedes the civil/legal service in import; it is this ritual that consecrates the marriage and marks the specialness and sacredness of the event. Usually, it signifies not only the joy and wish for fulfillment of the shared dreams of the couple but also the hopes of the new couple's respective families of origin. For all, potentially it means perpetuation of the family into the next generation.

All too often, the dream of the couple to "live happily ever after" does not materialize. They are disappointed in a marriage that does not fulfill their often unrealistic expectations. Disillusionment and despair replace optimism and love. No matter how hard they may try, the schism of distrust and chronic discontent widens. Efforts to "communicate better," to repair power imbalances, and/or restore to affection and intimacy lead to naught. Ultimately, the emotional estrangement is accompanied by a physical estrangement, and the couple separate. They may or may not seek assistance in marital and, later, divorce therapy. No matter whether the couple enters the adversarial system directly by contacting two separate attorneys to handle their divorce action or whether they decide to mediate the divorce, the process must culminate in court, and it is there they receive a judgment decree that legally grants the divorce. Generally, the legal process is cold, lonely, and characterized by anger and

F.W. Kaslow, *Divorced Fathers and Their Families: Legal, Economic,*   231
and Emotional Dilemmas, DOI 10.1007/978-1-4614-5535-6,
© Springer Science+Business Media New York 2013

hostility. The marriage that began with pomp, flourish, and a mass celebration formally ends with each former partner in a dreary courtroom usually alone except for his or her sole attendant, the attorney – who is paid to be there. The divorcing person is rarely accompanied by an emotionally supportive friend.

Over the years, scores of clients and friends have described the forlorn sense of alienation they experienced at the time of the legal ending of their marriage to me. Many expressed the desire to have their marital dissolution recognized and accepted by their church as their wedding had been. I have encouraged them to approach their clergy person and request that such a ceremony be developed and performed on their behalf. Some ministers assent; people who undergo this process report a new sense of closure. Over time a few clergy – therapist friends of mine have been receptive to the idea and have written ceremonies that they were willing to have me share and publicize and to use with members of their congregation.

It became obvious to me from researching the literature and discussing the topic widely that (1) only Orthodox Judaism has traditionally recognized the need for a divorce ceremony and promulgated one through the centuries, but this is only at the husband's request; (2) there is an enormous need for a divorce ceremony by thousands of couples to mark the ending of the journey known as the divorce process; and (3) many churches are still not ready to develop and/or utilize such a ceremony.

Therefore, around 1982, I created a quasi-therapeutic ceremony that is adaptable for religious purposes also. Since then, I have utilized it with countless clients and in the training of numerous other professionals in divorce therapy and divorce mediation workshops in about 40 countries. It has been refined, based on experience, and the current abridged version updated in 2010 appears below.

Therapeutic/Healing Divorce Ceremony

Those asked to be present: Ex-husband, ex-wife, their children, and a mutual good friend of each parent. (Their own parents may also be invited, if they so choose and will be asked to comment as appropriate.)

The adult participants are asked to stand facing each other, and the children stand facing me. We are in a square or rectangle, depending on the number of participants.

FK: Mr. Green, please thank your wife for the good years and happy times you remember.

Mr. G: (usually puzzled – pauses – chokes and responds – surprised at the positive memories this question evokes. He may say) I really had forgotten – amidst my anger – how much I once loved you. You were so lovely, talented....

FK: Mrs. Green, can you tell your husband about the good things you will always cherish about your marriage?

Mrs. G: (Often teary and barely audible, affirms the sharing, fun, and early realizations of her dream and how wonderful she thought he was).

FK: (To each of the friends separately) Please tell Mr. or Mrs. Green how you were prepared to be available to them during this difficult transition time, what their friendship means to you, and what you might offer now.

Friends: You can still call me at any time to talk, cry, go somewhere with you....I am here for you in any way that you need me because you are a super person and a wonderful friend. (Their comments usually reflect the length of time since the divorce – whether recent or many years prior to the ceremony.)

FK: (To children) Can you each tell your parents what it felt like to you when the divorce was first happening? How old were you then? Please be honest and not afraid to *say what is in your heart's memory.*

Each child reminisces – often amidst tears – about how confusing it was; their sense of sadness, loss, and lack of control; and their fears about the uncertainty of the future and grief that one parent was moving out.

FK: (To each parent) Can you respond to what you have just heard from your child (children) without blame or defensiveness? (They take turns doing so.)

FK: (To the children) Can you tell each parent what you want from them now and in the future?

Each child: (Something like) I am still sad that this happened, but I know you tried your best. I need to know that you will each continue to love me, take care of me, listen to me, and respect my needs, let me love and care about each of you, and see you as much as possible. Please do not ever ask me to take sides or interfere with my relationship to mom/dad. (This is usually said with great sadness, wistfulness, and through tears.) I need to know you can be at my graduation, wedding, etc., in the same room and not make anyone, especially me, uncomfortable.

FK: (To each parent) Can you tell your children how they were conceived (or adopted) in love, born at a time when you cared very much for each other, and were delighted to be having a family? Also, let them know what your thoughts are about your future relationship to them and if you can fulfill their request to be in the same room together for them and not create a sense of tension or unhappiness.

Each parent: (Tells in their own words what child has meant to them and affirms that their parental feelings and role will continue.)

(The room is usually pervaded by the strong feelings being exchanged. Often some in the audience are sobbing, especially those who also are divorced and become engulfed in the stark realism of the interchanges.)

FK: (To anyone else at the ceremony) Please tell Mr. and Mrs. Green what is in your hearts as you help them to feel some inner peace and some healing. Does anyone else care to add anything?

When everyone has said what they feel compelled to communicate, depending on the feeling tone being conveyed, I may ask if they all care to hug each other as a different goodbye to the family in its present form.

Prologue

Rarely can such a ceremony be effective prior to two years postdivorce. Before utilizing such a ritual, it is important to ascertain that the couple wishes to bring emotional closure to their marriage. Also, if either parent is involved in a new relationship, that partner should not be included as the need for further closure on the first marriage predates the new relationship existentially.

All of the families with whom I have utilized this intervention strategy have expressed appreciation for the release from the remaining unwanted emotional shackles it affords. Sometimes, one or both will spontaneously offer apologies for the hurt they caused or forgiveness for a betrayal. In acknowledging what was valuable in their relationship, they counter the feelings of failure carried for too long. In openly communicating profound feelings and memories with their children and finally listening attentively to what the children and friends have to say, a transformation of bonding begins. Amid tears of relief, this parting occurs minus anger and the desire for further recriminations and retribution, on a more positive trajectory.

© F.W. Kaslow, Ph.D. 2010.

Author Index

A

Abelsohn, D., 90, 117
Abt, L.E., 4, 6
Ackerman, M.J., 184
Ahrons, C.R., 8, 13, 34, 86, 139
Ally, G.A., 162, 164
Amato, P.R., 175, 177
Anderson, C.M., 3
Anderson, E.R., 164, 169
Angarne-Lindberg, T., 135
Antonovsky, A., 210

B

Baker, A.L., 12, 49, 60, 119, 207
Barker, R., 194
Bauserman, R., 175, 178
Beavers, W.R., 75
Beck, C.J.A., 164, 169
Ben-Ami, N., 12, 60
Benjamin, G.A.H., 161, 162, 164, 169
Bennett, L., 71
Bepko, C., 19, 108
Bernal, G., 31
Berne, E., 129
Bernet, W., 12, 42, 56, 127
Blakeslee, S., 200
Blau, M., 7
Bonach, K., 208
Bos, H.M., 13, 135
Bostwick, S., 141
Boumil, M.M., 129, 131
Braver, S., 162
Braver, S.L., 63

Brewster, K.O., 164, 169
Brooks, G.R., 11
Brown, E.M., 17, 74, 191
Byrne, K., 198

C

Carter, D.K., 171, 173, 178, 180
Charny, I., 138
Cirillo, S., 130
Clawar, S.S., 12, 46, 49, 55, 86, 118, 127, 159, 205
Coleman, M., 41
Coogler, O.J., 11, 141
Cox, M., 160
Cox, R., 160

D

Daley, D.C., 108
Donsky, T., 171

E

Ebling, R., 178
Egizli, J., 86, 154
Elkin, M., 148
Emery, R.E., 154, 160, 171, 175, 177, 178
Engel, M.L., 183
Erickson, E.H., 116
Erickson, S.K., 143, 144, 152
Everett, C.A., 40
Everly, G.S., 110

F.W. Kaslow, *Divorced Fathers and Their Families: Legal, Economic, and Emotional Dilemmas,* DOI 10.1007/978-1-4614-5535-6, © Springer Science+Business Media New York 2013

F
Fabricius, W.V., 175, 205
Fauber, R., 160
Ferstenberg, R.L., 141
Firestone, G., 205
Fisher, R., 141
Folberg, J., 6, 141–143, 153
Forehand, R., 160
Freud, A., 139
Freud, S., 2
Friedan, B., 2
Friedman, J., 129, 131

G
Ganong, L.H., 41
Garb, H.N., 164, 166
Garcia-Preto, N., 97
Gilbreth, J.G., 175
Glass, S., 62, 191
Gold, L., 29, 90
Goldstein, J., 139
Gollan, J., 161, 162, 164
Gordis, E.B., 173
Gould, D.D., 183
Greenman, P.S., 193
Greer, G., 2
Grossman, S., 191, 193

H
Hakvoort, E.M., 13, 135
Hall, J., 171
Halon, A., 163, 164
Harari, C., 171
Hawthorne, B., 194
Haynes, J.M., 11, 141, 142
Henry, W.J., 171
Hermanns, J.M., 13, 135
Hetherington, E.M., 173–175
Hetherington, M.E., 160
Hill, E.W., 208
Hodges, W.F., 4, 13
Hudson, B., 12

I
Insabella, G., 175, 178
Isaacs, M.B., 90, 117

J
Jacobson, G.F., 101
John, R.S., 173

Johnson, M.O., 183
Johnson, S.M., 193
Johnson v. Adair, 148
Johnson, W.B., 98, 192
Johnston, J.R., 173, 176, 178

K
Kaslow, F.W., 7, 8, 21, 27, 28, 40, 47, 57, 66,
     80, 83, 93, 95, 99, 101, 118, 127,
     138, 140–143, 145, 153, 169, 200
Kelly, J., 173, 174
Kelly, J.B., 138, 160, 162, 171, 173, 175, 177,
     178, 205
Kernberg, O., 65, 190Kessler, S., 141
Kirkland, K., 180
Kline, M., 176
Kopecky, G., 9
Kreger, R., 191
Kreston, J.A., 19, 108
Kruk, E., 100, 205

L
Lachkar, J., 190
Lansford, J.E., 160
Lee, R.E., 40
Leesa, N.R., 19
Lennings, C.J., 194
Levant, R.F., 9–11
Lindahl, K., 157
Linehan, M.M., 193
Little, T.D., 175
Long, N., 160
Lowenstein, L.F., 121
Luecken, L.J., 205
Lusterman, D.D., 11, 63, 99

M
Maccoby, E., 173
Margolin, G., 173
Maslow, A.H., 210
Mason, P.T., 191
McGoldrick, M., 3
McGreenery, C.E., 184
McHale, J., 157, 176, 178
McKnight Erickson, M.S., 143, 144, 152
Millar, P., 205
Miller, A., 60
Millon, T., 42, 91, 103, 110, 191, 193
Milne, A.L., 6
Minuchin, S., 56
Mitcham-Smith, M., 171

Mnookin, R.H., 173
Montalvo, B., 90, 117
Moore, C.W., 145
Murray, K., 98, 192
Myers, M.F., 26, 90, 129

N
Neville, W.G., 141
Nichols, W., 190, 192
Nurse, A.R., 194, 207
Nutt, R.L., 11

O
Orfanos, S.D., 79
Orford, J., 112
O'Sullivan, A.L., 183

P
Palazzoli, M.S., 130
Pearson, J., 178
Philpot, D.L., 11
Pica, D.A., 149
Pittman, F., 137
Polcari, A., 184
Pollack, W.S., 10, 11
Pruett, M.K., 171, 175, 178, 194
Pryor, J., 35, 67, 175

Q
Quinn, E., 118, 191

R
Ransley, C., 208
Reid, G.D., 3
Reiss, D., 71
Reskin, M.S., 108
Ricci, I., 27, 63
Rivlin, B.V., 12, 46, 49, 55, 86, 118, 127, 159, 205
Roberson, P.E., 8
Rodgers, B., 175
Rosen, E.J., 47, 69
Rotman, A.D., 184

S
Sabo, M., 8
Salem, P., 6
Samson, J.A., 184

Samuels, M.D., 184
Sartre, J., 126
Sbarra, D., 161
Scanlon, W.F., 19
Schneider, J.G., 59
Schwartz, L.L., 7, 8, 21, 27, 28, 40, 93, 127, 138, 184
Searles, J.S., 106, 111–112
Selvine, M., 130
Shapiro, E., 31
Sheets, V., 162
Sifneos, P.E., 10
Silverstein, L.S., 11
Simon, F.B., 107
Slater, E., 160
Smyth, B., 178
Solnit, A., 139
Solomon, M.F., 70, 111, 192
Sorrentino, A.M., 130
Spy, T., 208
Steinem, G., 2
Steinglass, P., 71
Stierlin, H., 107
Stuart, I.R., 4, 6
Sullivan, H.S., 2
Sullivan, M., 180

T
Taylor, A., 142, 143, 153
Teicher, M.H., 184
Tesler, P.H., 6, 12, 145
Thoennes, N., 178
Thompson, P., 6, 12, 145, 194, 207
Tompkins, R., 184
Tschann, J.M., 176
Tsemberis, S.J., 79

U
Ury, W., 141

V
Van Balen, F., 13, 135
Vassiliou, D., 12, 201

W
Wadsby, M., 135
Wallerstein, J., 138, 176, 200
Walsh, F., 3
Watzlawick, P., 190
Weinstein, J., 205

Weissman, H.N., 165
Weitzman, L.J., 13
Weltman, S.F., 47, 69
Wickel, K., 8
Williams, C.F., 11

Williams, T.Y., 175
Windle, M., 106, 111–112
Wolen, S., 71
Wright, T., 62, 191
Wynne, L.C., 107

Subject Index

A

ABA. *See* American Bar Association (ABA)
Abandoned father, 129
Abandonment, 14, 73, 143, 163, 164, 176, 177
"Abuse of discretion,", 149 151, 154
Abzug, Bella, 2
Ackerman, Marc, 184
ADR. *See* Alternative dispute resolution (ADR)
Adversarial divorce, 146, 207–208
Affairs, 5, 17–19, 26, 32, 38, 54, 62, 63, 70, 72, 79, 80, 84, 89, 91, 99, 126, 132, 137, 153, 159, 184, 187, 191
Affluence, 105, 115
Agreement for representation, 149
Alcoholism, 110
Alienation, 9, 12, 81, 119, 122, 127, 141, 150, 159, 198, 201, 205, 209
Alienation of affection, 81
Alimony, 12, 13, 20, 26, 33, 38, 47, 49, 55, 64, 81, 101, 108, 116, 122, 126–129, 131, 133, 134, 152, 204, 210
Alternative dispute resolution (ADR), 11, 12, 145, 163, 168–169, 171, 180
Ambition, 45, 57, 62, 85, 97
American Academy of Forensic Psychologists, 185
American Bar Association (ABA), 140
American Psychological Association (APA), 6, 199
Annulment, 32
Antisocial personality disorder, 123, 192, 193
APA. *See* American Psychological Association (APA)

Association of Family and Conciliation Courts, 199
Axis II personality disorders, 198

B

"Bad fathers,"46
Barracuda, 54, 132, 157
Berne, Eric, 129
"Best interest of the child,", 6–7 29, 39, 40, 76, 139, 144, 150, 166, 194, 202, 208
Betrayal, 5, 138, 160, 163, 175, 184, 201, 206, 208
    Arturo Miguel, 90, 91
    Blue Eyes, 22
    Hy Hopes, 99, 101
    Terry Kelly, 61–67
Bi-nuclear post-divorce family, 86, 139, 141
Bly, Robert, 9
Boarding school, 90, 92, 157, 158
Borderline personality disorder, 70, 76, 190, 192, 193, 210
Brain washing, 12, 55, 121, 127, 129, 198, 209
Brandeis, Louis, 6
Breadwinner, 55, 92
Brogan, Bill
    children, 53–54
    children's lives, contributions to, 58–59
    divorce
        experience, 58
        painful aspects, 56–57
    early postdivorce period, 55
    ex-in-law family/his family, postdivorce interactions with, 57
    finances, 54–55
    later postdivorce years, 57–58

F.W. Kaslow, *Divorced Fathers and Their Families: Legal, Economic, and Emotional Dilemmas,* DOI 10.1007/978-1-4614-5535-6,
© Springer Science+Business Media New York 2013

Brogan, Bill (*cont.*)
    legal divorce, 53–54
    marriage, 53–54
    personal history, 53
    poignant memories with children, 59
    retrospective, 59–60

C

Carrying grudges, 39
CASA. *See* Court Appointed Special
        Advocates program (CASA)
Cases, commentaries on
    child advocate
        in action, 185–187
        role of, 183–185
    collaborative divorce, 145–146
    contraindications, 144–145
    custody litigation, family evaluation in, 160
        ADR, for future concerns, 168–169
        comprehensive family evaluation,
            162–168
        lawyering, efficacious, 161–162
    divorce
        mediation, 140–144
        therapy, 137–140
    parenting coordination (PC)
        history and objectives, 171–172
        process, 172–180
        roles and function, 172
    right lawyer, 148
        child support, 151–152
        different result, 156–159
        judge and client, assessment of, 149–150
        mediation, 152–154
        pitfalls, avoiding, 154–156
        Relocation Statute, 150–151
Chicanery, 46, 133, 134, 138, 197, 202, 209
Child advocate, 141, 183–187
    in action, 185–187
    role of, 183–185
Childbirth without Fear, 3
Child custody, 4, 6, 8, 139, 183, 189, 193,
        199–200, 205
Child Protective Services (CPS), 19
Child rearing, 27
Children
    Ari Regis, 79
    Arturo Miguel, 89–90, 92–93
    Bill Brogan, 53–54, 59
    Blue Eyes, 17–18
    Bob Straight, 25
    of divorce, 13, 19, 27, 171, 201–202, 210
    Gene Goodman, 70
    Hy Hopes, 98

Jorge Garcia, 35
    life events participated with
        Ari Regis, 85
        Arturo Miguel, 93–94
        Hy Hopes, 102–103
    reaction to divorce
        Ron Dedicated, 48
        Terry Kelly, 63–64
    relationship
        Bob Straight, 28
        Gene Goodman, 74–75
        Zack Determined, 109
    Reuben Guy, 37–38
    Ron Dedicated, 45–47
    Scott Unlucky, 116–117
    Terry Kelly, 62
    Zack Determined, 105–107
Children's lives, contributions to
    Ari Regis, 85
    Arturo Miguel, 93–94
    Bill Brogan, 58–59
    Blue Eyes, 21
    Hy Hopes, 102–103
    Jorge Garcia, 34–35
    Reuben Guy, 41–42
    Ron Dedicated, 50
    Terry Kelly, 66
Child support, 4, 13, 33, 116, 117, 126, 129–131,
        133, 134, 151–152, 161, 200
    Ari Regis, 81, 84, 86
    Arturo Miguel, 92
    Bill Brogan, 55
    Blue Eyes, 20
    Bob Straight, 26
    Gene Goodman, 71, 73
    guidelines, 71
    Hy Hopes, 101
    Reuben Guy, 38, 39
    Ron Dedicated, 47, 49
    Terry Kelly, 64
    Zack Determined, 108
Child Support Calculation Sheet, 151
Citizenship, 99
Co-habitation, 47
Collaborative divorce, 6, 12, 137–146, 189,
        194, 207
Commentaries, on cases. *See* Cases,
        commentaries on
Compassion, 35, 39
Comprehensive family evaluation, 160, 162–169
    accurate results, 164
    evaluator, 167–168
    faulty clinical judgments, 164
    recommendations, 165–167
Conflictual parenting, 173

Coogler, Jim, 11
Cooperative co-parenting, 173
Co-parenting, 8, 139, 140, 171–173, 175, 205,
    208. *See also Specific* Co-parenting
Court Appointed Special Advocates program
    (CASA), 183
CPS. *See* Child Protective Services (CPS)
Crazy Love, 192
Criticality, 11, 19, 21, 26, 34, 49, 50, 65, 73,
    75, 83, 86, 93, 118, 122, 138, 153,
    155, 160, 175, 178, 203
Cultural beliefs, 31
Custody, 148
    child, 4, 6, 8, 139, 183, 189, 193, 199–200,
       205
    decisions (*See* Custody decisions)
    litigation (*See* Custody litigation, family
       evaluation in)
    sole *vs.* joint, 90, 116, 143
    and visitation plan, 11, 63, 100, 109, 203
Custody decisions
    "best interest of the child,", 6–7
    case studies, 13–14
    contemporary developments, 12
    divorce, alternative routes to, 11–12
    feminist revolution, 2–3
    industrial revolution, impact of, 1–2
    Kramer vs. Kramer, 8–9
    losses, 5–6
    men's movement, 9–11
    natural childbirth, 3–4
    "no fault" laws, 7–8
    rights and needs, 13
    sociolegal custody decisions, 4
Custody litigation, family evaluation in, 160
    ADR, for future concerns, 168–169
    comprehensive family evaluation,
       162–164
       components, 164–168
    lawyering, efficacious, 161–162

D

DCF. *See* Department of Children and
    Families (DCF)
Deadbeat dad, 129
Deceit, 138, 209
Deception, 91, 132, 193, 197, 208
Dedicated, Ron
    children, 45–47
    children's reactions and aftermath, 48
    divorce, experience of, 48–49
    "do no harm,", 45–51
    with ex-spouse and in-law family/his family,
       postdivorce interaction with, 49

    finances, 47
    legal divorce, 45–47
    life events participated with children, 50
    marriage, 45–47
    memories, 50
    personal history, 45
    postdivorce period, 47–48
    postdivorce stress, turmoil, illnesses, and
       scars, 50–51
    relationship to children, 47–48
    remarriage, 51
    retrospective, 51
Denigration, 40, 56, 66, 117, 139, 174, 186
Department of Children and Families
    (DCF), 118
Dependent personality, 12, 55, 84, 163, 191, 192
Depression, 116, 119, 141
Detachment, 120
Determined, Zack
    children, 106
    children's relationship, with subsequent
       partner, 109
    divorce, 106–107
       acceptance, 109
       children's reactions to, 109–110
       emotions, 108
       feelings about, 108
       painful aspects, 110
    ex-wife's family and postdivorce, 111
    finances, 108–109
    ideas about family, 110–111
    lifestyle
       changes in, 110–111
       subsequent changes in, 111–112
    marriage, 105–107
    personal history, 105
    personality, changes in, 110–111
    retrospective and prospective, 112
    sense of belonging, changes in, 110–111
"Devoted dads,", 13
Disappeared dad, 129
Disappointment, 86, 103, 209, 210
Disillusionment, 67, 103, 127, 137, 192
Divorce. *See also* Legal divorce; Postdivorce
    period
    adversarial, 146, 207–208
    alternative routes to, 11–12
    Ari Regis, 79–80
    Arturo Miguel, 89–91
    Blue Eyes, 18
    ceremony, 146, 209
    children, 13, 19, 27, 171, 201–202, 210
    child's reaction to, 63–64
    collaborative, 145–146
    emotional, 138

Divorce. *See also* Legal divorce; Postdivorce
        period (*cont.*)
    experience
        Ari Regis, 84
        Bill Brogan, 58
        Blue Eyes, 21
        Bob Straight, 28
        Gene Goodman, 74
        Hy Hopes, 103
        Reuben Guy, 40
        Ron Dedicated, 48–49
        Scott Unlucky, 120–121
    games played, exposition of, 130–131
    Gene Goodman, 70–71
    Hy Hopes, 99
    with integrity, 134, 135
    Jorge Garcia, 32
    legal (*see* Legal divorce)
    mediation, 140–144
    mediators, 197–198
    and multiple losses, 80–81
    painful aspects
        Bill Brogan, 56–57
        Blue Eyes, 21
        Bob Straight, 28
        Gene Goodman, 74
        Hy Hopes, 103
        Jorge Garcia, 33–34
        Reuben Guy, 40
        Ron Dedicated, 48–49
        Terry Kelly, 64–65
    postdivorce (*see* Early postdivorce period;
        Later postdivorce period)
    postdivorce interactions (*see* Postdivorce
        interactions)
    sequelae
        Reuben Guy, 42
        Terry Kelly, 66
    therapists, 197
    therapy, 137–140
    tragedy (*see* Tragedy of divorce)
    Zack Determined, 105–107
        acceptance, 109
        children's reactions to, 109–110
        emotions, 108
        experience, 110
        feelings about, 108
        painful aspects, 110
Divorced dads, typology of, 128–129
Domestic violence, 117, 118, 150, 158–160,
        168, 184
"Do no harm,", 45–51 202
Drug addiction, 19
Duplicity, 90, 209
Durational alimony, 12

E
Early postdivorce period
    Bill Brogan, 55
    Bob Straight, 26–27
    Gene Goodman, 71
    Scott Unlucky, 117–119
    Terry Kelly, 63
    Zack Determined, 108
Emotional divorce, 138, 192
Emotional train wreck, 94
Entitlement, 116, 122, 129, 192
Equal parental responsibility (EPR), 205
Equal Parenting, 205–206
Equitable settlement, 54, 168
Evaluator, 6, 164–168, 171, 183, 185, 189,
        193, 199, 203
Exploitation, 120
Ex-spouse and in-law family/his family
        postdivorce interactions with
        Ari Regis, 84–85
        Arturo Miguel, 93
        Bill Brogan, 57
        Blue Eyes, 21
        Bob Straight, 27
        Gene Goodman, 75–76
        Hy Hopes, 102
        Jorge Garcia, 34
        Reuben Guy, 41
        Ron Dedicated, 49
        Scott Unlucky, 119
        Terry Kelly, 65–66
        Zack Determined, 111
Ex-wives, 200–201
Eyes, Blue, 17
    addictions, 19
    child, 17–18
    children's lives, contributions to, 21
    divorce, 18, 21
    ex-spouse and in-law family, postdivorce
        interactions with, 21
    finances, 20–21
    marriage, 17–18
    personal history, 17
    postdivorce years, 19–20
    retrospective, 22
    separation, 22

F
False accusations, 58
False allegations, 117, 121, 130, 158, 204
    Bill Brogan, 56
    Hy Hopes, 99
False memory syndrome, 56, 59
False sexual abuse allegations, 56

Family
  law litigation, 160
  loyalties, 28, 36, 37, 49
  of origin, 41, 45, 49, 53, 57, 63, 93, 123
  reactions, 119
  relationship with, 100–101
  values, 192
Family court judges, 203–207
Family courts, 156, 164, 171, 179, 180, 203
Family evaluation, in custody litigation, 160
  ADR, 168–169
  comprehensive family evaluation, 162–168
  lawyering, efficacious, 161–162
"Family games: General models of psychotic
    processes in the family," 130
Father's rights, 13
Feminine Mystique, The, 2
Feminist revolution, 2–3
Final Judgment of Dissolution, 155
Finances
  Ari Regis, 81–82
  Arturo Miguel, 92
  Bill Brogan, 54–55
  Blue Eyes, 20–21
  Bob Straight, 26
  Gene Goodman, 71
  Hy Hopes, 101
  Jorge Garcia, 33
  Reuben Guy, 38–39
  Ron Dedicated, 47
  Terry Kelly, 64
  Zack Determined, 108–109
Financial manipulations, 64, 209
Florida Legislature, 12
Forgiveness, 207–209
Fraud, 69

G
GAL. *See* Guardian ad litem (GAL)
Game playing, clinical case illustrations of,
    131–135
Games divorced/divorcing people play, 129–131
"Games People Play,", 129
Garcia, Jorge
  actual divorce, 32
  children's gender and loyalty to mother, 35
  children's lives, contributions to, 34–35
  divorce, painful aspects of, 33–34
  early marriage and family, 31–32
  ex-spouse and in-law family/his family,
      postdivorce interactions with, 34
  finances, 33
  memories, 34–35
  personal history, 31

  postdivorce period, 33
  retrospective, 36
  worst memories, 35
Gender differences, 35
Gigantic losses, 5
"Goddess Consciousness," emergence of, 11
Goodman, Gene
  children, 70
  disturbing issues, 72–73
  divorce, 70–71
  early postdivorce period, 71
  events, 75
  ex-in-law family/his family, postdivorce
      interactions with, 75–76
  finances, 71
  ideas about family, changes in, 74
  marriage, 70
  memories, 75
  painful aspects of divorce, 74
  personal history, 69–70
  personality, changes in, 74
  postdivorce reactions, 72
  relationship to child, 74–75
  retrospective and prospective, 76
  sense of belonging, changes in, 74
  worst times, 75
Good stepmom, 18
Guardian ad litem (GAL), 73, 76, 141, 164,
    168, 176, 183, 185, 189, 203, 206
Guilt inducing, 64
Guilty father, 129
Guy, Reuben
  children, 37–38
  children's lives, contributions to, 41–42
  divorce, painful aspects of, 40
  ex-in-law family/his family, postdivorce
      interactions with, 41
  finances, 38–39
  legal divorce, 37–38
  long-term divorce sequelae, 42
  marriage, 37–38
  personal history, 37
  postdivorce changes in family, 39
  remarriage, wonders of, 40–41
  retrospective and prospective, 42–43

H
Haynes, John, 11
Healing, 138, 146, 194, 207–209
Heart connection, 55, 83
High conflict, 160, 161, 163, 164, 168,
    171–173, 178, 197
High conflict tactics, 160
Histrionic personality disorder, 65, 72, 191–194

Hoffman, Dustin, 8
Hung in for the kids, 54
Hy Hopes
    children, 97–98
    divorce, 97–99
    ex-spouse and in-law family, postdivorce
        interactions with, 102
    finances, 101
    greatest losses, 101
    ideas about family, changes in, 102
    life events participated with son, 102–103
    lifestyle, changes in, 102
    marriage, 97–99
    memories, 102–103
    personal history, 97
    personality, changes in, 102
    postdivorce, 100
    relationship with family, 100–101
    retrospective and prospective, 103
    sense of belonging, changes in, 102

I
Ideas about family, changes in
    Arturo Miguel, 94
    Gene Goodman, 74
    Hy Hopes, 102
    Zack Determined, 110–111
Incompatibility, 38
Industrial revolution, impact of, 1–2
Infidelity, 5, 64, 90, 102, 132
In-law family, 5, 21, 27, 41, 49, 57, 65–66,
        117. See also Ex-spouse and in-law
        family/his family
Innuendos, 141
Intergenerational transmission, 86

J
Judge and client, assessment of, 149–150
"Junk science,", 12

K
Kelly, Terry
    children, 62
    daughter's life, contributions to, 66
    divorce
        child's reaction to, 63–64
        painful aspects, 64–65
        sequelae, 66
    early post separation/divorce period, 63
    finances, 64
    in-law family/his family, postdivorce
        interactions, 65–66
    legal divorce, 62
    marriage, 61–62
    personal history, 61
    retrospective and prospective, 66–67
Kramer vs. Kramer, 8–9

L
Later postdivorce period
    Bill Brogan, 57–58
    Bob Straight, 27–28
Lawyer, 148
    child support, 151–152
    different results, 156–159
    judge and client, assessment of, 149–150
    matrimonial, 202–203
    mediation, 152–154
    pitfalls, avoiding, 154–156
    Relocation Statute, 150–151
Lawyering, efficacious, 161–162
Legal divorce, 5, 25–26, 37–38, 40, 45–47,
        53–54, 61–62, 115–117, 139, 142.
        See also Divorce; Postdivorce
        interactions
    Bill Brogan, 53–54
    Bob Straight, 25–26
    Reuben Guy, 37–38
    Ron Dedicated, 45–47
    Scott Unlucky, 116–117
    Terry Kelly, 61–62
Lesbian, gay, bisexual, or transgender
        (LGBT), 198
Life events participated with children
    Ari Regis, 85
    Arturo Miguel, 93–94
    Hy Hopes, 102–103
    Reuben Guy, 41–42
    Ron Dedicated, 50
Lifestyle, changes in
    Hy Hopes, 102
    Zack Determined, 110–112
Live in boyfriends, 27, 75
Long-term divorce sequelae.See
        Divorce:sequelae
Losses, 5–6, 40, 51, 80–81, 86, 101, 103, 139,
        145, 163, 176, 177
Loss of confidence and self-esteem, 209
Lying, 63, 64, 190, 191, 209

M
Maneuvering, 132
Manipulation, 64, 72, 120, 193, 209
Marital conflict, 72, 106
Marital counseling, 46, 62, 70

Marital paradise, 18
Marital settlement agreement (MSA), 4, 26,
        38–39, 46–47, 49, 51, 63, 64, 91,
        109, 117, 119, 127, 129, 131, 140,
        203, 207
Marriage
    Ari Regis, 79–80
    Arturo Miguel, 89–90
    Bill Brogan, 53–54
    Blue Eyes, 17–18
    Bob Straight, 25–28
    Gene Goodman, 70
    Hy Hopes, 97–99
    Jorge Garcia, 31–32
    Reuben Guy, 37–38
    Ron Dedicated, 45–47
    Scott Unlucky, 115–117, 121–122
    Terry Kelly, 61–62
    Zack Determined, 105–107
Matrimonial lawyers, 202–203
Mediation, 152–154
    assisting clients, 142
    custody decisions, 143
    direction of children, biased in, 142–143
    divorce, 140–144
    engagement, 141–142
    participants, 144
    principles, 141
    session, 143
    task orientation, 141
Memories
    Ari Regis, 86
    Arturo Miguel, 93–94
    Bill Brogan, 59
    Gene Goodman, 75
    Hy Hopes, 102–103
    Jorge Garcia, 34–35
    Reuben Guy, 41–42
    Ron Dedicated, 50
    Scott Unlucky, 121–122
Men(s)
    movement, 9–11
    reciprocal portrait, 191–193
Miguel, Arturo
    children, 89–91
    children's lives, contributions to, 93–94
    divorce, 89–91
    ex-spouse and in-law family/his family,
        postdivorce interactions with, 93
    finances, 92
    ideas about family, changes in, 94
    life events participated with sons, 93–94
    marriage, 89–91
    personal history, 89
    personality, changes in, 94

    poignant memories, 93–94
    postdivorce reactions, 91–92
    problematic sons, 92–93
    retrospective and prospective, 94–95
    sense of belonging, changes in, 94
Misrepresentation, 160, 163
Model Code of Professional Responsibility,
    140
Money and affluence, 105
Ms. Magazine, 2
MSA. *See* Marital settlement agreement
    (MSA)

N
Narcissism, 111
Narcissistic personality disorder, 62, 76,
    122, 191–194
National Organization for Women
    (NOW), 12
National Women's Political Caucus, 3
Natural childbirth, 3–4
"Nervous and scattered" personality, 108
"Nervous breakdown,", 108 112
"No fault" laws, 7–8
NOW. *See* National Organization for Women
    (NOW)

O
Obsessive-compulsive personality, 192
Out of control, 71, 110, 112
Over-involved dad, 129

P
Painful aspects, of divorce
    Bill Brogan, 56–57
    Blue Eyes, 21
    Bob Straight, 28
    Gene Goodman, 74
    Hy Hopes, 103
    Jorge Garcia, 33–34
    Reuben Guy, 40
    Ron Dedicated, 48–49
    Terry Kelly, 64–65
    Zack Determined, 110
Parallel co-parenting, 173
Parental adjustment problems, 161
Parental alienation, 12, 122, 127, 159, 198,
    201, 205
Parental deficit, 205
Parental prophecy, 17
Parentification, 19, 107, 199
Parentified child, 107

Parenting coordination (PC), 156, 163, 171–180
    development, 171
    history and objectives, 171–172
    primary intervention, 174
    process, 172–180
    roles and functions, 172
Parenting plans, 146, 155–158, 172, 173,
        178–180, 200
Paternal grandparents, 5, 47, 49, 118, 184
PBI. *See* Pennsylvania Bar Institute (PBI)
PC. *See* Parenting coordination (PC)
Pennsylvania Bar Institute (PBI), 183
Personality
    changes in
        Arturo Miguel, 94
        Gene Goodman, 74
        Hy Hopes, 102
        Zack Determined, 110–111
    disorders (*See Specific* Personality
        disorders)
    patterns, 189
        portrait of women, 189–191
        reciprocal portrait of men, 191–193
        reflections, 193–194
Physical abuse, 19, 130
Physically/sexually abusive man, 129
Pogrebin, Letty Cottin, 2
Poignant memories. *See* Memories
Political asylum, 98
Portrait, of women, 189–191
Post-divorce family, 6–8, 82, 135, 144, 194,
        202, 208
Postdivorce healing, and well-being, 207–208
Postdivorce interactions
    with ex-spouse and in-law family/his
        family
        Ari Regis, 84–85
        Arturo Miguel, 93
        Bill Brogan, 57
        Blue Eyes, 21
        Bob Straight, 27
        Gene Goodman, 75–76
        Hy Hopes, 102
        Jorge Garcia, 34
        Reuben Guy, 39, 41
        Ron Dedicated, 49
        Scott Unlucky, 119
        Terry Kelly, 65–66
        Zack Determined, 111
Postdivorce period. *See also* Divorce; Early
        postdivorce period; Later
        postdivorce period
    Ari Regis, 82–83

    Arturo Miguel, 91–92
    Blue Eyes, 19–20
    Gene Goodman, 72
    Hy Hopes, 100
    Jorge Garcia, 33
    Ron Dedicated, 47–48
    Scott Unlucky, 121–122
Postscript, 208–210
Prenuptial agreement, 82, 134, 157
Presumption, 4, 148, 150, 205, 210
Projection, 131
Psychiatric hospitalization, 116
Psychic Divorce, 208
"Psychology of Men and Masculinity, The,", 11

Q
Questionnaire responses (from dads), 125–128

R
Reciprocal portrait, of men, 191–193
Regis, Ari
    children, 79
    children's lives, contributions to, 85
    divorce, 79–80
        experience, 84
        and multiple losses, 80–81
    ex-wife and her family/his family,
            postdivorce interactions with,
            84–85
    finances, 81–82
    life events participated with children, 85
    marriage, 79–80
    memories, 86
    personal history, 79
    postdivorce period, 82–83
    remarriage, 82–83
    retrospective and prospective, 86–87
    worst times, 86
Rehabilitation, 7, 19, 71, 110, 133, 207
Rehabilitation alimony, 12
Reid, G.D., 3
Rejection, 14, 39, 40, 82, 102, 206
Relationship to children
    Bob Straight, 28
    Gene Goodman, 74–75
    Ron Dedicated, 47–48
Religious dictum, 38
Relocation Statute (Florida), 150–151
Remarriage, 169, 186
    Ari Regis, 82–83
    Jorge Garcia, 33, 36

Reuben Guy, 40–41
Ron Dedicated, 51
Re-petitioning the court, 203

S
Sacred covenant, 36, 201, 206
Sadness, 14, 18, 33, 42, 59, 85, 102, 118,
    119, 126
Self-centeredness, 103, 135
Sense of belonging, changes in
    Arturo Miguel, 94
    Gene Goodman, 74
    Hy Hopes, 102
    Zack Determined, 110–111
Settlement agreement, 54, 73, 169, 199
Settlement offer, 117
Social climbers, 115
Sociolegal custody decisions, 4
Sole *vs.* joint custody, 90, 116, 143
Splitting, 132, 140, 163, 190, 203
Splitting asunder, 138, 187
Stages of divorce process, 138, 189
Standardized psychological testing, 166
Steinem, Gloria, 2
Stepsiblings, 20, 33, 35, 36
Straight, Bob
    children, 25
    divorce experience, and relationship
        to son, 28
    early postdivorce period, 26–27
    finances, 26
    in-law family and his family, postdivorce
        interactions with, 27
    later postdivorce years, 27–28
    legal divorce, 25–26
    marriage, 25–26
    personal history, 25
    retrospective, 29
Streep, Meryl, 8
Substance abuse disorder, 5, 19, 76, 129, 150,
    168, 177
Substance abuser, 129

T
Temper
    outbursts, 91, 190
    tantrum, 71
Tender years, 4, 148
Theft, 55, 186
Threat of withholding access to children, 38
"Til death do us part," ,27 101, 126, 192
Time sharing, 12, 143, 148–152, 154–159,
    173, 174, 177–180, 207
Traditional wedding, 31
Tragedy of divorce, 197–210. *See also* Divorce
Trial separation, 106
Twelfth Judicial Circuit, 183

U
Unlucky, Scott
    children, 116–117
    divorce, experience of, 120–121
    early postdivorce period, 117–119
    ex-spouse and in-law family, postdivorce
        interactions with, 119
    family's reactions, 119
    legal divorce, 116–117
    marriage, 115–117
    personal history, 115
    postdivorce years, 121–122
    retrospective, 122–123

V
Value system, 28, 31, 115
Victimization, 168
Victimized dad, 129
Volatility, 65

W
Walking on eggshells, 71
Wars of the Roses, 14
Women, portrait of, 189–191
Worst memories. *See* Memories

CPSIA information can be obtained at www.ICGtesting.com
Printed in the USA
LVOW102135150213

320402LV00006B/93/P